Londoner Sean Egan has contributed to, among others, *Billboard, Book Collector, Classic Rock, Record Collector, Tennis World, Total Film, Uncut* and RollingStone.com. He has written or edited seventeen books, including works on The Beatles, Jimi Hendrix, The Rolling Stones, *Coronation Street* and Manchester United. His critically acclaimed novel *Sick of Being Me* was published in 2003, while his 2008 collection of short stories *Don't Mess with the Best* carried cover endorsements from Booker Prize winners Stanley Middleton and David Storey.

animal tracks

The Story of The Animals:
Newcastle's Rising Sons

Sean Egan

ASKILL
PUBLISHING

Originally published in 2001 by Helter Skelter Publishing
This revised edition published and copyright 2012 by Askill Publishing

A CIP record for this book is available from the British Library

ISBN (10) 0-9545750-4-0
ISBN (13) 978-0-9545750-4-5

table of contents

acknowledgements

I would like to express my thanks to members of The Animals — original and new — for giving me their time. Vic Briggs, Eric Burdon, Barry Jenkins, Zoot Money, Dave Rowberry, John Steel, Andy Summers, Hilton Valentine and John Weider all co-operated with this book. Without that assistance — all of which was unpaid — this book would not have been possible.

I am particularly grateful to two of the above: firstly, John Steel who, as well as putting up patiently with my damn fool questions, also gave me access to his private diaries so that I could ensure that dates were as accurate as possible, and secondly, Vic Briggs who — like John — allowed me to grill him for hours about his time in the band. Vic also gave me access to his uncompleted memoirs and provided me with press clippings.

The above list of Animals is, of course, incomplete. I did request interviews with Alan Price and Danny McCulloch but received no reply in each case. This inevitably causes a distortion in the story: their perspectives are missing. That being the case the offer remains open to them to give their opinions for any future editions of this book.

Note: Dave Rowberry passed away between the first and second editions of this book but I have retained references to his quotes in the present tense in order to make clear that they were provided specifically for this project.

I am deeply in debt to Dionisio Castello, author of *The Ultimate Eric Burdon Audio-Videography* (see bibliography) for compiling tapes of Animals rarities for me and to Phil Metzger of the Eric Burdon Connection Newsletter for putting me in touch with Eric Burdon.

My thanks also go to the following for providing more minor, but telling, assistance: Albert Lee, Mike Kraft of One Way Records, John Reed of Sequel Records and Andy Neill.

note on 2012 edition

This revised and expanded version of *Animal Tracks* differs significantly from the original one published by Helter Skelter in 2001 in several ways.

Naturally, it has been updated to reflect changes in The Animals' story since its first publication, limited though the developments in the story of a long defunct group may be. I have also taken the opportunity to correct errors pointed out to me by various parties.

The new edition is richer than the first one. My Helter Skelter editor cut out large chunks of my text, an act I considered unwarranted, and I have reinstated them. I have additionally instated many original quotes I secured from Eric Burdon which I did not use at the time. Interviews have been conducted with people to whom I did not manage to speak for the first edition: Barry Jenkins, Andy Summers and Rod Weinberg. Additionally, Hilton Valentine, John Steel and Vic Briggs gave me some new quotes and pieces of information. I have incorporated into this revised edition quotes given to me by Kathy Etchingham in approximately 2001 for my subsequent book on the making of Jimi Hendrix's debut album. As she is a friend of Eric Burdon and the former girlfriend of Jimi Hendrix, she naturally had a few insights to offer on The Animals and on their and Hendrix's mutual manager Mike Jeffery. Barry Mann and Cynthia Weil quotes relevant to 'We've Gotta Get Out of this Place' from my 2004 book on songwriters, *The Guys Who Wrote 'em*, are also newly included.

Finally, I have nipped, tucked and tweaked the text, having, I hope, improved as an author in the dozen years since I began work on the project.

introduction

In 1981, the disc jockey Paul Gambaccini wrote and presented a Radio 1 series of hour-long appreciations of major figures from rock history. His programme on The Animals began with mentions of The Hollies, The Lovin' Spoonful and Creedence Clearwater Revival, groups he considered in the same bracket as The Animals on the grounds that, though they made great music, their lacking a certain charisma and their failure to revolutionise popular music meant that they were rarely the subject of radio shows or books. He had a point. Though they put out many classic records — including in 'The House of the Rising Sun' one of the greatest ever made and one which, because it convinced Bob Dylan to go electric, changed the course of rock forever — The Animals have been the subject of just one proper biography, discounting this one and Eric Burdon's memoirs. Burdon himself is now an almost forgotten figure. Once hailed by many as the greatest lead vocalist of all time, he was nowhere to be found in a list of one hundred great singers produced by a 1998 survey of fellow vocalists conducted by *Mojo* magazine nor included in a 2011 listing of "Great British R'n'B Voices" printed by similarly retro-rock themed *Uncut*.

This neglect is an inevitable consequence not just of remarkable ignorance on the part of music journalists who are paid to know better but also the inconsistency of the various bands that from 1963 to 1968 (plus later reunions) traded under the banner "The Animals." It must be conceded that The Animals — either the original R&B-purveying Geordie ensemble or the American-based group who had Eric Burdon's name and an ampersand in front of their moniker — never made a classic album. The original line-up were hampered by their blues purism: twelve-bar blues songs get repetitive when stretched over an entire album, even in the case of a band far more capable than most of transcending the genre's rigid conventions. Eric Burdon & The Animals, meanwhile, embraced the new age represented by the Haight-Ashbury hippie scene so unequivocally that some of their product — especially the elongated, free-form material — has dated quite horribly. Yet adjudging a band lightweights because they couldn't quite manage to sustain brilliance over the forty-minutes playing time that made up an old vinyl LP is short-sighted. Almost every one of the nine British singles released by the original Animals (not one of which appeared on a UK album) was a classic. In addition, at least half of every Sixties Animals album is utterly magnificent. Equally short-sighted is to invoke the facts that the original Animals didn't write their own songs and that Eric Burdon & The Animals often merely imitated, rather than innovated, in the psychedelic sphere as a reason for consigning them to the ranks of Minor Artists. Whether it be 'The House of the Rising Sun' or 'Sky Pilot' (one a cover version, one an original; both epic and exquisite), whether it be the Geordie mob's sultry shiver-inducing version of Ray Charles' 'I Believe to My Soul' — made immortal by its universal sentiments as well as its musical excellence — or the psychedelic group's 'San Franciscan Nights', a song so of its place and time as to be as dated as 'I Believe to My Soul' is timeless but in no way musically inferior to the Charles cover, The Animals' music was of a quality which ensures that it is still giving huge pleasure more than four decades after it was first heard.

This book examines that music in unprecedented depth. Even those music critics who are fans of the band have stopped short of analysing their output to a degree they would not balk at if the band were The Beatles or The Rolling Stones. The assumption has seemed to be that it's somehow slightly ludicrous to studiously examine the art of either a covers band or a band whose records, however enjoyable, often come perilously close to being period pieces. Yet great music deserves to be put under the microscope to find out what gives it its special quality, whatever its origins or nature. And, after all, we are not talking about Milli Vanilli. Both versions of The Animals were comprised of supremely talented musicians and *they* were ultimately responsible for the brilliance of the records they made, not their producers nor even the people who wrote their non-original songs. (If you don't believe the latter, compare Frijid Pink's or Bob Dylan's versions of 'The House of the Rising Sun' to Burdon and co's.)

There are some who will take exception to this book's treatment of every band who had "The Animals" in their title as being equally deserving of attention. It's certainly true that when Eric Burdon retained the Animals name for his new group following the dissolution of the original Animals in 1966, it amounted to nothing more than persisting with a franchise: in sound and in spirit, the New Animals (as they were billed on the cover of their first album, *Winds of Change*) had nothing in common with their predecessors except Burdon's membership. So why not simply write a book about Eric Burdon, from The Animals to the present-day? Well, because unlike everything he did subsequently (with the possible exception of War), Burdon's involvement with both line-ups of The Animals constituted something profoundly more than him bossing around a back-up band. Though none of the first incarnation of The Animals except Alan Price was Burdon's equal as an artist, they could stand their ground with him simply because he was not an idol to them: they had become stars together. Consequently, all five of them contributed ideas and all had to a certain extent a creative veto, a situation far more conducive to aesthetic excellence than if they were simply taking their cue from the front man. That egalitarianism was even more pronounced in Eric Burdon & The Animals, who were all exceptionally accomplished musicians. War excepted, Burdon has simply not been able to have that kind of healthily democratic musical dialogue since: whatever good intentions he may have (and despite some occasionally fine records), every band he ever employs contains at least a couple of members to whom he is a god. Reverence from colleagues is not a recipe for great music. Nor are the limited budgets with which Burdon has had to contend since losing the perception of commercial viability The Animals' name gave his projects: a franchise might not be able to generate great art in itself but it can certainly provide the resources and conditions that make great art more likely. For all those reasons, limiting the story to those parts of Eric Burdon's career when he happened to be trading under The Animals' title is in no way meaningless.

One of the aims of this book is to stake a claim for The Animals (both sets) as great *bands*, each in their own way amongst the finest of the 1960s, a decade when great groups were not exactly thin on the ground. It is for this reason that their music will *still* be giving pleasure more than four decades hence.

chapter one

'When I Was Young', the debut single by the 'new' Animals in May 1967, featured what seemed a clearly autobiographical lyric from Eric Burdon.

Its opening verse talked of rooms being cold, his father being a soldier and times being very hard when he was young.

The stuff about his father can be put down to poetic licence. "He was actually a conscientious objector," he explains. "It didn't do much good as they sent him to Southampton which was considered a war zone, I guess — it was called the 'home front.'" However, Burdon's childhood was certainly marked by the kind of poverty — of both finances and culture — that was the lot of many English children in the infancy of the welfare state, and furthermore exacerbated by the austerity of the post-War years and the fact of being located in a part of Britain where being poor has always bitten deeper. The inhabitants of Newcastle — Geordies — in many ways have more in common with Scots and Scandinavians (with whom they have strong historical connections) than with their countrymen. John Steel, Animals drummer, says, "The North-East corner where we come from is a bit isolated from the rest of England." When he and his contemporaries were growing up, "…it was still a heavy industry-type area where people still remembered hard times from the Thirties. No different from a lot of the North of England but there'd always been a strong coal mining tradition, ship building — all the big dirty jobs." Although it was nothing like as cosmopolitan as ports such as Liverpool, Steel reveals that Newcastle's poor-relation status to other English cities gave the musicians of the locale in the early Sixties a bond with their counterparts in far flung places like Mississippi: "We just had an instinctive emotional identification

with black American blues." Burdon would become one of the
definitive white English blues singers, which term he fully appre-
ciates is for many an oxymoron. "My roots aren't really the blues,"
he concedes. "I interpreted the blues. But then again, what's the
root of all of us? I was doing a session with a percussionist friend
of mine who's white but he plays like an African and his house is
full of African artefacts. He said, 'Have you always felt an affinity
with Africa?' I said, 'Yeah.' He said, 'It's funny, so have I.' And here
we are two Anglo-Saxons talking about Africa. Why? Ultimately
why, because now we're beginning to find out that centuries ago
Africa was the birthplace of it all. That's where life began. So
who's to say what your roots are?"

Eric Victor Burdon was born on May 11 1941 in Walker, a
district of Newcastle upon Tyne. He was therefore of the right
age to be caught up in the Angry Young Man culture of Great
Britain in the late Fifties. He has spoken in interviews of the
way that he, and people of his generation, were inspired by the
likes of John Osborne's ground-breaking play *Look Back In Anger*
and so-called Kitchen Sink literature like Alan Sillitoe's *Saturday Night and Sunday Morning*. The heroes of these dramas were
young, working class men who were determined to have a better
life than their fathers and were contemptuous of the "Not for the
likes of us" supineness that had hitherto prevented the British
proletariat from getting its fair share. It was this, perhaps even
more than his love of the blues, that inspired Burdon to want to
be a professional singer.

Yet his was by no means an upbringing of unrelieved grimness.
Burdon speaks fondly of growing up in a locale with a rock-solid
sense of neighbourliness where people felt able to leave their doors
unlocked. "We all live in a world that's lost its sense of community," he laments, although he adds, "but I think I've gained a
spirituality since I left England so many years ago." John Steel, a
friend of Burdon's from the age of fifteen, describes Marondale
Avenue, the sleepy Walker cul-de-sac where Burdon grew up, as a
very pleasant place. "It wasn't leafy suburbia — they were council
houses — but everybody took pride, the area was clean and well
looked-after," he says. Elsewhere, Burdon has admitted that he

had parents who spoiled him and gave him just about anything he wanted. This included being allowed to travel to Paris and Spain before he was eighteen (unusual for those days) and being indulged in his decision not to immediately leave school for the world of work. "Just a very decent, ordinary, God-fearing, law abiding working class family" is John Steel's verdict on Burdon's folks. He also adds that despite their tolerance of his maverick spirit, "His parents were a bit too protective of him. When I met Eric, I had much more freedom than he had for going out and staying out late, sleeping over without my parents having to know where I was. If Eric stayed out, he was in big trouble when he got home."

Though short, Burdon is a pugnacious character. "I've spent a lifetime trying to quell my anger," he admits. "I can become extremely agitated, extremely angry, extremely violent. It's all got to do in part with my own physical constitution. Asthmatics tend to get angry faster than other people do and maybe the cause of the asthmatic condition is triggered by the anger."

In 1956, at the age of fifteen, Burdon decided to take the same option as did — independently of each other — many of his British musical contemporaries. Like fellow future rock'n'roll stars Ray Davies, Jimmy Page, Pete Townshend, Phil May, Keith Richards, John Lennon and Eric Clapton, Burdon became an art student, in his case enrolling at the Newcastle College of Art and Industrial Design. On his first day there, he met a smiling-faced, snaggle-toothed student who attracted his attention by asking the class if there was anyone present who liked jazz. Burdon answered said student — John Steel, born on February 4 1941 in Gateshead, County Durham — in the affirmative. He could have added that he liked any music that was black and American. Steel says, "I started in my very early teens with an interest in jazz. My first instrument was the trumpet. Trumpet was the guitar of its day. It was just about the dawn of rock'n'roll. When I first started playing, it was about 1955. Jazz was the dance music of the time — trad jazz — for young, rebellious-type persons. It was either that or go to the Mecca ballroom type places where you danced to watered-down swing. If people wanted to jive, you'd jive to jazz. The summer that I left school without any O-levels or

A-levels or anything, it was straight into art school, and that was the year Lonnie Donegan had 'Rock Island Line' come out and the summer Elvis Presley put out 'Heartbreak Hotel'. The year before that was 'Rock Around The Clock' with Bill Haley. It was new music basically, based on very old music. As a jazz and blues fan, I wasn't surprised by it because it was the gritty bits of jazz and blues that were being amplified." As for Burdon's penchant for jazz, Steel says, "He very soon discovered that rock'n'roll was his preference. He sooner than most realised that this was where his heart lay." What were Steel's first impressions of a character who would become such an important figure in his life? "Very likable bloke, full of passion and mischief, really lovely fella. Bit hard to handle sometimes. We became instant friends. We were big movie fans. We spent half our time at art college in the cinema in the afternoons watching movies."

Steel and Burdon teamed up with two other like-minded students, Blackie Sanderson and Jimmy Crawford, for jam sessions in the college's common room. Steel played trumpet (though only in B-flat), Sanderson played drums — on a kit which consisted of a snare drum and a hi-hat — and Crawford played four-stringed banjo. Burdon sang and played trombone. Steel: "He couldn't play trombone to save his life but he had to have something to do." The four styled themselves The Pagan Jazzmen and performed material like 'Frankie and Johnny'. They sounded, according to Steel, "terrible." "We were fans," Steel says. "We were listening to this stuff and rather than just sit listening to them doing it, we thought, 'Why don't we do it as well?' It's not a big deal because everybody in the country seemed to be doing the same thing at the same time. It seemed like a spontaneous thing. I've always said it was skiffle that did it. When Lonnie Donegan recorded 'Rock Island Line' that's when everybody realised that 'I can do that.' Three chords on a cheap guitar. And when Elvis Presley came out with 'Heartbreak Hotel' and sounded so black, that's when everybody realised, 'Well, fuckin' hell, why can't us white kids play blues, play rock'n'roll?'"

The first configuration of the Pagan Jazzmen didn't last very long. Reveals Steel, "Suddenly Eric just decided, very sensibly, he didn't have a career on trombone and decided he wanted to sing. We all did a switch around. Jimmy moved from banjo to guitar. Alan Sanderson just switched from drums to bass and it was like a duck to water. You could do that when you were a kid in those days. It was just 'Alright, I'll play this and you play that then.' I just took over the drums. When I look back on it, it was really weird." Steel's jazz leanings led to him developing a style quite different to the majority of drummers in British rhythm'n'blues and beat groups of the era. Chas Chandler, Animals bassist, once said that Steel's playing, which tended toward subtle cymbal work rather than muscle, gave The Animals a unique 'swing'. "I've heard Chas said that and with hindsight I guess it's true," says Steel. "I wouldn't know what to do if I didn't have a ride [cymbal]". However, Steel remains modest about his abilities: "I was never a great technician. I was listening to guys like Elvin Jones. They were my heroes — what I thought of as real musicians. I could never aspire to play like that. I was quite happy to play a simpler kind of music."

Meanwhile, Burdon's first ventures into singing produced a pleasing revelation: although it took him a while to develop the style with which the world would become familiar upon The Animals achieving fame, he transpired to possess a booming, world-weary voice identical in sound to those of the black vocalists he idolised. There has been surprisingly little discussion of this amazing, almost supernatural coincidence by rock critics. As Burdon said in another autobiographical Animals song ('New York 1963-America 1968'), "The negro was my hero — I tried my best to sound like him." Indeed. When, many years later, he made an album with blues legend Jimmy Witherspoon, it was literally often impossible to tell the voices of the two apart. Even Burdon himself seems to have accepted his classic blues voice as good but unremarkable fortune, dismissing it in his 1986 autobiography *I Used to be an Animal, but I'm Alright Now* as merely "...the talent to get drunk enough or out of my mind enough to climb onto a stage in front of a club full of people and sing with emotion..." Some might be inclined to consider his gift almost on the level of a miracle. Pressed on this, Burdon says, "I can recall my first

vocal experience in copying the sound of the coal man who used
to come round selling coal from the back of a donkey and cart. He
used to shout '*Cooooal!*' and I used to shout '*Cooooal!*' back. That
was just a step away from singing the '*Bluuuues*'! But, yeah, maybe
it was a miracle. If it pays off it'll be a fucking miracle, that's for
sure." "He just opened his mouth and out it came," says Steel. "In
a way we just used to take this sort of thing for granted. The arrogance of youth. We just tried it and we thought, 'Oh, we can do
this — great.' It surprised other people, mind you." Burdon says,
"My biggest influences as singers was Joe Turner, Jimmy Witherspoon, Ray Charles, Joe Williams, Billie Holiday, Chuck Berry."
Steel cites Burdon's becoming a fan of Ray Charles as the turning
point in his journey to status of great vocalist: "That is the point
where Eric realised a style. He never tried to sing like Ray Charles
but that's when it gelled for him." Steel says that it was from Joe
Turner that Burdon picked up much of his sense of timing.

One of the reasons his colleagues weren't as overwhelmed by
Burdon's voice as critics is possibly technical deficiencies that
only musicians tend to notice. Burdon has never sung from the
diaphragm, for instance. Dave Rowberry, who replaced Alan Price
in The Animals in mid-1965, not only says, "I never heard him
as black," he also states, "I'm not being detrimental here: I never
thought of him [as] a singer. I thought of him more as a shouter.
But it came from the bollocks, that's what counts. When I first
heard the band in London, it was one of the most exciting things
I'd ever seen. You knew it was coming from the heart, the bollocks. He just gives it so much enthusiasm. He's steeped in it."
Zoot Money, long-time Burdon friend and member of the last
Animals line-up, agrees: "He's a blues shouter. He doesn't actually sing as such. He's not aware of the sonorous resonance that
you get when you sing long notes, notes that are really resonating
with the instruments." Did Money ever try to correct Burdon's
technique? "Yeah, I made suggestions, but you couldn't tell Eric
what to do. Nobody can tell Eric what to do." Money feels that
Burdon has stuck with his 'wrong' approach partly because he
fears the outcome would be inferior: "Oh, he definitely would
have lost it. Lost whatever he had. It was a guttural effect. He

would be the first to say to you that he is not a singer, even though he's done some melodically great stuff. It was a question of there was a bigger need inside to express something than there was to worry what you sounded like."

By March 1959 the art school band had graduated from rehearsing in the common room to the first rung of the concert ladder: playing support in uninspiring surroundings to bands of an only slightly less nobody status than them. One such public performance took place that March at Headlam Street Church Hall in a rough area of Newcastle called Byker. The act for whom they were playing an interval spot were called the Frank Hedley Trio. "By this time it was not the Pagan Jazzmen but The Pagans, R&B band," recalls Steel. This denoted a more populist direction, rhythm'n'blues being an umtempo, more commercial variation on the blues, if still more gritty than straightahead rock'n'roll. Steel: "Frank Hedley was a piano player who based his whole set on Jerry Lee Lewis. We were watching them and it was boogie-style stuff. It was okay, it was quite good. Better than us because he seemed to have more instruments. We were still just four and occasionally five. We had a kid called Dave Ashcroft who came in on rhythm guitar and a bit of jink-jink-jink piano, really limited Little Richard stuff. We were attempting to play anything from Joe Turner, from the *Boss of the Blues* album. *Boss of the Blues* was a big thing Eric discovered at the time. It's still a cracking album: Joe Turner with basically a band from the Count Basie band. It was good kind of city blues. It really struck a chord with us and we were doing quite a bit of that, plus whatever rock'n'roll appealed to us at the time. We went on to play the middle spot and this guy from this other band came up after we'd played a couple of numbers and said 'Can I sit in?' It was like a church piano, upright out-of-tune piano. He'd been playing rhythm guitar in Frank Hedley's band but he just sat down at the piano and started playing amazing boogie. We thought 'Whoa! He's gotta join us.' Simple as that. We just made that instant decision and said, 'Do you wanna come and be with us?'"

The young pianist who so impressed the band was named Alan Price, born April 19 1941 in Fairfield, Durham. Contrary to some reports, this was the first time either Steel or Burdon had met their future fellow Animal. Although Steel and Burdon to this day are in awe of Price's keyboard skills, neither of them ever counted him as a genuine friend. "Kind of a strange fish," says Steel. "I never really, really got on on a personal level with Alan. It's something about him. He was stiff and prickly and defensive. I could never sort of hang loose with him. He didn't know who he wanted to be, I think. He had a bit of a difficult upbringing and it affected his character." Price's musical tastes also created a barrier. Steel: "He just wasn't kind of hip enough, if you'll pardon my arrogance, for the time. Eric and me instantly had a thing: we loved the same kind of music and we loved the same kind of movies, in a broad stream. I went much more extremely in one direction to jazz and Eric was less interested in jazz and much more extremely interested in R&B and rock'n'roll. We had a great big area in the middle where we could meet. But Alan seemed to be a bit…I dunno. His hero at the time — as well as Jerry Lee Lewis — was Buddy Greco. That might tell you something. I think he imagined himself as a kind of lounge player. With that knowledge, you can see exactly why he's doing what's he's doing now." Some might consider it appropriate that Price was such a fan of Jerry Lee Lewis. The 'Great Balls of Fire' man is also known for a combination of personal prickliness and breathtaking skills — a tortured genius of the keyboard. "He could have been Britain's Jerry Lee Lewis," says Burdon. "I don't know about being a tortured genius, but, yeah, he seems to be tortured. He *should* be fucking tortured."

With Price on board, the art school band continued refining their abilities. "The Pagan Jazzmen lasted a matter of months and The Pagans maybe a year," Steel remembers. "We didn't do a lot of gigs, we were rehearsing, mostly at my house on a Saturday night. Then we started to get some gigs. We had the Kansas City Five and the Kansas City Seven. The Kansas City Seven was kind of an attempt at Ray Charles' band sound, with brass. We had two trumpets, alto and tenor. There's no record of it anywhere in the world. If I heard it now it'd probably sound pretty crappy. We loved what we were doing. We never really pulled any great crowds but we enjoyed ourselves. Danny and Pat, the trumpet players, moved back to Manchester where they'd come from and it suddenly became the Kansas City Five, which was a Louis Jordan-ish kind of outfit with one tenor player and Alan Price, anybody who could play bass (we never really had a regular bass player), me on drums, a guy called George Stoves on rhythm guitar and a bit of lead, Jeff Hedley on tenor and Eric. We were called the Kansas City Five because we were still hooked on this rolling R&B shouting thing that Joe Turner and Joe Williams and people like that were doing. We didn't think of it as a living or a career or anything. It was just something that we wanted to do." In their free time, the Five attended a university jazz club located above a pub called the Gardener's Arms in Newcastle. During the day, the club was a dance studio. The club reportedly had no licence but as long as the rent was paid, no questions were asked by the owners about what took place there. This shady scenario was typical of the man who ran the club, Londoner Mike Jeffery, who would be a hugely important figure in The Animals' story.

Jeffery, as if to live up to the villainous reputation he was already acquiring, perpetually wore dark glasses. Although almost all of the musicians who would play in The Animals refer to him as Mike *Jeffries*, signed legal documents reveal "Jeffery" as the correct spelling of his name. To add to the confusion, his name is also often rendered as "Jeffrey". Though the mispronunciation and misspelling was probably accidental, Jeffery was unfortunately the kind of character who would probably have found it convenient for there to be confusion over his name/identity, something The Animals would learn to their considerable cost in the future. Burdon admits, "I knew all along that Mike Jeffries was trouble." Burdon was commissioned by Jeffery to design the interior of his Club A'Gogo: "This was after me turning down several good positions that the college had offered me. My involvement in music was pissing my parents off because they'd put me through art school at great expense." At this point, Burdon's electrician father told him of his suspicions about Jeffery. His father had worked on another of Jeffery's clubs called the Marimba where there had been a fire. Burdon says, "Although on one level, my old man was saying to me, 'Well I'm happy that you've got yourself a job, son', on another level he said it was his electrical cables that were blamed for the fire and he knew that it wasn't the cables that were at fault. He put the cables in two days before. So my father knew that Jeffries had set fire to that club in order to make money to open the Club A'Gogo. We knew he was a bad guy, but when you're young and dumb and full of come, you're attracted to the Jesse Jameses of this world."

After getting to know Jeffery through his jazz club, the art school graduates helped him decorate yet another of his clubs called the Downbeat, which was soon to open on the top floor of an old warehouse. They were rewarded with a regular Friday night gig there. "Then one night Pricey just didn't turn up," says Steel. "We thought 'What the fuck's going on here?' Couldn't ring him. He didn't have a phone in those days, and we didn't have one. Subsequently we found out that he'd been poached by The Kon-tors. I'd never heard of them. They were basically a cover band that played all the pop hits to kids at the Co-Op halls. These sort of gigs that were sprouting up all over the place that young people would rather go to than go to a dance hall. Pricey just defected without even telling us. So that was it. The Kansas City Five just collapsed." Though Steel hadn't heard of the band, he did know The Kon-tors' bass player, Bryan 'Chas' Chandler, born on December 18 1938 in Heaton, Newcastle. Chandler had actually previously rehearsed on an informal basis with Price, Burdon and Steel. At those rehearsals, Chandler, a big, burly man of 6' 4," towered over Burdon, who it was now apparent was never going to grow beyond his diminutive 5' 6". "Chas was a big guy," says Burdon. "He was too big for me, that's for sure." He adds, "I'm only small when I'm standing up. When I'm lying down, believe me: I'm tall. As they say: 'Big man, big cock. Little man, all cock.'" Animals roadie Tappy Wright corroborated Burdon's vainglorious claim in his 2009 memoir *Rock Roadie*, wherein he described the singer's trousers "straining with the largest cock I'd ever seen."

Steel recalls his first impression of Chandler: "Big, red-headed, lanky, big-boned bloke. He had a terrible hangover, I remember.

He loved going out for several jars of beer and he was very keen on playing darts." Despite Chandler's decidedly un-intellectual appearance, Steel reveals, "Chas was always a reader and I always had a book in my pocket and we'd say, 'What you reading?'" In fact, The Animals were quite a literate band, with Burdon also a keen reader and Price a white-collar worker. Steel: "We never considered ourselves to be intellectuals but we were all pretty bright and we hung out with people that we recognised as similar characters. We didn't just talk about football and tits and things." Chandler's musical tastes were far more mainstream than those of the avid jazzman Steel and the Ray Charles fanatic Burdon, something reflected in the chart-oriented approach of The Kontors. "He was mostly into good quality popular music," recalls Steel. "Sam Cooke, that sort of thing. He wasn't into jazz. He just recognised good pop music when he heard it. He was absolutely potty about The Beatles. As soon as they appeared on the scene he was absolutely crazy about them. He knew which direction he was going in." Steel accepts that this may have helped make The Animals a bit less precious about R&B than their contemporaries. "All these little things come into the melting pot," he says. "It wasn't planned. We drifted this way and that way. Chas had his contribution and with hindsight it was probably very significant. He was very hip on the kind of pop music that Eric and me could agree with."

That, however, was in the future. With the dissolution of the Five, Steel drifted into bread-and-butter drumming jobs: "I just played working men's clubs and any sort of stuff like that I could get. And then eventually I got into supper club work, where you had a resident trio with bow ties playing 'Fly Me To The Moon'." As for Burdon, Steel explains, "Eric was just jamming around. He didn't have a band. He got up and sang regularly with a band called the Mighty Joe Young Jazzmen. The trumpeter of that incidentally was a guy called John Walters, who became John Peel's producer. It was like a big band based mostly on Duke Ellington and Count Basie. It wasn't a job. Eric [would] get up and do a couple of numbers in the middle of the spot for them." Steel also depped on a few occasions for The Kon-tors. Although Steel was at least able to make a living from his drum work, Burdon was having to support himself with labouring jobs, despite possessing a National Design Diploma. Burdon also went down south to check out London's flourishing R&B scene.

Although The Kon-tors were very successful as a live act and even cut a demo at one point, their members were prepared to bluesy-up their commercial, chart-oriented style for gigs at clubs with less pop requirements. Before long they had formed a sort of splinter group called The Alan Price Rhythm and Blues Combo, whom Eric Burdon initially joined as an occasional member but soon became a permanent fixture of. They featured two saxophonists, Jeff Hedley and Nigel Stanger. (The latter would, many years later, set up the live venue the Newcastle Arena with Chas Chandler.) The parallel bands often played separate venues on the same day. Burdon's tastes inevitably pushed the splinter group into a grittier, more blues-based style. Gradually, the Combo became more important, and more lucrative, than The Kon-tors. One of the Combo's regular venues was Mike Jeffery's new club, the Club A'Gogo. It was a happening venue by anybody's definition. Legendary bluesmen and jazzmen like John Lee Hooker, Brownie McGhee, Sonny Terry, Count Basie and Sonny Boy Williamson played there, as did soon-to-be legends like The Yardbirds and The Rolling Stones. "We used to go there socially," says Steel. "There was a great room called the Jazz Lounge and there was another room, the Young Set, and bands like The Gamblers and The Kon-tors played at the Young Set. Mike and Ian Carr played in the Jazz Lounge, and tenor players from London: Tubby Hayes and Tony Coe and people like that. It was a great scene for that time. It was bloody exciting. There was really good music going down."

John Steel's drift into musical mediocrity was halted in late August 1963 by Chas Chandler who had decided that the Combo's drummer, Barry Preston, would have to go because of a bad attitude. "I'm playing in this club called Emerson's in Newcastle," remembers Steel. "One day I'm walking down the street and Chas stops and says, 'You know Eric's playing with us now?' I'd heard this. Chas said, 'Do you fancy playing with us?' By this time I'd turned professional. I'd quit my little job selling wallpaper and

I was making fifteen quid a week playing this nightclub. I said, 'Chas, I'd love to but I can't afford it. It's me living now, I'm making fifteen quid a week.' And Chas says, 'Well, hell, we're playing seven sets a week and we're picking up fourteen, fifteen quid a week as well.' And I thought, 'Well, fuck me.' I said, 'Can you almost guarantee that?' He says, 'Yeah, we're playing six nights. One's a double: you play the A'Gogo for two sets early and then you go down to the Downbeat at midnight and you play 'til three in the morning. Mondays off. Tuesday's at the Old Vic in Whitley Bay (which was a big pub room upstairs). And the rest of the nights are at the A'Gogo, either in the Jazz Lounge [or] the Young Set.' So I said, 'Right definitely, you're on. Who's in the band?' He said, 'Well, me and Eric, Pricey...' I said, 'What about guitar?' and he said, 'Well we're getting this guy from a band called The Wild Cats.' I said, 'I'm going on holiday to Ostend for a week', and he said 'Okay, well come back and we'll start.'"

Steel's first gig as a member of The Alan Price Rhythm and Blues Combo is retrospectively important because it marked the completion of the classic Animals line-up of Burdon, Price, Chandler, Steel and Hilton Valentine. It straddled Saturday 7 and Sunday 8 September 1963, the Combo playing the Downbeat Club's midnight-to-three late session. These dates are from John Steel's contemporaneous diaries. By now the saxophonists were gone for good, except for the occasional guest blow from Nigel Stanger, who was too busy pursuing his studies at Oxford to devote much time to music. The gig occasioned the seat-of-the-pants approach which The Animals would employ throughout their career, both in terms of gigs and the records they would one day make. "I turned up on the night," says Steel. "No rehearsals, never even met. That's where I was introduced to Hilton Valentine. 'This is the guitarist.' 'Hello, how you doing?' I think it was either Hilton's first night or his second gig. We thought, 'What we gonna do?' So we wrote a few numbers out. We got up and played and the place was *packed*."

Hilton Valentine was born on May 21 1943 in North Shields, Northumberland. Not only was he heartthrob material, the newcomer had the perfect surname for a would-be rock star, almost like something British Fifties pop Svengali Larry Parnes might have invented for one of his stable of singers (Billy Fury, Johnny Gentle, etc.). However, Valentine was actually the name on his birth certificate, as was his unusual Christian name: "I was named after an uncle," he explains. Valentine started playing guitar at around the age of thirteen. He recalls, "Rock'n'roll was just starting to happen. Chuck Berry and Lonnie Donegan probably were the greatest influences." It was no easy matter for a working class child to afford a guitar in those days. "First guitar I had was from a newspaper, on the payments," he says. Valentine was mostly self-taught ("I had about three or four lessons in the very beginning and that was it") and was in bands virtually from the moment he started playing the instrument. In fact, Valentine was one-up on his new colleagues in that he had actually made an album, albeit in acetate form. The record in question was by his previous group, The Wild Cats, an ensemble with a frequently changing line-up who covered songs from the more commercial end of the musical spectrum. *Sounds of the Wild Cats* was a 10-inch LP recorded in Spring 1963 when one of the band's members was Tappy Wright, who would later become The Animals' roadie, go-fer and general connection with reality. Chandler saw the band in action and approached Valentine about his commitment to music and was impressed enough to ask him to join his band. Valentine: "There was a local venue called the Rex Hotel and The Wild Cats played there on a weekly basis and he came down to see me play with them and he invited me to see *them* play. I wanted to get out and tour and play music for a living but the rest of The Wild Cats didn't so when this opportunity came along...Plus after I'd seen the band, particularly Eric singing. I didn't know what it was — it was just amazing, that's all I thought." Did Valentine get the feeling that the man with his name in the title was the creative power in The Alan Price Rhythm and Blues Combo? "No. He did the administration, he was the one that got the money and divided it out, but Eric always seemed to be the dominant one." Despite the fact that Steel was technically the last to join the Combo, Valentine felt that it was he who had the status of new boy: "'Cause John had played with Eric and Alan prior to all this."

The capacity crowds that Steel was amazed to see generated by a band that didn't go for the easy option of covering chart hits were the result of both the musical excellence of the Combo and a previously undetected market. "In the year or so that I'd been playing these nightclubs, they'd developed into this band that was the most original band in the area," Steel says. "There was a lot of bands but they were all just playing cover versions of the charts. Eric wouldn't do that. If he was going to be in a band it was to sing stuff that he liked. Suddenly there was enough people that liked the same kind of stuff. It was stuff like 'Roll 'Em Pete', Chuck Berry material, Bo Diddley material, Sam Cooke, Ray Charles, 'Night Time is the Right Time', that kind of stuff. Very jazz-influenced, blues-R&B. If we played rock'n'roll it was Fats Domino or Little Richard rather than Elvis Presley or [Eddie Cochran]. We were playing the black end. I think what it was, the fans who used to dance to jazz became the kind of people who got into rock'n'roll but still had that jazz direction. Young kids came along, a few years earlier if they'd been that age they would have tended towards jazz but just as they were becoming fifteen or sixteen there was this music put in front of them and they went: 'Whoo! This is where we wanna be, we don't want Cliff Richard.' They didn't want The Shadows — you wanted Ray Charles. There's always that stream of kids who won't go in that pop direction. They want a bit more meat to it." "There was some kind of purity," Hilton Valentine remembers. "The kind of stuff we were doing at the time was not in the charts. Most people didn't really know who Jimmy Reed or John Lee Hooker were. They knew about Bo Diddley and Chuck Berry 'cause they had hit records. But that's what became popular. That's why we were playing in front of beatniks and arty students. The rest of the bands up here, including The Wild Cats, were playing the stuff that was in the charts. I came into The Animals and this was all new to me: I'd never heard of Jimmy Reed or John Lee Hooker." However, Valentine emphasises that the Combo were not utterly purist. "It wasn't so much the blues, it was rhythm'n'blues that The Animals were about. That takes it up from just 12-bar blues into a much more exciting kind of

music. It was very, very close to rock'n'roll. That's what we were:
an out-and-out, rock and blues/roll band! It's a very fine line.
Chuck Berry isn't rhythm'n'blues — that's rock'n'roll. The difference between rhythm'n'blues and rock'n'roll? First of all, it
was very unusual to hear a white man singing rhythm'n'blues but
there were white men singing rock'n'roll. Then you had Elvis who
was taking stuff from country-western *and* blues, so it was just a
big melting pot under the name rock'n'roll. Bill Haley — there
isn't any touch of rhythm'n'blues in that: *totally* country-western."

Barry Preston, the drummer Steel replaced in the Combo,
went on to take over the drummer's stool in The Gamblers,
an ensemble who became Billy Fury's backing band. That The
Gamblers' other members were Blackie Sanderson and Jimmy
Crawford, the fellow students who had been party to Steel and
Burdon's first musical fumblings in the common room back in
art school, gives an indication of the incestuousness of the Newcastle music scene at the time. This incestuousness — born out
of a much smaller population than a city like London — helps
explain why Burdon and Price were prepared to work with Alan
Price after his previous discourteous defection from the Kansas
City Five. "Whether or not you liked him it didn't really matter to
us," says Steel. "We could live with that as long as he played good
piano. We were pretty ruthless about things like that." However,
Steel does add this qualifier about their antipathy toward Price:
"We weren't exactly enemies with the guy, we weren't just best
buddies sort of thing. We used to socialise as well. I mean, I've
slept in the same bed with Alan Price." Oh? "When he missed his
last bus home, he would come over to my place. You didn't think
of things like that. We didn't know what homosexuals were then.
If you were stuck for a bed for a night you just piled in." Considering the difficulties (including the loss of vast sums of money)
that would arise for Burdon and Steel — as well as Chandler
and Valentine — from their professional association with Price,
it could be suggested that the two might have been better off
taking the Kansas City Five incident as a warning. There again,
it could also be that without Price they would never have enjoyed
the commercial success they did. In possessing arguably the finest

singer of his generation in Eric Burdon, the Combo/Animals were lucky indeed. In having both Burdon *and* Alan Price they were truly blessed.

Alan Price built his reputation as one of rock's greatest ever keyboardists on an instrument obtained for convenience, not sonic quality, and which at least one of his colleagues has serious misgivings about. Price was still playing club pianos as late as 1962. Sometime during that year, he purchased a Vox Continental electric organ. Valentine: "Alan primarily is a piano player. He always has been. In them days if you wanted to play piano in a band, you had to have a few people with you and a van to carry an upright piano with you. When the Vox Continental came out, you didn't have the problem of miking it up, you would go straight into an amplifier." Burdon says, "I hated the sound of the fucking Vox. I hated it. That's where Pricey and I parted, musically, when he bought that frigging Vox. It's just the chintziest, wheeziest sound. It's due to the records our ears became tuned to it and it became a very affectionate sound signal to a lot of people but I never liked it at all. I wanted Pricey to stay on piano. It was out of convenience that the Vox organ became a part of The Animals' musical line-up."

Yet the sleek electric organ playing which gave the original Animals a signature sound was not just remarkable for the technical brilliance that one would expect of a musician of Price's prowess, but for the fact that it was unique: nobody in the world played organ with the blurred-fingered style of Price. The piano is an instrument whose keys have to be struck in quick succession to sustain continuous sound. The electric organ is an instrument which only requires the placement of a finger on a key to generate uninterrupted sound. By the time Price switched instruments, his style had been set in concrete. He proceeded to play the Vox as if it was a piano, striking the keys instead of pressing them, thus creating an intriguing and singular little twig on the tree of music.

With regard to the balance of the band in terms of characters, Steel says, "We were all fairly strong personalities in the sense that everybody had opinions but obviously some people tend to be drivers and other people go along for the ride. Myself, I'm a drummer and I'm quite happy to sit and watch what's going on, but at the same time, I put my two penn'orth in if I felt somebody was out of order or whatever. Chas was a very strong personality. He was a trade union shop steward in Parsons factory before he finally burnt his boats, so that will give you a little bit of an idea of Chas. Alan was a civil service/taxman-type. Desk bound job. Eric was a flaky romantic would-be artist-cum-singer. Colourful sort of bloke. Hilton was a bit of a naïve, simple sort of guy in a way that everything was exciting to him. In a pretty unsophisticated way he just hurled himself into it, shook his head around and loved doing it. He didn't carry an awful lot of weight early on in the sense of what made the band tick." And the other, far more important, alchemy? "The chemistry as far as the performances and the music, it was ideal," says Hilton Valentine. It needed to be, for eight days after the new line-up played together for the first time, they were involved in their first recording session.

chapter two

It was clear from the very beginning that the new line-up of The Alan Price Rhythm and Blues Combo had the makings of a great band. So clear that the disc they cut just over a week after playing their first gig was a thoroughly enjoyable listening experience, and remains so to this day. Steel says, "Again, it was Eric driving us: 'We gotta get in and make a record.' 'Cause he was really into the story of Elvis Presley and Memphis and Sun studios. He lived that kind of world. He read avidly about that kind of stuff. It was always Eric who was driving the band in the direction he wanted to go in. So we found ourselves in the studio to knock up a few tracks. By that time Mike [Jeffery] was our main employer, apart from the one gig at the Victoria. I can't remember precisely whether he paid for the session or not. I think he organized it. He wasn't our actual manager at that time but he was our employer basically, so he might have paid for it. I haven't even got a copy myself."

The recording took place on Sunday September 15 1963. The official title of the four-track EP the session produced is *I Just Wanna Make Love To You* but it is commonly referred to as the "Graphic Sound EP" after the studio where it was recorded. (Contrary to some reports, it wasn't recorded at Mortonsound studio — that was where The Wild Cats had recorded their record and The Kon-tors a demo.) The disc was pressed as a one-sided 12-inch record rather than the more logical double-sided seven-inch. Jeffery even gave it a catalogue number: ALO 10867. "It certainly captured what The Animals were about," says Valentine. If the EP is a superb representation of the sound the crowds at places like the Club A'Gogo were hearing at the time, it is simply because the band used the same techniques in their debut recording session as they did on stage. Steel: "It was just the way we played. It was all one-take mono stuff. There was no double tracking or anything. You just sat in the studio and played your live set. There was no attempt to try and change the music. Fortunately the guy who recorded us had more of an idea what to do than anybody else in Newcastle at the time. Phil Woods. He owned the studio, he did everything. It was a one-man business." Woods was quite a local character: "He was the first gay guy we ever knew," says Steel. "He had a gimpy leg as well and drove quite a big Citroën." Such was the extent that the EP froze in time the band at a particular point in their development that on a couple of tracks the strains of a melodica (sounding remarkably like a harmonica) can be heard. This was an instrument that no longer figured as part of the band's sound by the time they signed a proper recording contract. "It was a peculiar little thing that you blew down but it had a keyboard," Steel remembers, "and that was Pricey. John Walters played one of those as well. I can't remember whether Pricey pinched it from John Walters or vice versa. It was a sort of white cream plastic device, about a foot long and on one end you had a mouthpiece that you just blew into and down the right hand side there was a short keyboard, maybe one or two octaves or an octave-and-a-half. Black-and-white keys. We used to use it in numbers like 'Pretty Thing'. We used it on a few numbers during the live set, just experimenting with it. It was just another thing to try."

The greatest irony of the original Animals' career is that for all their subsequent commercial and artistic success, they may well have peaked on this record, at least in terms of achieving a sound they considered true to their nature. The band's ambitions for the session were more practical than artistic. They were recording a demo for the purpose of playing to people who might be able to get them performing work in London, becoming known in which was essential to attracting the attention of record labels. Additionally, it was hoped that their loyal Newcastle following would purchase copies. The latter ambition was certainly realised. "We sold it round the club," says Steel. The pressing (500, possibly more) was a sell-out, the band unknowingly pre-figuring the tactics and philosophy of indie labels by some fifteen years. (The EP clearly had a second pressing, as copies have turned up bearing the credit "The Animals", a name they didn't acquire until further on into that year.) Whether the EP got them work in London is a matter of dispute but for an artefact born out of such functional intentions, the Graphic Sound EP was, aesthetically, a quite incongruously grand achievement. Many of The Animals' professional recordings by the mighty EMI (including versions of songs here) sound rather stiff compared to these four galvanising shots of rhythm'n'blues. The record opens with 'I Just Wanna Make Love To You'. The Animals' version of the Willie Dixon classic written for Muddy Waters is classier and sultrier than the rendition to be heard on The Rolling Stones' first album. Whereas Mick and the boys go for metallic punchiness, the Tynesiders exhibit more of a swing. Price is on piano rather than organ. One of The Animals' favourite artists, as least as far as covering his songs goes, was John Lee Hooker, the so-called King of the Boogie, whose guitar sound is considered the dirtiest on record until The Kinks' 'You Really Got Me' appeared. The Animals would make several recordings of Hooker's 'Boom Boom' over the years, the first of which is the EP's next track. On it, the band ensure that the EP has an overall variety of tone by using a guitar break instead of a keyboard solo. Burdon's vocal is impressively phlegmy. The subsequent 'Big Boss Man' is a Jimmy Reed number which laments the aggravations of unskilled labour and the petty humiliations of proletarian life. More sonic variety is provided by Price's melodica. The EP's stand-out track is the closing 'Pretty Thing', written by Bo Diddley. It contains the chunka-chunka rhythm that was a feature of so many other Bo Diddley songs, played by the Combo with an emphaticness that packs a real punch. Most impressive feature of the track is some lovely melodica. The latter here sounds very much like a harmonica but the imaginativeness of Price's playing deftly sidesteps the echoey, wailing mouth harp clichés to be heard on so many R&B records of the era.

Things moved astonishingly fast for the Combo in their first few weeks of existence. That very month (Thursday September

19 — Steel's diaries), the band auditioned for BBC radio at a Leeds studio. The audition tape would be transmitted on the show *Saturday Club*. Although Steel's diaries don't reveal a date for this broadcast, some sources state it as being December 27 the same year. (The band each received a cheque for £10 as payment for the broadcast the following January, a tidy sum in those days.) "In between September and December of '63, we just became the hottest thing in Newcastle," says Steel. "Everywhere we played was absolutely jammed. It was in that period that we discovered that we had an audience and it was like, 'Wow.' Those Saturday night sessions at the Downbeat and the A'Gogo were absolutely *steaming*. We'd do two or three or hours at the A'Gogo, then go down and play at the Downbeat from midnight 'til three in the morning. We were absolutely drenched but it was such a buzz. The audience were absolutely great." Valentine agrees: "I don't think there was really any competition, not with the kind of stuff we were doing. There were other bands doing that kind of stuff but I don't think they were in the same league."

Chas Chandler was convinced that the Graphic Sound EP secured the band the ten days' work they fulfilled in the capital at the end of 1963, "…ten days in London that turned into over twenty years." John Steel disagrees, pointing to the importance of an unconnected visit to Newcastle by Graham Bond. "I don't think that EP ever got any further than Newcastle at the time," he says. "My memory is it was Graham Bond who talked to people and we had the great visit from the big city." A saxophonist and keyboard player, Bond had been one of the founding fathers of the British R&B scene and was responsible for bringing on several future superstar musicians such as Ginger Baker, Jack Bruce and John McLauhglin. Tragically, he died under the wheels of a train in 1974, probably through suicide. Steel says, "The big turning point was by this time the A'Gogo had a policy of putting on some really good R&B. We backed Sonny Boy Williamson and John Lee Hooker and stuff like that and also the visiting band. One of the bands was the Graham Bond Organisation, which was Graham, Jack Bruce, Ginger Baker and Dick Heckstall-Smith. Great band, you can imagine, but he loved our band. So we were playing in the Young Set when he was playing and then we'd come through and play the interval spot in the Jazz Lounge. He got up and started jamming with us, playing alto. Graham was a good sax player. There was one night where he was playing within a reasonable distance and he actually came to the club, pulled his Hammond in — his fucking big Hammond organ! — just to come and jam with us. Graham went back to London and talked to somebody. Next thing, there was somebody from London — The Smoke! — in the club checking us out. It was one of Ronan O'Rahilly's people from the Scene Club talking to Mike Jeffries, and next thing we knew Mike's got a contract for us to sign for him to be our manager. We thought, 'Ooh!' He said, 'We're gonna go someplace with this.' We thought, 'Right.' So we signed this — we'd sign anything then, absolutely green as grass.

"By this time, that summer we'd seen The Rolling Stones playing support to Bo Diddley at the Odeon in Newcastle. Here was this band — same kind of guys as us — on stage, at the Odeon cinema! Capacity of three-and-a-half thousand, something like that. It was Bo Diddley, the Everly Brothers and the last spot before the interval was The Rolling Stones. They came round to the A'Gogo afterwards. They seemed to like us. I remember seeing Brian Jones dancing about on the floor in front of the bandstand. They'd just put out 'I Wanna Be Your Man'. That was what they were promoting on the tour. Eric had gone down to Alexis Korner's club to check that out. He'd heard the story, read it in *Melody Maker*, *NME*. He'd made the pilgrimage. So we knew something was going on, Eric more than anybody else, and Mike suddenly began to realise that something was going on as well… Things were starting to really happen. All of a sudden groups like us were in the charts. It was a sort of 'Fuck me!' moment. 'Maybe there's more to this than playing a load of gigs.'" Were any of the Combo thinking of music as a long-term career at this point? "I would think Eric," says Steel. "Eric left art school and his idea of a career was to someday be a singer. By this time I was fully committed because I'd been a professional musician for a year or so before this band but I wasn't particularly imagining being a pop star or anything like that. This was what I was doing and I would go wherever it took me. Chas was probably realising the potential. He was such a big Beatles fan, he knew the history. Chas realised about that time this is more than just a part time job [or] pastime. Things were beginning to dawn on us gradually, but basically we were just driving along with all that youthful enthusiasm and ignorance."

Mike Jeffery went to the capital to see about furthering the career of his charges. Steel recalls what transpired on his return. Steel: "He said, 'Right, we've got a thing set up. There's a band called The Yardbirds who've taken over from The Rolling Stones doing a lot of gigs, Ricky Tik, Eel Pie Island, stuff like this. I've been talking to this guy called Giorgio Gomelsky and also this guy Ronan O'Rahilly. Ronan O'Rahilly's got a club called the Scene Club which is just off Piccadilly and that's where we're gonna be playing late night and we're gonna be doing all these Rolling Stones gigs. The Yardbird gigs early in the evening.' He set it all up. The deal was he'd take The Yardbirds and put them in all our gigs. So right up to practically the day before Christmas, we had these ten or so days lined up where we'd play these small clubs, pubby-type gigs in the early part of the night, eight o'clock to ten, ten-thirty, and we'd zoom into London down to the Scene Club and start there about midnight 'til two in the morning. And he said, 'Oh, and by the way, the name's been changed. You're now The Animals.' And everybody went, 'What!'"

In the July/August 1964 edition of the EMI house journal *EMI News*, Alan Price is quoted as saying of the name The Animals, "How it began we never could find out. Maybe it was because we looked the part in those days. We couldn't afford smart mohair suits…" Burdon offered, "The name was probably an association with the kind of music we play." However, the latter idea that the band were given the name — to their surprise — by fans galvanized by their gutsiness and wild stage antics, repeated endlessly in press and biogs since, would seem to have been an invention by the marketing men. Unfortunately, there is disagreement amongst the band members as to the genuine origin of the name. Burdon maintains that the band sat down in a pub and agreed to give themselves the name "The Animals" after a local character whose untamed and hedonistic attitudes summarised what they wanted to put across with their music. "Animal Hogg was a member of a gang, The Squatters, who we used to hang out with," he says. "He was the oldest and most revered member of the group and had seen action in Cyprus with the British Army and he had his mind blown by that experience. He lived out on the road along with his dog who he used for body heat on cold nights. He just used to sleep in a sleeping bag and I thought he was quite a character and he became the basis for the name of the band. That's the way I remember it but nobody else remembers it that way." Indeed. John Steel says, "That was a bullshit thing. That was the story that was made up for the Maureen Cleave interview when we had our first interviews when things started to happen in the charts. It was Graham Bond suggested the name. He said, 'You can't have these guys called the Alan Price Rhythm and Blues Combo. Christ — what a mouthful.' Which was eminently sensible. He had suggested that name and Mike came back from London and said, 'How about that then?'" So why the alternate versions of the source of the name? Steel: "Eric always had a phenomenally weird way of remembering things. You'd meet Eric and the guys in a pub before a gig and he'd say, 'I've just seen this fantastic movie…' And he'd tell you this whole story and you'd go to see the movie and Eric's version of it was so distorted and exaggerated. If he felt that something should have been done differently, he would just include that in his memory of it. If the guy was shot and fell down and didn't splurt blood all over the place, Eric would put that in because that's what should have happened. He was seeing Sam Peckinpah movies before it was ever allowed in his mind. I think Eric just preferred that story to the reality. We came up with this story for Maureen Cleave initially and then it became part of the legend. If he could make it more interesting by telling a few porkies, he will. He likes a good story, bless him. He's harmless. He's the kind of guy who'd probably defend to the death that it was fact now 'cause he believes it himself. It's part of his character. Take everything he says with a pinch of salt. And he's got a terrible memory anyway. The reason I can remember most of this stuff is because I actually jotted things down in little diaries. I've actually got dates and things. It's amazing how a simple little entry like 'Played the Ricky Tik, got thirty bob for it' is a good little memory-jogger." Zoot Money concurs about Burdon's memory. "If anybody's got the right to forget the Sixties, Eric has," he says. "But in his case it sort of continued into the Seventies and the Eighties. He loves to story-tell and he doesn't necessarily remember it the way it was. He constantly phones me about things, asking me what happened in Australia when we were down there. I've never been to Australia. It's Danny McCulloch he means. But that is all part and parcel of knowing Eric and loving him for the fool he is." On the same theme, Steel describes Burdon's autobiography *I Used To Be An Animal* as fiction. Burdon offers, "I have a photographic memory. Not for names and dates but for colours and faces and actions and reactions."

Following the band's initial shock at the Combo's new name, they started to like the idea. Steel recalls, "Chas immediately said, 'Well right, fair enough: The Beatles, The Animals, whatever.' Eric and me thought it was great. It sounded at the time outrageous." There was one dissenting voice, though — that of the man whose name would no longer be in the group title. "I remember Alan Price wasn't happy about the fact," says Valentine.

Though he may not have provided the band's name, Jackie 'Animal' Hogg was a real person and for a time a fixture in the band's collective life. Steel: "Animal used to go off into one of the little villages with a sleeping bag on a weekend and tear up the place. [The Squatters] were a pretty wild bunch. We were kittens compared to them. They were what nowadays would be Hell's Angels but they didn't have motorbikes. We used to go along as almost groupies to them. They loved us because Alan could get on the pub piano and Eric would sing and I'm on tabletops and stuff…" Burdon says of Animal Hogg, "I've no idea what's happened to him. Probably still in his sleeping bag covered in snow on the outskirts of Hexham with a new dog." (One Jacqui Lamb posted a message on *http://ericburdon.ning.com* in 2009 stating, "My dad who I must say drowned before I was born was Animal Hogg.")

The visit to the capital in December '63 was an occasion of no little excitement for the band. "It was a childhood dream for me to actually get out on the road" says Valentine. "Everything suddenly started to happen so fast," says Steel. "One minute we're the hot band in Newcastle, next minute we're down playing all these London venues. These were days when London was a different country, almost. There was a different culture, a different lifestyle. All things were new. [We said to] the girl at the Scene Club, 'Oh, we'd love to play The Cavern…' And she picked up the phone and phoned The Cavern. We thought, 'Fucking 'ell, it's amazing!' And she got us in. So we zoomed off and did that. It was astonishing. We just couldn't believe it was happening. Suddenly everything seemed possible." Of the audiences they played to down south, Valentine says, "I don't think they were that different except there were the mods. We were playing the places where the Manfreds were playing, The Yardbirds, Stones, Georgie Fame, and them audiences were mod-type people. Purple heart pill pushers. The mod situation wasn't happening in Newcastle at the time, only seemed to be happening in London. But we found them great audiences, very enthusiastic."

Following The Animals' return to the North-East, they naturally resumed playing the local venues. On December 30 1963, the band played two sets at the Club A'Gogo, one in the afternoon, the other in the evening. The evening session was divided between supporting legendary visiting bluesman Sonny Boy Williamson II and playing their own set. Both performances were taped by Giorgio Gomelsky, who was, like Bond and O'Rahilly, a pivotal figure in the early-Sixties British blues scene. Gomelsky had neglected to bring a tape recorder with him but borrowed one from Philip Woods, owner of the Graphic Sound studio. He proceeded to capture on the Ampex temporarily in his possession a superb and invaluable snapshot of The Animals' pre-recording contract stage act. Without this tape (which wasn't to be released on record until several years later), posterity would have lost the fact of just how raw and exciting the band were outside of a studio. This recording manages to both constitute a worthwhile listening experience and capture the atmosphere of a gig in a small club:

most live recordings do one or the other but rarely both. "Again it was representative of what we were doing at the time," says Valentine. The most striking thing about these performances is the suggestion that Hilton Valentine was a more important part of the band's stage sound than the records The Animals later made would suggest. Whereas on disc Price's organ was the most noticeable part of The Animals' sonic landscape, here Price is matched and often overshadowed by Valentine's mellifluous and raucous playing. (For his part, Valentine says, "I always thought the keyboards was quite a dominant part of the sound.") Meanwhile, Burdon's wild vocal improvisations and extemporisations are things that could not be replicated in sessions designed to produce recordings of a certain structure and length. Gomelsky eventually licensed the tapes to the French-based BYG label which split the recordings between those featuring Williamson and those not and released them as *Faces and Places* Vol. 1 and 2 in the early Seventies. American labels Wand and Springboard did something similar not long afterwards but it wasn't until 1976 that any of the recordings were issued by a British label. These performances have been endlessly repackaged and re-licensed down the years, with some of the records/CDs on which they have ended up shockingly sloppy in either content (arbitrarily dropping tracks) or presentation (passing off the recordings as rare when they are anything but and offering no explanatory sleevenotes) or both. For the purposes of this book, the British Charly CD *The Animals With Sonny Boy Williamson* has been chosen as the definitive collection of the pertinent performances: not only does it round up all the tracks from that evening (including ones Burdon doesn't sing on: most leave those out) but it boasts informative sleeve notes from John Platt.

'Sonny's Slow Walk', 'Pontiac Blues', 'My Babe'. 'I'm Gonna Put You Down' and 'Fattening Frogs for Snakes' are songs sung by Sonny Boy Williamson with musical backing by The Animals. 'I Don't Care No More' and 'Baby Don't You Worry' are Williamson solo performances. 'Night Time is the Right Time' is a duet between Burdon and Williamson of a Roosevelt Sykes song which would also feature (as 'The Right Time') on the first

Animals studio LP. Burdon's impassioned vocal outshines that of the older man, although it should be acknowledged that if Burdon had had only one tooth his singing might be just as impenetrable as Williamson's. The following 'Nobody but You' is actually Ray Charles' 'Talkin' 'Bout You', here credited to one "W. Spriggs." It's another Burdon-Williamson duet, this one to the backing of stomping, rabble-rousing percussion that puts one in mind of Slade, the band The Animals' bassist would one day manage. The farewell to the (temporarily) departing Williamson of 'Bye Bye Sonny Bye Bye' features some cranked-up, static-raising guitar from Valentine. The spoken-word tribute to Sonny Boy from Burdon must have been as impenetrable to Williamson in its dense Geordie as Williamson's singing had been to the Tyneside crowd. This segues into 'Coda', which is supposedly a separate track but which seems to have been divided up on CD/record to provide a publishing royalty for "H. Young." The Animals' own set starts with a rip-roaring version of 'Let It Rock'. This thundering complaint of a railway worker hankering for pay day and leisure time is almost certainly Chuck Berry's greatest song but paradoxically was originally published under the pseudonym "E. Anderson," something which is possibly responsible for the surprisingly few cover versions of the number by British R&B bands who flogged everything else in the Berry catalogue to death. The Animals' version is stunning, particularly the piercing guitar work, and makes one wish they had made a studio recording of it rather than of over-familiar Berry numbers like 'Sweet Little Sixteen' and 'Memphis, Tennessee'. The following 'Gotta Find My Baby' is another Berry number. It's an excellent collective performance, especially the interplay between guitar and organ. Burdon's vocal makes it sound as though he's polished his throat with sandpaper. If one thinks about it too much, the entire concept of doing a version of Diddley's eponymous, vainglorious anthem is ridiculous (would Bo Diddley have done a cover of 'Eric's Blues', if Burdon had ever written such a thing?) but The Animals' version of 'Bo Diddley' is no less delightful for that fact. Price starts out playing the chunka-chunka rhythm in tandem with Valentine, then during the instrumental break abandons the guitarist as he sets off into the stratosphere. Burdon rouses the crowd by getting them to participate in call-and-response routines, then engages Price in similar activity: making bizarre noises with lips and throat and daring Price to try to imitate them on his keyboard. Price turns out to be game. 'Almost Grown' is another number from the prolific pen of Berry. The backing vocals of the band are surprisingly dulcet on this exploration of the transitional period between playground and matrimony. The lecherous 'Dimples' is a John Lee Hooker number that would be revisited by the group on their debut album, its most notable feature here the crawling king snake guitar copped from the song's author. 'Boom Boom' is the second and best of four recordings The Animals would make of this Hooker song. That it has the same riff as 'Dimples' is more than made up for by sublime playing by Valentine in the instrumental passages, him alternating between skilful picking and powerhouse riffing, all done at high speed. During the track, Burdon pays another tribute to Williamson. The bluesman's reaction to Burdon's invitation to "climb upon my knee" can only be wondered at. Burdon's and Steel's jazz roots are showing in the closing 'C Jam Blues', a Duke Ellington song whose authorship is credited on some releases of this material to "The Animals". Sonny Boy Williamson plays drums and doesn't do too badly for someone who's clearly as pissed as a fart.

Burdon says of the night of the recording, "It was a great experience at the time but I might add that Giorgio Gomelsky has never paid us a fucking dime for those recordings and still continues to evade paying any sort of royalties. Last time I saw him, I met him in a club in New York and I asked him why he hadn't paid any royalties and he just smiled like an idiot and we had to call the New York City Police Department and we had him thrown out of the gig. So fuck him and the horse he rode in on." If true, this would make Gomelsky simply the first of many to exploit The Animals' talent and leave them with nothing to show for it.

chapter three

In January 1964, The Animals moved down to London permanently. They'd made the decision to do so during their ten-day visit the previous month. They'd already known that the capital was where they needed to be to attract the interest of record companies, so the fact that it had become obvious that they could make a living from gigs in the Smoke sealed the deal.

Some of the first gigs they performed that year, though, were in Scotland and it was during this sojurn that an attempt was made to oust Chas Chandler from the group. Chandler's hair-trigger temper and his disinterest in most R&B had rubbed the others up the wrong way too many times. Steel: "There was some friction. Chas didn't seem to be in the same direction as us musically. Nothing to do with his bass playing. His taste *and* his personality. He just seemed to be on a different wavelength to us. We talked and said, 'Can't we get somebody we can get along with better?' Everybody agreed to do the dirty deed and it was on the van in Scotland. He was stunned by this. I wouldn't say he pleaded but he wanted to talk us round. And that's when Alan did a complete about-face. He turned it round completely and said, 'Well, I don't think we should do this.' We just went: 'What!' Because he had been very supportive of the idea. So we just left it at that and didn't pursue it any further. From that point on, Alan had Chas in his pocket. They chummed up and in London they shared a house together. From then on it was Hilton and Eric and me with Chas and Alan on the other side. Two factions. I think he was being a bit manipulative. He saw a way of getting a lever on Chas by stepping in." In a way, it's a surprise that it wasn't Chandler's musicianship that led to the attempt to sack him. Burdon is on record as saying Chandler's bass playing — at least at this point in time — was "dreadful." Dave Rowberry, who worked with Chandler at a stage where it might be assumed his technique would have improved, is equally scathing about his abilities: "He wasn't a musician. I used to get his bass and tune it up before a gig and he would come onstage and say, 'Dave, give us a "G"' and I'd try and ignore him, try and pretend I was doing something else 'cause I knew the bass was perfectly in tune. He'd be plucking one string and turning the hammer on another one. By the time the curtain went up, the bass was out of tune." Valentine, however, disagrees. "I thought Chas was a good bass player," he says. "I didn't always like the sound that he got: like a *donk! donk! donk!* sound. But when it came down to playing rock'n'roll and walking bass lines, I thought he was good." Perhaps the last word on whether Chandler was a good bassist should be left to his partner in The Animals' rhythm section. Steel says, "I think Chas was a pretty decent bass player in his limited way."

The exposure given the newly-christened Animals by them playing London venues had the desired effects rather quickly. By the end of January 1964 the band had signed up to the renowned Don Arden agency for live work and to an independent record producer called Mickie Most who was intending to attempt to get them a recording contract. Steel states that signing to Arden and to Most "…seemed like a package," starting with the night — Sunday January 12, according to his diaries — Most and Arden's booker Peter Grant came together to see the band perform at the Eel Pie Island Hotel. "Mike Jeffries brought them," says Steel. "There's a bit of a myth about him [Most] coming to see us at the A'Gogo but my memory is the first time we met him was at Eel Pie Island, which would definitely stick in your mind because it was the first time we'd played these type of gigs outside of the North-East. It was a time of everything happening for the first time. Peter Grant was brought in to look at the band with an eye to putting us out on the road and Mickie Most knew Peter. So he turned up and Mike said, 'This guy's gonna record ya.' We thought, 'Great, bloody hell — recording!'"

Arden and Grant were known as music industry figures who could Make Things Happen, something underlined by the phenomenal success they would later achieve as managers of the Small Faces and Led Zeppelin respectively. During the band's first meeting with Arden, he made their wildest fantasies come true at a stroke. Steel recalls: "Mike took us up to this big plush office in Mayfair. He was a real West End, showbiz agent-type guy: little stocky, good-looking, hyper Jewish guy. We sat down in this big office with this big hardwood desk. Don Arden's got this cigar and a mohair suit and says, 'I've got Chuck Berry coming over on tour.' Chuck Berry was a *god* to us, an absolute god. And he says, 'He's gonna tour the UK for the first time. It's a three-week tour and I've got the Nashville Teens signed, Carl Perkins as well — and you're gonna be second.' We thought this was tremendous. He says we're gonna be playing…He started reeling off these dates. And Hilton whips out his little gig diary and says, 'Hang on a minute!' and kneels on the floor and puts his diary on Don Arden's desk and says, 'What are those dates again?' So uncool!"

Of course, the ultimate objective of any band was to secure a recording contract. Following their acclaim in first Newcastle and now London, were The Animals confident of realising that objective? "You thought, 'Well why not?'" says Steel. "Seeing as The Beatles had done it and now the Stones have done it. We weren't particularly confident but by this time we had something that people were excited by. 'It could happen to us too.' But it wasn't a masterplan." "We never really thought about it" says Valentine. "We were playing in Newcastle, enjoying our music. Wanting to get out, take the music further and go to London — but we weren't thinking of being in the hit parade or anything like that. It just seemed to happen: click, click, click, click. You didn't have time to think about it."

That Mickie Most was planning to take The Animals into a studio wasn't quite the same thing as being told that they had a recording contract. Mickie Most had persuaded Jeffery that he could get the coveted deal for him by recording the band first and then selling the distribution rights to the result. Most (born Michael Hayes in June 1938 in Aldershot) had started out as a recording artist and had had phenomenal success in South

Africa, where he'd gone to live because of his South African girlfriend in late 1958. It was while recording in that country (where he had eleven consecutive number ones, mainly covers of standards like 'Rave On') that he decided to be a producer, although 'producer' in his case seemed to mean little more than 'hit-maker'. He had no pretensions of fulfilling a Phil Spector auteur role. Steel: "Mickie had had this idea — brilliant when you think about it but at the time it was just another new thing to happen — of recording a band and then taking the completed tape to a major label rather than us go to a major label and then do all the stuff. He was the first independent producer." Though time has spectacularly proven Most's concept to be visionary, did the band not worry at the time about the fact that he was a nobody and his idea untested? "The thing is, we didn't really know anything," says Valentine.

There has often been confusion about when The Animals' first recording session with Most took place and what precisely was recorded. This confusion has only been added to by the release in 1990 of a double CD called *The Complete Animals* which attempted to round up everything the Tynesiders laid down under Most's aegis. It contained liner notes that cited a session on January 22 1964 which produced recordings of 'Boom Boom', 'Talkin' 'Bout You', 'Blue Feeling' and 'Dimples'. Only three weeks later at a far more successful session, according to the liner notes, was their first single recorded — along with 'The House of the Rising Sun'. But Valentine avers, "When we first went in the studio with him he had this record, 'Baby Let Me Take You Home', which he gave to us in consideration for playing and we played it. That's all I can remember. I can't remember any other session before that." John Steel's diaries favour Valentine's recollection. His entry for Wednesday February 12 1964 states that the band made their first Mickie Most-produced recording session that evening and laid down 'Baby Let Me Take You Home' and 'Gonna Send You Back To Walker', the A- and B-side respectively of their first single.

Confusion also surrounds the source of the song on the A-side of that first 'proper' Animals record. Some say it's a version of a blues song called 'Baby Don't You Tear My Clothes'. Mickie Most claimed that he discovered the song on a single he picked up at Chess Records in Chicago, possibly a Rufus Thomas release. The majority of sources claim that the band took their cue from Bob Dylan, whose debut LP featured a variation he called 'Baby Let Me Follow You Down'. Chas Chandler insisted that it was on a Josh White album that The Animals first came across this public domain number. However, Valentine recalls quite vividly the track Most played the band: "'Baby Let Me Hold Your Hand' by a guy called Hoagy Lands." "We went in a studio called De Lane Lea," says Steel. "I think Mike paid for it, but it was pennies. It was only a mono studio. We just went in and recorded exactly as we had done the EP. Just set up, played live. We knew the song from Bob Dylan's first album. [Mickie] had picked up a 45 in the States or somewhere and it was a sort of black pop version of it. We recognised it from the Dylan version on the first album so that was okay by us 'cause we loved that album."

There would later be much rancour about Most's commercialism: Burdon and Chandler particularly came to resent what they felt to be the producer's inability to understand their music and his relentless pursuit of high chart figures, but Valentine claims, "When we started recording with Mickie Most it was discussed that he would pick the songs, because for singles we had to try to be a bit more commercial, but we could do what we wanted on album tracks. It was stated. I didn't have any gripes about doing 'Baby Let Me Take You Home'. Maybe some of the other guys did." In any event, the band did their own thing with the song. "It's nothing much like the version that Mickie had played to us," Steel says. "We just grafted and kicked it around ourselves and that's what came out."

Once having supervised the laying down of two satisfactory tracks, Most's task was now to persuade a record company that they were a commercial proposition. He didn't seem to have much trouble on that score. "I think he just went straight to EMI," says Steel. "EMI was the hottest company in the country, if not the world, by that time because they had The Beatles. Mickie just got this deal, which is a ballsy thing to do really." Most's negotiations with EMI for records to be released on their Columbia label (not to be confused with what was for many years the US version of the CBS label) were not so impressive, at least from the group's perspective. Valentine reveals, "The deal that he did with Columbia was for six per cent: two to him, two to Mike Jeffries and two split between us [The Animals]." At the time, naturally, the band were not going to worry about how the pie was divided. They were simply ecstatic to know that they would be releasing a record, which duly appeared in the UK on March 27 1964. It had been trailed by press interviews at EMI's offices in London's Manchester Square beginning on Wednesday March 11 and TV appearances on the BBC's *Top Of The Pops* (Thursday March 19) and ITV's *Ready Steady Go!* (Friday the 20th), all these dates recorded by the meticulous Steel.

The record made for a fine entrée. Valentine's guitar rings clear and true on the song that The Animals re-named 'Baby Let Me Take You Home' (Russell/Farrell). The propulsive rhythm, meanwhile, is truly galvanizing (especially as it jumps into double time at the end) and Eric Burdon starts his recording career as he means to continue with bellowed vocals that leave no doubt about the depths of his passion for the girl to whom the song is addressed. The B-side also sees The Animals tweaking with a title. A cover of 'Gonna Send You Back to Georgia' by Timmy Shaw (written by Matthews/Hammond Jnr.), the band substitute the Newcastle district of Walker where Eric Burdon grew up for that better known southern American state in this depiction of a man disgruntled with the airs and graces of a woman who's had her head turned by the big city. It's a fine punchy number, deftly arranged, with some velvet-throated backing chants. The single reached a respectable number 21 in the charts.

May 9 saw the start of the package tour on which The Animals supported the legend whose songs had long studded their stage sets. The first of 21 gigs in 21 days was at the Finsbury Park Astoria. Of Chuck Berry, Steel says, "He was a very hard guy to get to know, very prickly sort of a fella, but we all got on well with him. We loved him. We were fans. He didn't speak too much to anybody. Very withdrawn. Kind of reserved and dignified and a little bit intimidating. You didn't just go up to him and chat to him. But if you did, you found that he wasn't completely aloof. But you never felt really comfortable with him." He adds, "Carl Perkins was a beautiful fella, lovely guy. We had a marvellous time. We were playing for the first time two- or three-thousand venues, seated audience."

The format of the package tour — then standard, now absolutely obsolete — involved multiple acts performing short individual sets and the headliner closing the show with a longer performance. The Animals decided to use the tour to try an experiment. "We knew that if we were gonna stand out we had to do something dramatically different," says Steel. "That was why we were working on 'House of the Rising Sun'. And the reaction we were getting from that song!" Valentine: "We thought it would be a good number to put in the Chuck Berry tour because everybody was playing rock'n'roll so we thought this would be a good number to do different. Judging by the reaction we got from doing it, this would be a good thing to record." Steel: "We loved the song. We loved that first [Dylan] album. 'House of the Rising Sun' was to us the outstanding track from that album and that's where we got it from." And the common belief that it came from Josh White? "Again, that was another fairytale from Eric... Even though Bob Dylan was really fresh and new then... we'd much prefer it to be thought that we were delving into some really obscure stuff." Valentine agrees. Dylan's rendition of this public domain song was, "The first version I heard — Eric was aware of the song before that — and basically it was the Bob Dylan version that we took the chord sequence from. He strummed it — it was only him, guitar and harmonica." Valentine decided to use arpeggios rather than strummed figures. It was a crucial decision, for those relentlessly repeated arpeggios gave a tranquil, winding feel to the arrangement that was ultimately hypnotic. So simultaneously arresting and simple are they that they have become a staple of instruction manuals for beginners on guitar. "I don't know why," Valentine says of his decision. "I just started doing it and it seemed to work. Nobody was aware in them days that it was going to be such a huge hit and still last

and encouraged a lot of guitar players to start playing the guitar."
"We were rehearsing it at the Club A'Gogo before we went on the
road with it," says Steel, "and Alan absolutely detested Hilton's
idea of that guitar. I don't think anybody else had heard it other
than Bob Dylan's version which was purely acoustic and, because
of that, that's the way Alan wanted to play it, with acoustic guitar,
strumming." Of the arpeggios ("Absolutely Hilton's idea"), Steel
recalls, "We were a hundred per cent in agreement with him
except Alan. And Alan stormed off in a huff because we said,
'No, no, no, that's the way it's gonna be, it's gotta be that thing
that Hilton's doing because we're not doing an acoustic version
we're doing a fucking electric version' — and by the time he came
back after his sulk we had worked it out and all he had to do was
drop in that organ in the middle. And then he got the credit for
the whole thing! It was the way it was on record by the time we
took it on tour. The reaction blew a few minds. We could tell.
We could sense it coming back. 'We've got something here.' It
was dramatic." Ironically, Price's organ work on the single was
stunning. "Oh, absolutely," Steel concedes. "I wouldn't take that
away from him. It was brilliant. But Hilton's guitar thing made
it. Practically everybody in the world who's picked up the guitar
for the first time started on that." If Valentine deserves the credit
for most of the musical power, Burdon deserves credit for his own
piece of modification, one which ensured that the song actually
got played on the radio. In his hands, the lyric was transformed
from a tale of a prostitute into a song about a gambling den.
Although it must be assumed there were also practical aesthetic
reasons behind this (Burdon convincing as a hooker?), there was
also anxiety over a possible ban. Steel: "To make it a record or
to get across anybody at the time, you couldn't go singing about
a bloody brothel, not to an audience of kids, mothers, whatever.
It was the way of the time." Burdon claims that the disreputable
house in question genuinely exists and that he had the privilege
of visiting it in March 1999. "It was both legally and illegally a
bordello but it's not now," he says. "It's a piece of New Orleans
history. It's a museum. The woman who owns it is one of the
biggest attorneys in Louisiana and she owns a lot of buildings in

the French Quarter and she's got all the city papers to document that it is the real place." However, Alan Price told *Saga* magazine in 2009, "It was a song about a brothel in Soho, and it was taken in the sixteenth century across to America." He added, "It was a tune based on 'Greensleeves'."

Those problems ironed out, there was another one with which to deal. "Mickie Most didn't want us to record 'House of the Rising Sun'," says Steel. Most instead wanted the band to issue their version of Ray Charles' 'Talkin' 'Bout You' as their second record. This was quite understandable. TV pop programme *Ready Steady Go!* had decided that a version of this track by The Animals would be their new opening theme song, a quite astounding stroke of luck for the band with massive potential commercial benefits. That recording was precisely why The Animals entered a studio at this juncture. "Mickie had us going into the studio in the middle of the tour," says Steel. "Things were that crammed. We were playing every bloody night. The chance to do a thing for *Ready Steady Go!* was a big deal. Every time it come on on a Friday night, the whole of the young population of England were watching it, so that kind of exposure was great." Even so, the Animals pressed the case for 'Rising Sun'. Steel: "We said, 'Mickie, we've got to record this.' He said, 'Well, put it on the B-side.' He didn't see it at all." Steel's diaries show that Most's grudging recording of 'The House of the Rising Sun' took place in the early hours of Monday May 18 1964 following a dash to London (De Lane Lea again) from Liverpool, where the Chuck Berry tour had stopped off on the 17th. This refutes the suggestion in the *Complete Animals* liner notes that 'House' had been recorded at the same session as the first single. Also incorrect, says Steel, is another legend that the recording took place at around 8am on the 18th: "More like about 3am," he remembers. "We recorded 'House of the Rising Sun' first because we had to get the sound balance sorted out. [Most] said, 'Run through to get the balance' and we played half of it and he said, 'Okay I've got it, we'll go for a take.' So we played it. We played it once and Mickie said, 'I think that's it.' He played it back and said, 'Yep, that'll do.' One take. The whole bloody process took about ten minutes. He played it back and that was the moment when he realised it was a single. That was the first time he accepted what we were saying. *That's* when he said, 'How long is it?' And Mickie said, 'Oh what the fuck, we'll still go with it, you can't take anything out of that.' That was a tremendous decision."

The answer to Most's question about the song's length, given by engineer Dave Murphy, was four minutes and twenty-seven seconds. This would make it, if issued commercially, one of the longest singles ever released up to that point. "In the broadcast world everybody's mind was set on that length of a 78 record," Steel explains. "It was practically carved in marble that you couldn't have a song longer than three minutes and we said, 'Oh that's a problem.' But Mickie, he's gotta get points for his balls. He said, 'No, bugger it. We'll go with that.'" However, the astuteness of The Animals in realising that something so different could be so successful should also be noted and for Steel the member who they had so recently tried to get rid of deserves most of the credit. "This had a lot to do with Chas' way of thinking," he says. "His input was more calculated than ours. Eric wanted to be a success more than anything in the world but he didn't know how to do it. I just went along with anything that sounded good that I could live with quite happily. But Chas actually thought things through."

Following the session, the band went off to get some sleep before travelling down to Southampton where the Chuck Berry tour was playing the town Odeon that evening. Subsequent to this historic recording session, Most got a taste of the doubt he had displayed to The Animals when they had first suggested recording 'House'. EMI were initially not convinced that radio stations would play a record that was literally more than twice as long as a lot of other records in the charts. Most claimed he convinced them with the logic that a two-minute song can be boring and that the quality of the actual performance is what makes a record tedious, not its length. EMI conceded the point. Before the single was released, though, there was one other matter to attend to — one which is a bone of contention to this day, and a disfiguring scar on the face of The Animals' story.

It was an established custom that publishing royalties from new renditions of songs so old as to be out of copyright should be divided equally amongst all of the recording personnel. Said financial arrangement was reflected in the parenthetical information to be found beneath a song's title on the record label, with "Arr." (for arrangement) signifying this was not an original composition. Mike Jeffery, however, advised the band that the label arrangement credit should only bear one band member's name and that the one credited should subsequently divvy up the proceeds. And the identity of the person who would receive the arranger's credit? None other than Alan Price, who, according to the others, is the individual least deserving of that accolade. This, Hilton Valentine is convinced, is down to some kind of shady agreement struck beforehand between Price and Jeffery, who were friendly. He says, "Looking back on it, it must have been quite premeditated because the excuse, or the reason, given was that there wouldn't be enough room on the record to put 'Traditional: arranged by…' and put our five names on, so Mike Jeffries turned round and said, 'We've just had to put Alan's name on but it's understood that the royalties will be shared.' We should have just put, 'Traditional: arranged by The Animals'." It does seem surprising that it apparently didn't occur to anybody that something like "Arr: The Animals" would have only occupied the same amount of space on a label as "Lennon/McCartney" — a *fairly* frequent publishing credit at the time. "We were suspicious but we were stupid," says Burdon. "We trusted Alan Price and we trusted Mike Jeffries. Why, I don't know, but at the time it seemed like a good idea because he was the only guy that could get us out of Newcastle, or so we thought. You live and you learn and what seems to be so obviously stupid now, at the time it seemed like the right thing to do." Consequently, due to Price's failure to share the publishing cheques that came his way (except, possibly, with Mike Jeffery), Burdon, Valentine, Chandler and Steel never saw a penny in publishing royalties from one of the biggest-selling and most broadcast records in history. "He knows that he didn't arrange it" seethes Valentine, bitter to this day. "No matter how much he wants to try to convince himself that he did, he didn't. It was agreed verbally and understood that them royalties would be shared. That's the thing that he can't deny." If anything, Burdon is even more bitter than Valentine: "He and Jeffries had a relationship of sorts and the bottom line is that Pricey scarpered off with the proceeds to the funds forthcoming to the band collectively for the recording of 'House of the Rising Sun'. We all could have made, not a comfortable living, but we all could have had a bit of extra money over these years and it would have avoided lots of confusion. Certainly, Alan Price has no right whatsoever to claim that he wrote — as it says on the sheet music — and arranged — as it says on the records — 'House of the Rising Sun'. It was me that found it on the first Bob Dylan album. It was at my suggestion that we do it on the Chuck Berry tour. And I hope he fries in fucking hell."

At the end of May, The Animals started filming a United Artists movie called *The Swingin' UK* (aka *Go Go Big Beat*). Press reports beforehand had announced that the group would be performing three numbers in this tacky movie, whose pop-group-cameo format was common for the time, but in the end only a mimed rendition of 'Baby Let Me Take You Home' was included.

From the ridiculous to the sublime. June saw the release of 'The House of the Rising Sun', quite simply one of the greatest records ever made. Even today, the recording sounds remarkable. In 1964, Valentine's stately, circular arpeggios rising from the speakers at the beginning were the start of an experience that for pop consumers was unbelievably exotic. Price's organ throughout the record is superb, alternately pulsing away like a heartbeat under Burdon's brooding, bitter reading, then heightening the drama with spectacular crescendos as Burdon's emotions boil over. Price also provides a conceptually perfect ending, his final shimmering wash conjuring an image of the first rays of dawn creeping over the horizon.

The rendition of 'Talkin' 'Bout You' on the record's B-side is one of several Ray Charles songs The Animals recorded at this stage of their career. It's not one of Charles' best and the track is not one of the band's better interpretations. A pleasant surprise, though, are the background "Hey-hey-ey" chants, which are rather pretty for a band who, unlike The Beatles, were never renowned for their harmonies. This track is an edited version of a far longer — and more enjoyable — recording which eventually appeared on *The Complete Animals*. That CD also featured a track called 'F-E-E-L' which is a blatant rewrite of 'Talkin' 'Bout You': it could conceivably be the case that 'F-E-E-L' was the track intended to be the one used as the theme for *Ready Steady Go!* In the event, and whichever the track offered, *RSG!* passed, making The Animals' insistence on 'House' as their second single seem almost eerily prescient. Having said that, it's interesting to realise that, initially, EMI's fears about the record not receiving radio exposure were proven right: the BBC, which literally had a monopoly on radio broadcasting in those days, wasn't playing it. It was the band's performance of the track on *Ready Steady Go!* that made the record a commercial success. Without that invitation to appear on the programme, history might have been totally different. "It could have sunk without trace," Steel admits. "But the song had been so well-received during the Chuck Berry tour that it only took one break on television to give it that boost." The Animals would enjoy a very special relationship with *RSG!* over the years. "*Ready Steady Go!* loved us," says Steel. "We were practically the resident band there. We could play live and they never had to worry about fuck-ups, cameras, stuff like that. They could put the cameras on, turn the sound on and that was it — we'd deliver."

'House…' shifted a quarter of a million units in its first three days of release and by July 11 had topped the charts. "It was like an electric current that just ran out," Steel says.

chapter four

That summer, The Animals set about the task of following up a single that had both been acknowledged as an instant classic and catapulted them to a pop stardom that saw them acquire all the benefits of that status: screaming girls, pop magazine colour spreads and persona-most-grata status at London nightclubs.

Bravely, they decided that the successor to 'The House of the Rising Sun' should not be another cover version, however customised. Instead, they concluded that they could generate a hit on their own. "Chas, being a real Beatles fiend, knew the story," says Steel. "He knew everything about them and how they developed as songwriters and stuff like that. It was probably Chas who said, 'We should be writing our own material, that's what The Beatles do.' Alan was the obvious choice because it wasn't like he was The Animals' arranger but he was the one who could play the piano and lift something off a record and say, 'This is the guitar line, this is the bass line and these are the guitar chords.' We pinched stuff, basically. Very little original stuff. And Eric would say, 'How about this for a lyric?' and they would thrash it out a bit. Unfortunately it never really developed much beyond that."

Around this time, the band also recorded their debut album. Laying down a long player was no more a sophisticated process than recording the singles had been. Valentine says, "That first album was recorded one song after the other. It had to be right all the way through, 'cause if you fucked up in the middle then you would have to start again."

August saw The Animals maintaining a heavy schedule. They embarked on a sixteen-day British tour (including the Isle of Wight), the day after the end of which they performed on The

Beatles' radio show *From Us To You*. Shortly after that (August 24-26), they filmed two mimed cameo performances for another trashy movie, *Get Yourself a College Girl* (English title: *The Swingin' Set*), the tracks in question being 'Around and Around' and 'Blue Feeling'.

In August, following the phenomenal domestic success of 'House…', MGM released the track on single in America. However, the label were even more apprehensive about the length of the song than EMI had been in the UK and insisted it be edited. The result was butchery. Price's organ solo is reduced to the fast, high-pitched part and is shortened with such clumsiness that it almost sounds like a joke or a deliberate attempt to draw attention to the tweaking. In addition, (and insanely, for it made almost no difference to the length), Price is faded out just as he begins his final, sublime organ wash. The uncut version of the song would not be released in America until the following year and even then there was no fanfare attached to its appearance: it appeared on a Various Artists compilation called *Mickie Most Presents British Go-Go*. Nonetheless, the butchering did the trick. 'House' received US radio play and replicated its British chart-topping success. America suddenly had another British Invasion group to take to its hearts. The Animals were the first British band to secure a US #1 after The Beatles, discounting duo Peter & Gordon's 'A World Without Love', which in any case almost certainly only made the pinnacle because it was a Lennon-McCartney composition. The Animals — only the fifth British act in all to secure a US number one — were stunned. Nobody had ever said playing that playing R&B — a form of music recently obscure in Britain and outmoded in its native country — would lead to Transatlantic chart domination. "The stuff that was chart material was changing," Valentine says. "It wasn't so much that bands that were true to what they were doing were trying to change to be poppy but the pop scene was changing from the schmaltzy rock'n'roll to a hard rhythm'n'blues. The Beatles were like chalk and cheese compared to Cliff Richard: raw vocals and raw rock'n'roll. To have that number one record in America, that's what made me think, 'Crikey, this *is* big.'"

Needless to say, the success of 'House…' engendered the re-promotion of the band's first single, which had initially flopped in the States. However, the radio stations preferred to play the flip and it was 'Gonna Send You Back to Walker' which eventually made the Hot 100, peaking at number 57. A visit by The Animals to the States was inevitable. When it occurred at the beginning of September, it occasioned the kind of massive hype that only Americans can organise without feeling ashamed of themselves: air balloons emblazoned with 'The Animals Is Coming' and a fleet of Triumph Tiger cars — complete with scantily clad young women wearing tiger heads, whiskers and tails — to ferry them from their press conference. There were no screaming teenagers awaiting the band's arrival at JFK airport, though: the mayhem of The Beatles' visit had caused the authorities to put the kibosh on that scenario. The latter wasn't as pleasant a trip as might be imagined, for it was on this journey that The Animals discovered that the version of 'House…' that had taken the American charts by storm was not the one that been such a success in their home country. Valentine: "It was very distressing. When we heard it for the first time we couldn't believe it. On the radio, in the car, going from the airport to the hotel. We thought, 'Christ, they chopped out half of the fucking organ solo!' Total shock." Steel says, "They hacked it to bits. The Americans at that time were still so far behind in their thinking. We were still having to deal with Fifties mentality, with the suits and the agents and the rest of it. They made us go and get suited up on our first visit to the States. This was Don Arden: 'That's the way they do things in America.'" Burdon says, "We were manipulated I would say more by the agency than Jeffries. Don Arden and Peter Grant… tried to dress us up in fucking monkey suits, Beatle suits, get your hair cut, don't say a fucking thing about Vietnam when you get to America. Meanwhile the Stones were realising the bad boy image was the way to go. Originally, The Animals were that naturally."

The Animals were booked to play ten days at Times Square's Paramount Theater, five shows a day. Confirmation of their new star status was provided by the fact that on some dates they were supported by their heroes, Little Richard and Chuck Berry.

According to Valentine, the latter was admirably philosophical about playing second fiddle to the men who covered his songs and over whom he had been headlining in Britain only four months previously: "We said to him, 'Well this is really strange' and he said, 'Well, that's the way it goes, man.'" The dates were a roaring success, as was the visit in general, despite it being restricted to New York. "Fantastic. Totally amazing," Valentine recalls. "As soon as I found out that there was a possibility that we were going to America, that was just something that was beyond my dreams." One sour note, though, was what The Animals considered the astonishing ignorance of the Americans about their own musical heritage. Valentine: "People said, 'What's the source of your material?' We said, 'What do you mean? It's American music.'" Steel notes, "In the UK, we always attracted a 'laddish' audience, to use the current phrase. It was more of a boys' band than a girls' band. But in America it seemed to be all girls. Screaming and doing all the bit — I think they were just programmed. We were just another one of the British bands."

One of the things The Animals most wanted to do in America was to meet another of their heroes, Bob Dylan. Now beginning to realise that they possessed the star status that could make such fantasies possible, they made enquires. A meeting was arranged between The Animals and Dylan in the New York home of Dylan's manager, Al Grossman. It took place in the room that was immortalised the next year by being depicted on the front of Dylan's *Bringing It All Back Home* album. The Animals met someone very different from the rough-hewn character they assumed the artist to be from his Voice of the Common Man music. Steel: "It was a bit of a shock just physically to meet him. He was a really great-looking guy but he was so fine. It seemed to me his skin was almost transparent. He had this mohair-type jacket and shirt cufflinks — really sharply turned out. This wasn't what we expected." He adds, "He was very nice." Just as shocking was the fact that it turned out that the admiration felt for Dylan by The Animals was mutual. Dylan had been so impressed by The Animals' version of his arrangement of 'The House of the Rising Sun' (which, incidentally, Dylan had stolen from fellow folkie Dave Van Ronk), that it caused a switch in Dylan's musical perspective, one which would have momentous consequences for pop music. This has long been a source of dispute but Steel says, "That is from the horse's mouth. That is what he told us. He said he was driving along in his car and ['House…'] came on the radio and he pulled the car over and stopped and listened to it and he jumped out of the car and he banged on the bonnet. That gave him the connection — how he *could* go electric. He might have been heading that way already but he said that was a really significant thing for him." Dylan then proceeded to reveal to the band the first fruits of his electrification. Steel: "He said, 'This is what I've just recorded' and he played us 'Subterranean Homesick Blues'. He said, 'What do you think?' We said, 'You're doing so well with the acoustic folk stuff, you're taking a chance with that, aren't you?' It sounded a little bit like Chuck Berry."

Although 'House…' had been knocked off the top of the US charts by The Supremes' 'Baby Love' in the week they arrived, The Animals returned to the UK in triumph. Not surprisingly, considering both the gruelling workload they'd had to endure at the Paramount (and the no doubt just as gruelling acquiescence to the overtures of young American womanhood post-show), they were exhausted. However, they had a new single to promote. 'I'm Crying'/'Take It Easy' had been released at the beginning of September. In addition, they had to undertake a 28-day UK tour. Discussing the Price/Burdon composition 'I'm Crying' in 1995, Price told journalist Dawn Eden, "We were being harassed into producing material, as everybody was in those days. At that time, we'd just toured Britain with Carl Perkins. We all became extremely friendly with him on the tour bus, and he showed me that chord sequence." Price — who said that Perkins picked up the lick from the Everly Brothers — learned how to play it on the piano. He recalled that The Animals' next stop was a gig in Blackpool, Lancashire. "During sound check I played that riff for Eric and he made up all the words," Price told Eden. "And that was 'I'm Crying', really. It was just a throwaway attempt at a song, without any conviction whatsoever." Perhaps it shouldn't come as a surprise that Price is dismissive of the composition — he replied to Eden, "None whatsoever" when she asked him The Animals songs of which he was most proud, claiming, "We had a missionary zeal about blues music, and I felt, particularly, that Mickie Most was attempting to homogenize, sweeten, and make it accessible for the mass market." However, he is completely wrong about 'I'm Crying', which is a top-class record. It also manages to sound as authentic as any of the R&B standards in The Animals' repertoire while adroitly side-stepping the easily-made mistake of regurgitating the biggest clichés of the genre. A spurned lover's lament, its two biggest assets are a breakneck pace appropriate to the narrator's desperate mood and backing vocals any choir of an Alabama church would be proud to claim as its handiwork. In the easy-rolling flip, 'Take It Easy', Eric and Alan again pay homage to the masters of the music they love without mindlessly aping their mannerisms.

The single reached number eight in Britain and number 19 in America (where it was released in October). Valentine notes, "The fact that we followed one of the biggest records ever, actually to get the next single in the charts was like a relief: 'Fucking 'ell — at least we're still in the charts.'" Both artistically and commercially the band would seem to have been vindicated in their decision to write their own material for their third single. Yet they were never to write another A-side. One wonders how different history would have been if The Animals had developed their songwriting. The Rolling Stones started from exactly the same place as The Animals: rhythm'n'blues fanatics content to cover (if imaginatively) the songs of others with little confidence in their own compositional abilities. Possibly with some justification: 'The Last Time' — their first self-written A-side — was a rip-off of a Staple Singers song (itself adapted from a spiritual), 'May This Be the Last Time'. Yet three months later, the band's Mick Jagger and Keith Richards had written the immortal '(I Can't Get No) Satisfaction' and were well on the way toward a totally self-reliant recording career with all the financial rewards and enhanced artistic fulfilment that entailed. In terms of technical ability, The Animals were arguably the Stones' superiors: Mick Jagger's vocals sounded like those of an ingénue compared to Burdon's grizzled tones, while no one in the Stones possessed the musical virtuosity of Price. The Rolling Stones, though, had something The Animals lacked in the form of their manager Andrew Loog Oldham. The latter dismissed their scepticism about their own talents and famously (if apocryphally) locked Jagger and Richards in a room until they'd come up with their first song. Burdon flippantly says, "I don't think that Price and I could have developed like Mick and Keith as writers because I'm not Mick and he ain't Keith," but we will never know what would have happened if The Animals had been surrounded by people who believed in them as much as Oldham believed in his charges. Steel says, "I think things would have been an awful lot different if we'd developed a songwriting team in the band. It's not fair to say we didn't get the time because nobody was busier than The Beatles but McCartney and Lennon always found time to knock out a song. The opportunity would have been there if we'd had the mind to do it. It might have been the glue that held the band together." "I don't think Mickie Most ever tried to stop them," says Valentine of Burdon and Price. "I think it was themselves. They should have kept writing stuff together but they didn't. It was their own fault. What's to stop two people getting together in a room and writing stuff?" Valentine, who says he never thought about writing songs when in The Animals himself, provides his own answer when he cites bickering in the band — even at this early stage — for the paucity of original songs: "I guess people just didn't really want to get together when they weren't working." Steel agrees. "The probable reason that it didn't develop was the fact that Alan and Eric didn't particularly get on together on a personal level," the drummer says. "With Lennon and McCartney, they were great buddies. I don't think Eric particularly liked Alan as a person." He adds, "But we were loving what we were doing and excited by it and things were happening very fast and we were just kind of along for the ride. My personal guess at the time — I remember saying it to some friends — was, 'Oh, give it a couple of years, then I'll have to find a job.' I don't think anybody really realised how long it could have. I think basically it was laziness and lack of direction that we didn't have a really good shot at forming a songwriting partnership of some kind."

The band were back in America by late September for a proper tour. On Sunday October 18 they appeared on The *Ed Sullivan Show*, an American national institution, knowledge of which had crossed the Atlantic when The Beatles' appearance on the programme on February 9 1964 had attracted 73 million viewers, the largest in television history. "It felt great to do it 'cause we knew it was a syndicated show," Valentine says. However, he adds, "It was a funny show. They had elephants on and fire-eaters and comedians. It was a family-type show. When you did *The Ed Sullivan Show* you got the feeling that you were accepted by middle America, grown-up America."

October 1964 saw the British release of The Animals' eponymous debut long player, which would peak in the charts at number six. As with many albums of the day, it contained none of the singles that had made the artists famous. In America (where it had actually been released in September and would reach number seven), that wasn't the case. There was no way the record company in the US was going to forfeit the umpteen million extra sales that 'The House of the Rising Sun' guaranteed. 'Baby Let Me Take You Home' was also included, as well as the excellent 'Blue Feeling' (which would only be released in Britain on an obscure Various Artists soundtrack). As with all British Animals albums with an American counterpart, it is the British configuration analysed herein as the edition constituting an organic entity representative of the band's artistic vision.

When the album was first released, the opening 'Story of Bo Diddley', a tribute to the one-time Ellas McDaniel, bore the sole publishing credit "Burdon". These days Diddley takes 50 per cent credit, which attribution is somewhat debatable as the main basis of Diddley's claim to have had any hand in the song's origin is simply that it employs the shave-and-a-haircut-two-bits rhythm that he admittedly made his trademark but which he most certainly didn't invent. The song makes for a fun and unusual first track. During its very long by 1964 standards 5:14 playing time, Burdon tells not so much the story of Bo Diddley but the story of rock'n'roll itself, from its raw and galvanizing beginnings, through its early-Sixties nadir (Burdon sneers through a snatch of Bobby Vee's 'Take Good Care of My Baby', one of the syrupy hits of that era) and onto its rejuvenation by The Beatles. The playfulness is a refreshing contrast to the over-earnestness that could sometimes afflict Burdon's singing. The lyric impresses for the fact that, despite its extreme discursiveness, it rhymes, at least most of the time. As Burdon quotes from Vee and others — sometimes approvingly, sometimes dismissively — Steel keeps a straight face as he maintains a nice pattering beat behind. Valentine reveals of the song, "That didn't come about in the studio. That came about at gigs, when we were doing 'Pretty Thing' or 'Bo Diddley'. Eric was great at ad-libbing and great at creating stuff on the spot. He could just go where he wanted to go and we would just follow him. If he was wanting to tell a little bit of a story, we would just bring it right down and let him tell the story until he was finished and he wanted to come back into the song. We could feel when it was going to happen." Diddley is done something of an injustice by the song's surprise ending in which Burdon recalls him putting down his English admirers in the presence of his maracas player Jerome Green and sister The Duchess at a visit to the Club A'Gogo. Valentine: "That [song] came about after Jerome Green came to the Club A'Gogo. It wasn't Bo Diddley. I'm not sure if the Duchess was there either. The excitement of that night, that came out in Eric's creativity. Within weeks of that night he probably started putting things in the live shows." The track was edited when released on the American *Animal Tracks* album because Burdon sardonically and potentially libellously refers to the black Johnny Otis as a "white guy" in reference to his supposed lack of soul.

'Bury My Body' carries the same "Trad: Arr. Price" publishing credit as appears on 'The House of the Rising Sun'. Hmm…This is one of the album's better tracks and would be even if it didn't prove just how sincere was the group's love of and knowledge about black music: it's difficult to imagine The Rolling Stones covering a Negro spiritual in which the narrator displays an equanimity about death because he knows his reward is going to come in heaven. (Valentine does admit, though, "I had a version of that on a Lonnie Donegan LP.") The performance is sinuous. 'Dimples' follows. Not one of John Lee Hooker's greatest, Valentine's endearing flat guitar twangs and Burdon's dependable passion distinguish what would otherwise be an unremarkable reading of a slight song. The Club A'Gogo version is much better. A rare, for an Animals record, female chorus appears on the cover of Fats Domino's 'I've Been Around', which had been a minor American hit for its author in 1959. Enjoyable, innocent fun. 'I'm In Love Again' is another Fats number (written in collaboration with his producer Dave Bartholomew), underlining that the band's (or perhaps Most's) vision of R&B encompassed good-time lyrics and New Orleans boogie-woogie as much as come-in-my-kitchen gutsiness. This song was originally released in 1956, when it took Fats to number twelve in Britain and three in the US. That it's not sequenced separately from 'I've Been Around' is lazy but it's a rollickingly good rendition, with a piano break from Price that challenges even Domino's keyboard prowess. 'The Girl Can't Help It' (Troup) was probably an unwise choice, on the grounds that anyone covering a song when the routinely berserk Little Richard has been there first is on a hiding to nothing. The Animals can only try gamely on their version. John Lee Hooker's 'I'm Mad Again' illustrates the way The Animals managed to deal during their career with a fundamental flaw in the music they loved. The 12-bar blues is a format heavily reliant on the cleverness of artists to provide colouring with virtuoso technique or arresting lyrics. Great boredom is the consequence for the listener if those things are not provided. Perhaps the greatest defiance of the limitations of the 12-bar structure is The Jimi Hendrix Experience's 'Red House', the highlight of their 1967 debut album *Are You Experienced*, wherein Hendrix contrives to cram into the most restrictive of all musical genres more than was ever meant to go, stretching the plodding 12-bar format to its very limit as he peels off notes at impossible speed. His daring becomes ever more outrageous the longer the song continues. The aural equivalent of a cheeky schoolboy making obscene gestures at a venerated old timer, it's almost hysterical stuff. The Animals do something similar (although of course on nothing like as grand or virtuoso a scale) on 'I'm Mad Again'. Valentine provides menacing guitar lines before handing the spotlight to Price, who hunches over his organ with gritted teeth as he produces some furious, stabbing phrases, which in turn inspires some wonderful staccato fretwork from Valentine. 'She Said Yeah' (Jackson/Christy) is another Stones/Animals overlap. This time, the Stones walk away with the honours of best interpretation, their buzzsaw-guitar augmented rendition from the following year's *Out of our Heads* easily topping a broadly unremarkable, if jolly, rendition by The Animals. 'The Right Time' is another track decorated with distaff backing vocals. Unfortunately, they run, repetitively, throughout the song and only serve to underline the monotony of the 12-bar format. 'Memphis Tennessee' is uncharacteristically downbeat and saccharin for a Chuck Berry song. It's also not a song whose nature — which relies for any impact almost exclusively on its convincing domestic notes and cute twist in its tale — gives much room for a band to stamp its identity upon it. The Faces, with their restrained, plaintive reading on *A Nod's As Good As A Wink…To A Blind Horse* (1971) were one of the few who managed. The Animals sadly weren't. 'Boom Boom' sees The Animals revisiting a song from the Graphic Sound EP. This is a better version (although not as good as the storming Club A'Gogo performance), mainly due to excellent playing from the two quietest and least celebrated Animals: Valentine comes up with some exquisitely mellifluous guitar lines while John Steel lays down a formidable steamhammer rhythm. On the closing 'Around and Around', The Animals purvey an okay version of a Chuck Berry song already squeezed dry by every R&B combo anybody ever heard of and quite a few no one did.

It's striking that despite the excellence of the 'I'm Crying' single, there are no original songs here. Even 'Story of Bo Diddley' doesn't really count, on the grounds that a monologue over a riff associated with another artist featuring snatches of other people's songs is hardly a composition. Despite having the entire R&B corpus to draw upon, the song source of *The Animals* is rather narrow and gives little indication of just how extensive the band's knowledge of the genre was: including three numbers by John Lee Hooker, two by Fats Domino and two by Chuck Berry is rather unimaginative, especially as some of the selections were tediously familiar staples of British beat group repertoires. "Yeah, you're right," accepts Steel. "The only time we made something calculated, like on 'Rising Sun', those were the odd exception. Our minds didn't work like that very much. It was a band that liked to party and hang out. We didn't really take ourselves as seriously as we should have and I think it shows in things like that, where we'd go into a studio and knock out a few tracks. 'Fancy doing this?' 'Oh, I haven't done that for bloody years. Well give it a shot.' We never gave any thought to the composition of the album. We just used to lash out a few tracks and walk out of the studio and go and get pissed or something and Mickie would put it together in some kind of running order. We were definitely a one-take band." The album also suffers from an overabundance of songs with stop-start rhythms. The cumulative effect is rather jerky, the band not flowing in the way the live Newcastle show recorded not too long before proved they could. By no means a great album then, but it is one with enough good material to make it a perfectly respectable debut — and one which would have been far more than that had the trends that prevail now for including hits on albums then been the norm.

In November, 'Boom Boom' was released as a single in America. The Animals didn't promote it, seeing as it wasn't their idea, and it reached a paltry number 43. Yet the record is of marginal interest because it features on its B-side a track which (apart from the album soundtrack to *The Swinging Set*, released the following year) wouldn't see the light of day in Britain for 26 years when it was included on the *Complete Animals* compilation. It's mystifying as to why 'Blue Feeling' (J. Henshaw) wasn't released on a British Animals record proper. In particular, it would have strengthened their first album quite considerably. It's an excellent uptempo track, the most delicious aspect of which is the way Burdon's voice is mimicked by Valentine's twanging guitar when the singer calls out the title phrase. To add insult to the injury of British fans not hearing this gem for a quarter-century, another version of it (almost imperceptibly different) ended up on foreign albums *All About The Animals* (Japan, date unknown) and *The Animals* (Argentina; 1966).

chapter five

The first month of 1965 (February in America) saw the release of a New Animals 45 that was a huge artistic step forward.

'Don't Let Me Be Misunderstood' — written by the team of Bennie Benjamin, Sol Marcus and Gloria Caldwell — had become well-known through a Nina Simone version, which had been an R&B, though not a pop, chart hit. Most may have chosen the song because he considered it commercial but The Animals retained its pop hooks without sacrificing an iota of their natural grittiness. What resulted was another classic. The record immediately grabs the attention with a militaristic riff played, in synchronisation, on guitar and organ. (Bruce Springsteen would later purloin that riff for his equally brooding 'Badlands'.) Enter Eric Burdon to enunciate a lyric that constitutes a startlingly honest depiction of love, the kind of which audiences of the day were used to hearing in neither rose-tinted pop songs nor braggadocio R&B numbers. Its narrator is a man agonising over the dismissive way he frequently treats his lover but who knows he is powerless to change his behaviour. He is aware of the hurt his moodiness causes her but, he tries to explain, it's because he has so much on his mind, so much in his life he's not satisfied with. Burdon's adoption of this persona is utterly convincing: his cracked-voiced insistence in the silence of a musical respite, "'Cause I love you," is enough to induce goosebumps. In its vulnerability and its acknowledgement of the complexities of love, the whole thing could not be more removed from the swagger of the numbers that made up the bulk of The Animals' material.

The power of the record is in no way diluted by a couple of glaring musical errors: a backing vocal which wanders out of tune at one point and an alarmingly shrill organ swoop. Burdon has said that these errors are present because the version released is an outtake. Ironically, another version of the song which cropped up on a Japanese compilation titled *Rock 'N Roll Best 20* (1977) also sounds like an outtake. The backing vocals are more choir-like than on the familiar version while the guitar is spikier, especially during the middle-eight. Unlike on the single version, there are no musical fluffs, although there are a couple in Burdon's vocal, which itself is not quite as thrillingly world-weary as on the single.

On the Burdon/Price-written flipside 'A-Go-Go', the band borrow the riff of Muddy Waters' 'Mannish Boy' (and who didn't back then?) to celebrate the Newcastle venue that helped catapult them into the big time. Burdon provides a litany of the artists who performed on its two stages, ones whose collective charisma have supposedly made his baby steal all his money and take up with a boyfriend called Big Joe. Price's piano pounds quite fearsomely in the verses.

Though the record only reached number fifteen in the States (barely better than 'I'm Crying'), it climbed as high as number three in Britain. Its popularity amongst the public was not matched by its reception from Simone, who publicly criticised the band's faster arrangement. "We were outraged by that," says Steel. "We were the ones who had a hit record. She didn't write it, so I don't know what she was getting her knickers in a twist about. Eric told her so to her face when we met her in the States and had a right shouting match with her and she eventually said, 'Okay, maybe you aren't so bad for white boys.'"

The Animals' and Most's tastes may have converged on 'Misunderstood', but Most's suggestion for the next single, 'Willow Weep For Me', a jazz song that had been around since before the Second World War, horrified them. (Price, though, would later record it as a solo artist.) Yet the record that eventually emerged at the beginning of April in Britain and a month later across the Atlantic seems only a shade less mercenary than Most's first choice. Cutting a version of Sam Cooke's 1962 single 'Bring it on Home to Me' (a number thirteen in his native US) was hardly in keeping with The Animals' policy of recording singles which were obscure or in some way unusual. Even 'Don't Let Me Be

Misunderstood' fitted that category, being well-known but not a chart sensation, and having been given a new spin by the band delivering it from a male perspective. 'Bring It on Home to Me' was a song already familiar to millions and very much in the mainstream. Nevertheless, what resulted was yet another great record. In addition, the group's incremental musical development was once again evident. Their latest step of progression was substantial overdubbing: Price is often heard simultaneously on the doomy, resounding piano which runs through the track and the organ swells introduced at various points for tone and shade. The Animals' version of the song is altogether darker than the sad but sweet number the composer laid down. Burdon's vocal is one of his very finest (and is helped in no small measure by the affecting call-and-response "Yeah"s between him and the band). The lung power he puts into telling his estranged love that he will be her slave even when dead and buried in his grave is the best moment of a vocal performance so wonderfully touching that it tops even Cooke's original. Whether the track as a whole is better than the Cooke template is a difficult one to call but what can confidently be said is that because of their evident love and respect for the song, The Animals would have alienated none of the song's many existing admirers. On the B-side is 'For Miss Caulker', a smoky, 12-bar Burdon original the soulful performance he invests in which is, for once, not the result of his ability to empathise with a fictional narrator's feelings. The song is part-autobiography, Doreen Caulker being the name of a young black woman with whom Burdon had been romantically involved. "That was Eric's big love," says Steel of Caulker. "They were a very heavy couple. Doreen was a really smashing girl. Good fun, great looking, one of the gang. She moved to London and she got some pretty lucrative work as a croupier." Caulker died of breast cancer in the mid-Nineties. As Burdon laments Doreen's absence, Price provides some moody supper club backing on piano. It's another track whose absolute authenticity (which is not even spoiled by one badly fluffed line) refutes the assertion famously made by some in the era that White Men Can't Sing the Blues. 'Bring It on Home to Me' reached a respectable number seven in the UK.

Its peak of number 32 Stateside was a bewilderingly poor performance, but the band soon had far bigger problems on their minds.

On April 28, The Animals were shocked to their roots when
Alan Price abruptly disappeared and subsequently explained that
he wouldn't be returning to the line-up: shades of his unexpected
and unannounced departure from the Kansas City Five several
years previously. "A hell of a shock because there was no warning
at all," Steel recalls. "We were literally gonna fly off that day for
a Scandinavian tour and Alan was nowhere to be found. Chas
was sharing a mews house with him in Holland Park and Chas
didn't even know where he'd gone. He just pissed off." The penny
didn't drop for a long time — even years — but Chandler became
convinced that there were reasons for Price's going AWOL very
different to the fear of flying explanation with which he eventually came out. In November 1994, Chandler told *Record Collector*
magazine that it was 'The House of the Rising Sun' royalties that
prompted Price's action: "…I woke Alan up, went into the shower,
had a shower, got out of the shower, and Alan had just gone, he'd
disappeared. And I never saw him again for eighteen months. I
believe the first cheque had come that day and he just walked
out the door with it." However, Burdon asserts, "It goes beyond
the nickage of the royalties for 'House of the Rising Sun'. I don't
think that AP could deal with me as front guy. His attitude is,
'Here I am, I've studied piano all my life, I'm the musician in the
band, and this fucker's out front getting all the adulation.' The
guy's got problems. Always has had problems." However, Burdon
has the good grace to admit, "Great player, no doubt about it. He
was The Animals to a certain degree."

Looking for Price wasn't an option. "We didn't have time," says
Steel. "We had a plane to catch. We just had to leave it with Mike
Jeffries to organise things… We suddenly had to fill this hole in
the band and we knew a guy called Mickey Gallagher who was
playing in a band in Newcastle that we liked. Good kid. And we
just told Mike to fill the hole and get on with the job. Poor kid.
We flew him out from Newcastle. He knew some of our stuff and
where we came from. Give him his due, he did a tremendous job
of filling a gap. We had a very successful tour as it happens. I work

in Scandinavia quite a lot these days and people still remember that tour and say, 'Wow, that was fucking great, man.'"

However, perhaps because of his tender nineteen years Gallagher (who would later play with The Clash amongst others) was not considered suitable as a long-term replacement. That role eventually went to Dave Rowberry but Burdon's old mucker Zoot Money reveals that, following a discussion between Burdon and Chandler, he was approached first. Money had known Burdon since '64 when The Animals were living near him in a communal flat after making the move to London. "I was first choice I think it's fair to say," Money says. "They knew that if there was going to be anybody that could fit in it was going to be me. I had the same drinking habits as Eric and Chas for one, which always helps if you are socialising. At that time, Chas phoned me, said, 'Alan has gone, do you want to…' I just couldn't do it at that time. They were a little embarrassed to ask me in a way, because I was forging my own way with The Big Roll Band. It was doing alright and for me to have given that up at that time would have been silly, really." Were Chandler and Burdon shocked at the refusal? "No, I think they understood. I was tied into being the leader of a band as opposed to being just the piano player. In Eric's band I wouldn't have been able to sing. They were in quite a good position to be looking for people, very high-profile and very successful, so there was no shortage of people to fit the bill. It was just a question of who could put up with the, shall we call them, artistic differences."

"For whatever reason, we couldn't have Mickey permanently replace Alan," says Steel, "but we knew Dave Rowberry and we just automatically decided that Dave was the guy we wanted. So we made contact with him and poached him out of The Mike Cotton Sound. So he came straight in, slotted in. He'd been to university in Newcastle and he'd played the same kind of venues as John Walters and people like that. He played in jazz and blues groups rather than rock'n'roll. That's why we felt he'd be right for us. He started to develop quite quickly. He was a better backing vocalist than Alan. I don't want to keep knocking Alan down but I never liked his voice. Quite often we used to not have his mike on because he often sang so flat it was horrible in the backing vocals. We used to get Tappy to make sure his mike wasn't on."

Dave Rowberry was born on July 4 1940 in Nottingham, where he was also raised. He'd attended Newcastle University because he felt that being so far from home would mean he wouldn't be distracted from his physics course by musical pursuits and that he could make the choice between the two disciplines once he had obtained his degree. "It was a misguided idea, 'cause I was already a musician," he says. "The second day I was in the local college band playing in the women's hall of residence. Also, I went to Mike Jeffries' club and there were great musicians like Mike and Ian Carr. I had my own band at Newcastle University and Eric came to sit in with my band." Was it a fairytale to be asked to join a hugely successful band like The Animals? "I wouldn't say 'fairytale.' I was in a successful band, the Mike Cotton band, backing people like P.J. Proby, Tom Jones." Demonstrating this is his prosaic attitude when the overture was made: "I was doing a gig somewhere and I got a phone call: Would I go and see Mike Jeffries when I got back to London? He asked me to sign there and then and I said no 'cause the lads were away in Scandinavia at the time. 'I want to talk to them. What's their musical policy? 'Cause I'd like to add brass or sax or something to the band. I want to talk to them before I join.' He was quite perturbed by all that. Obviously he wanted to get it signed, sealed, delivered, in the papers…It was almost as though I was saying, 'Well I'll think about it.' That wasn't what I was saying. I was being quite genuine. I want to clear one thing up. The *My Generation* programme [Channel 4]. This is as much to The Animals as anyone else who's interested but I was misquoted, or mis-edited. They said to me, 'What was the situation with the band when you first joined?' And I said, 'They were fucked up.' That comment was not about The Animals, it was about the finances. The money situation was fucked up but I didn't know it at the time. They just edited that bit out and put it into a totally different context."

The inevitable rehearsals to acquaint the newcomer with the band's repertoire followed, although they weren't particularly intensive. "I'm a very quick learner," Rowberry says. "Obviously

I knew most of the songs anyway. The one single thing I imitated with Alan was 'House of the Rising Sun', the arpeggios, because that was part of the song. I play me. I've never listened to people's solos and tried to copy them. I go on stage and I never know what I'm going to be playing. I'm an improvisational musician."

The Animals are divided as to whether Price's departure made a big difference. Steel says no: "On a personal level, he wasn't a big miss. On a professional level, Alan's disappearance didn't really affect us as a band." Valentine agrees: "Dave Rowberry was a good choice. Quite honestly, when I listen to the songs with both guys on I can't tell any difference." However, Burdon maintains, "Dave Rowberry wasn't that big an influence in the band. In fact, he was more of an Alan Price lookalike than a soundalike and we was stupid enough to go for that. We thought it would sit better with the American audiences who wanted to look at The Animals as a group. As soon as Pricey went, as soon as John Steel went, the magic went." Whatever the truth, keyboards would never again be as big a part of the The Animals' sound as they had been when Price was in the band. Steel puts this down to factors other than Rowberry's abilities or unwillingness to impose himself: "I think with Alan out of the picture, Eric became more dominant in material and Hilton, because he'd already had the experience and everything, blossomed a bit more because he wasn't the new boy anymore."

While this upheaval was going on, *Animal Tracks*, The Animals' second UK album, recorded before Price's departure, hit the shops. An album of the same name was released in America four months later in September but that was not the equivalent of the British album: the second American album, containing much the same material as the British *Animal Tracks* (with an edited version of 'Boom Boom' and a different take of the other John Lee Hooker composition, 'Dimples') as well as the 'I'm Crying' single, was released in March 1965 with the misleading title *The Animals On Tour*.

Although The Animals were sticking to their R&B roots for their second album, *Animal Tracks* displayed a definite broadening and deepening of their sound. There's much

four-o'-clock-in-the-morning moodiness in evidence in a generally downbeat platter. The greater darkness and sophistication of
the music is reflected in the way that the tone of the sleeve is the
complete reverse of the grinning gormlessness of the first album's
cover shot. The sleeve is the result of a triple pun, the word "tracks"
alluding to the bands of an album, railway lines and the marks
left by jungle beasts. All these things are combined, in a rather
confused way, in a monochrome picture showing the band sitting
on a railway line wielding guns and dressed in soldier's helmets. "I
don't know how so much military stuff got involved," says Steel.
"Eric always loved military memorabilia. For a pacifist he always
had this fascination with military bits and pieces." Meanwhile,
Valentine insists that there was no grand plan behind the darker
musical tone: "I don't think many things were conscious. It was
just a natural progression. We just did things." The supper club
sophistication is both a good and bad thing. Despite the undeni-
able quality of so much of this record, after the umpteenth smoky
lament one can't help but long for a little of the dash and colour
of the pop evident on the singles.

The album gets off to a rather hesitant start with the merely
okay 'Mess Around' (Ahmet Ertegun, writing under his backwards Nugetre *nom de guerre*), a song which makes a lacklustre
attempt to artificially create a dance craze a la The Twist. The
first of the sultry piano pieces, 'How You've Changed', follows,
another decision by the band to opt for a downbeat Chuck Berry
number *a la* 'Memphis Tennessee'. It's good stuff, with Price —
in many ways the star of this album — putting in an effortlessly
slick performance of high drama. 'Hallelujah I Love Her So', a
number five R&B chart hit in America for its author Ray Charles
in 1956, is a gloriously euphoric track that captures perfectly the
giddiness of being in love. Rarely has Burdon sung with the kind
of twinkle in the eye he exhibits on this celebration of romance
between next-door-neighbours. The band's performance is spot-
on, its playfulness and deftness of touch striking exactly the right
tone, from Burdon's 'brr-brr-brr' imitation of the sound of his
girlfriend calling on the phone to Steel's rat-a-tat-tat rendering
of her knock on the door. *Animal Tracks'* second Ray Charles

number couldn't be more different. 'I Believe to My Soul', is a brooding, atmospheric dissection of a relationship that is falling apart due to a woman's fickle behaviour. It is the album's highlight. Burdon's performance perfectly evokes the state of mind of a haunted man who is angry about the cavalier treatment he receives but leery of confronting his lover for fear of losing her altogether. Price's piano playing constitutes quite possibly his finest Animals studio performance, his breathtakingly rapid fingerwork underlining the broiling uncertainty in the tormented narrator's mind. John Steel makes his own valuable contribution with subtle, superbly judged ride cymbal work. Big Maceo Merriweather's 'Worried Life Blues' presents another man in torment in another drink-sodden, world weary mood piece. Variety is provided by Price switching from piano to organ. 'Roberta' (Smith/ Vincent), one of the closest things The Animals recorded — at least in the studio — to a rock'n'roll (as opposed to R&B) song, sees Burdon's case-hardened Geordie colleagues providing him cooing vocal back up as sweet and harmonised as that of The Picks, who augmented Crickets records. (The backing vocals were mixed out on the American *Animal Tracks*, weakening the charm of the song considerably.) The most interesting observation that can be made about the lacklustre 'I Ain't Got You' (Arnold) is the way its upbeat instrumentation contrasts with the sad spirit of its lyric. The song, though, had special memories for Eric Burdon as it was the first he sang on stage in London in 1963 after travelling down to check out the blues scene. According to Burdon, he shared the microphone on that occasion with a young R&B wannabe called Mick Jagger. The version of Jimmy Reed's 'Bright Lights Big City' — a song very similar in theme to a previously released Animals cover, 'Gonna Send You Back to Walker' — is competent. 'Let The Good Times Roll' (Lee) is a fine, fun track, especially Burdon's coy "Rock me all night lo-o-ong" in the lulls. 'For Miss Caulker' represents the first of only two occasions that a track from a single was placed on an original Animals UK album during the Sixties. Its inclusion turns out to be a bit of a mistake, for it serves to show how a different context can diminish a song. 'For Miss Caulker' impresses less here than it does as a self-contained B-side due to a melancholia overdose. There's no doubting The Animals' ability to put on a performance of convincing desolation but after the identical moods of 'I Believe to My Soul', 'How You've Changed' and 'Worried Life Blues', the formula is becoming wearying. Happily, things pick up with a cover of Bo Diddley's 'Roadrunner'. Though this song was covered by dozens of English beat and R&B combos in the early-to-mid-Sixties, The Animals' version is the best of them all, and it's almost all due to the performance of Hilton Valentine. He distinguishes the Tynesiders' rendition from all the others floating around at the time by scraping his pick against his bass string to brilliantly imitate a roadrunner's dust-raising velocity. Beep beep!

May 1965 saw the start of a court case which threw interesting light on the investment Mickie Most and Mike Jeffery had made in The Animals. Leslie Elliott and Harvey Lewis, two men involved in property development, claimed that they had financed The Animals, The Nashville Teens and Herman's Hermits after Most and Jeffery had realised they didn't have the money to exploit the contracts they held with those groups. All four were to be directors of a company called Warrior Records. According to Elliott and Lewis, Most and Jeffery had not honoured their agreement to pay proceeds from 'The House of the Rising Sun' into their bank account. Most and Jeffery eventually lost the case. "I remember it being a really heavy thing for Mike especially," says Steel. "He did get alopecia at one point." Were the band themselves not bewildered by the case? Steel: "We generally just tried not to think about that kind of stuff. All we wanted to do was play, record, get about, have a good time. People are a lot more streetwise about it nowadays."

In mid-May, The Animals embarked on a tour of America that took in Deep South locales like New Orleans, Birmingham and Alabama. Rowberry recalls, "Mike said to me, 'By the way, how are you about flying?' Obviously Alan had said he was giving up because he couldn't fly (if you believe that you'll believe anything). 'Oh, no problem.' At that point I'd done one flight in my life — which was Dublin and back. I shat myself all the way there and I shat myself all the way back. And there is my first major gig: live at *The Ed Sullivan Show* in New York. I had nightmares. But I made it and to this day now I love flying." Rowberry was somewhat underwhelmed by the show's legendary status: "He's like a piece of wood, Ed Sullivan. He hasn't got a bit of soul in his body."

Late May saw the purveyors of 'The House of the Rising Sun' visit the Land of the Rising Sun for ten days. "I absolutely loved it," says Steel of Japan. "It was the most alien country any of us had been in. Again, we were hit by a wall of young teenagers, mostly girls. Like a repeat of the American stuff, except with that Japanese reserve. They'd scream and scream and scream but they wouldn't actually touch you. We played about ten dates, just doing the major cities." "I thought it was very good," agrees Rowberry. "I wasn't looking forward to it, to be honest, but I came away loving the place. We were the first major band there." As well as live shows, the band made TV appearances. Rowberry: "I remember the organ broke down in the TV studio and I took the top off. Next thing, I couldn't get near it." John Steel chuckles at the memory. "Sixty-five was still early days in that technological revolution," he says. "He took the top off and there was a sudden flurry of black heads — all these heads were straight in there, looking into the guts of this Vox, trying to see what made it work." Of one television appearance, Steel remembers, "There was one overhead mike. They lined us up. We just did the number, presuming this was the first run-through. And then they started to clear up around us. We said, 'Hang on, that was just a run-though, wasn't it?' They said, 'No, it's gone out.' Apparently it was very good."

The first Animals record to feature Rowberry's playing was 'We've Gotta Get Out of this Place', a single released in early July in Britain. A totally different take of the song was released in America in September. Cynthia Weil has described The Animals' version of the track she wrote with husband and professional partner Barry Mann as her least favourite rendition of any of her songs ever attempted, although there are extenuating circumstances for this ostensibly rather puzzling position on a great record.

It was the Righteous Brothers that the songwriting pair had in mind when they devised 'We've Gotta Get Out of this Place', Weil as usual devising the lyric and Mann the melody. Mann, however, was so pleased with his demo of the song that he decided to release it as a single under his own name on Jerry Leiber and Mike Stoller's Red Bird label, to which he was signed as an artist. Unfortunately, as Mann explains, "Somehow we had given the song to Mickie Most and forgot about it." Weil says of Most, "He never said anything. Next thing we knew, it was number two in England, so that killed Barry's record…Had Barry's record come out and been a hit, our whole landscape could have changed."

To add salt to the wound of Mann's solo record — and ultimately possibly solo career — being aborted was what The Animals had done with the song. As ever, The Animals added their own personal stamp, but on this occasion this meant not tweaking the melody or arrangement but dropping an entire verse of Weil's lyric. "I just felt that what they did was right for themselves but a lyricist deserves the respect of being consulted," laments Weil. "If they had said, 'Look, this doesn't work for us… We'd like to change it to this…How do you feel about it?' I think we could have worked together and gotten something that might have pleased both of us. I felt that it was great disregard for what I did to just drop a verse and change things and not even say anything. 'House of the Rising Sun' is one my favourite records ever so I was so thrilled that he was doing it and then when I just heard this I just felt so bad." The fact that the record was a Transatlantic hit (thirteen in America and number two in Britain) softened the blow a little for the pair. With the passage of time, they have also gained enough distance to see The Animals' recording the way many others do: as a brilliantly gritty evocation of the working class experience with a soberingly authentic vocal performance by Burdon. "It was a terrific record," Weil concedes. "He's a great, great, great singer." In a postscript to the whole saga, when Burdon recorded the song again in 1990 with Katrina and The Waves, he sang Weil's original, unexpurgated lyric. "Listen to that — you'll hear the right lyric," says Mann. "He made up for it."

Not only is 'We've Gotta Get Out of this Place' a great record, it's one whose sepia-toned proletarian spirit and sheer belligerence accomplish the improbable effect of making a song written in New York's Brill Building the perfect summation of the Geordie grit that was uniquely Animals. Even the uncelebrated Chas Chandler puts in a bravura performance with lugubrious bass lines that serve as the song's riff and that — played in isolation at the beginning — herald a truly gut-wrenching band performance. Burdon is alternately desperate, determined and wistful: you can feel the spectres of the Tyneside unemployment queues and the building site jobs he was taking only a couple of years before nagging at his brain as he sobs, "Girl there's a better life for me and you…" Valentine: "It might have been a bit more poppy but at the same time, them lyrics are really hard-hitting."

"I came up with the harmony line on the song," Rowberry reveals. "It's the only track I've ever sung on. I like the song. Eric put his usual heart and soul into it." However, he adds, "The backing vocals were out of tune." Weil's antagonism toward the Animals' version is more understandable if, as is possible, she only heard the version released in America. Although it followed two months after the British record, it sounds like a rejected earlier take.

On the B-side Eric is lamenting the absence of a female again (perhaps it's even another number about Miss Caulker). The track is called 'I Can't Believe It', writing of which is credited to Burdon alone. On first hearing, it feels like a collection of standard blues chord progressions and mannerisms but successive listens reveal it to be a thoroughly absorbing and atmospheric track, particularly Burdon's vocal. Best of many fine moments is when Burdon hauls himself up the register to imitate (in synchronisation) Rowberry's keening organ.

On August 8 the band played at the fifth Richmond Jazz and Blues Festival. Despite a star-studded bill (The Who, The Yardbirds, The Spencer Davis Group, Manfred Mann and Georgie Fame were amongst the other acts appearing there), The Animals' performance must have been the most interesting of all. This event saw the one and only stage appearance of The Animals

Big Band: namely, the Animals plus three trumpeters (one of whom was Ian Carr), three tenor saxes and one baritone sax. The 20,000-strong audience received it rapturously. One of the songs performed was the Leadbelly number 'Rosie', which, in altered form, would eventually see release as the Animals single 'Inside — Looking Out'. "It was just a one-off idea," says Steel. "I think the idea originally came from Eric. Eric loved that thing of getting the brass behind him or backing singers. He had definite ideas about developing himself." Valentine recalls, "I was a little wary at first but as it happens I really enjoyed it." It seems a pity that The Animals didn't decide to capitalise on the good reception to this experiment by making an album along these lines. "We should have done," says Steel, "but when I think about it, it would basically have been a repeat of Ray Charles' couple of albums around about the time he did the Newport Jazz Festival. Basically that's where all the material came from." The closest The Animals came to making a record in this vein was when they and the same augmentation recorded a session for the BBC shortly afterwards. "I've often considered putting a horn band together," Burdon says. "I still would like to do it but it's an expensive proposition — very expensive — and one has to make money, unfortunately, to stay alive. A dream is a dream."

From October 10-12, The Animals filmed *The Dangerous Christmas of Red Riding Hood* in New York. This was an ABC television special written by Jules (*Funny Face*) Stein first broadcast on November 28 that year. The lead parts were taken by Vic Damone and the up-and-coming Liza Minnelli. The Animals' role in this musical comedy involved three hours in make-up for an appearance as wolves. They also performed one song, 'We're Gonna Howl Tonight', which appeared on the special's US-only soundtrack album in November 1965, which failed to chart. Though it would have made an appropriate bonus track on *The Complete Animals*, it's yet to be released on CD. However, the show itself has been the subject of both VHS and DVD releases. The track opens with somewhat hammy horror movie chords and is not exactly infused with the grit of the blues. It's as fleeting (1:39) as it is lightweight. That said, it's enjoyable and

The Animals' professionalism shines through: Valentine's guitar and Burdon's vocal are particularly good.

"It was a bit silly," says Steel of the programme. "We kept looking at each other thinking, 'What are we doing here?' [In] America they have bizarre ways of doing things where you think, 'This is so old-fashioned.' I really don't know why we just didn't turn round and walk out of that. There must have been a lot of money in it or something." "It seemed like a good idea at the time," says Rowberry. "The longer it went on, the more disenchanted everybody got with it. It was abysmal: it goes on and on and on, same damn thing every day. The actual plot of it was intriguing, I think, 'cause the wolf was played by an English ac-tor. He was the gentleman and the whole idea of the story was that the wolf wasn't the evil one, the wolf was the gentleman and she was a right slag." There have been reports that Chandler struck up something of a friendship with Liza Minnelli, but Rowberry says, "If anything, I did. She struck it up with me. Quite taken with me. She was Red Riding Hood. She wasn't my type. Too American. Miss Showbiz. She wasn't Gladys Knight, that's for sure. She didn't have any soul." He adds, though, "She liked a drink."

This programme was the closest the band came to making a feature film. That The Animals were one of the few British Sixties groups not to shoot a movie is all the more strange for the fact of Burdon's long-time ambition to be an actor. Both Steel and Rowberry recall the idea of the band appearing in their own motion picture being floated several times.

Valentine describes the deal The Animals had signed with Mickie Most in 1964 as "atrocious." It did at least have the merit of being short: it was soon to expire. With them both very successful and out of contract, it was inevitable that The Animals would leave Most's stable and sign directly to a record company.

The Mickie Most era of The Animals' career came to an end with 'It's My Life', released in October 1965 and two months later in America, yet another record that proved that — whatever his motives — Most was adept at picking songs Eric and company could turn into classics even though they might not have chosen to cover them. The track, written by New Yorkers Roger

Atkins and Carl D'Errico, is once again an excellent blend of pop sprightliness and bluesy grit. The sound is big and brawny and sets a trend for the relatively minor role of keyboards that would be a feature of Dave Rowberry's days with The Animals. In fact, there don't seem to be any keyboards on the A-side at all, leading to a more metallic and beat-group-like affair than anything they'd previously put out, though Rowberry says, "I was on the recording. I do remember doing that one, 'cause I disliked it so much." Valentine adds, "You can hear a keyboard on the intro: *dang*! A very distinct piano chord." The song's title at first seems to be a simplistic attempt at capturing the Sixties rebellious zeitgeist, but a closer listen reveals a song as layered and honest ("Show me I'm wrong!") as 'Don't Let me be Misunderstood'. A pleasing call-and-response between bass and guitar is the cherry on the cake. In the Burdon-penned B-side 'I'm Gonna Change the World', Eric expresses the same Angry Young Man sentiment as (ostensibly) informs the A-side in his best song to date. Frustratingly, some fine, stabbing organ work by Rowberry during the instrumental break is buried in a poor mix.

Rowberry feels that 'It's My Life' illustrates Mickie Most's shortcomings: "Can't stand that song. It's so angular and American. It's not the blues. It's nothing. I'm sure we could have found something better to record. A commercial song was not what The Animals needed at the time. They needed a song to sell, but that to me is pure crass commercialism." Burdon actually expressed similar sentiments at the time, telling a journalist that he didn't like the disc but that he was getting used to it. Valentine disagrees, both about 'It's My Life' ("I thought it was a good record") and about Most. "There was nothing that we did as singles that he *made* us do," he insists. "It wasn't: 'You've got to do this.' He brought stuff in for us to listen to and say, 'Yea or nay?' When you look back, he brought 'Don't Let me be Misunderstood', 'Baby Let Me Take You Home…' and these songs were hits and great records. Who's to know what would have happened if he hadn't have done that and we'd said, 'Oh no, we're gonna do what we wanna do and put out stuff like 'Dimples' as a single'?" "He was learning as we went along like everybody else," says Burdon of

Most. "He was good for us at the time and was smart enough to make a lot of money out of the business and best of luck to him. It's strange that the people with least talent make the most money. That's the name of the game because if you've got less talent you've got more time to study the business and figure out how you can get ahead. Mickie Most was a great picker of songs. That was his great talent. Not only for The Animals but for the other acts that he had." But Chas Chandler, when asked by *Record Collector* in 1994 whether Mickie Most understood The Animals, spat: "Not a clue. If he did understand, he would have stayed with us. He was such a shallow person, really. We didn't want him anyhow. We wanted Ian Samwell to be our producer, and then we found we had Mickie Most. It was like, 'Who the hell is he?'" Steel, though, agrees with Valentine: "Mickie really had a good commercial ear. He could predict that a record would be a hit and he was usually right. We had to give him credit for that when he presented us with material, but at the same time we wouldn't do *anything* that he said. At the time, when you compare what we were playing live, things like 'It's My Life' and 'We've Gotta Get out of this Place' weren't typical Animals songs, but by God they were anthems and they were hits. Mickie knew that and recognised that. We went along with it because we agreed with him. They were real grown up songs — and they still are today."

In any event, musical considerations were by now dwarfed by financial ones.

chapter six

The Animals' new record label was Decca, which — though not as big as EMI — had a certain prestige by virtue of being the home of The Rolling Stones. The band's record label in America continued to be MGM. Supposedly, the move to Decca would bring an advance of £100,000 while MGM would pay £90,000 upon The Animals signing directly to them (as opposed to being licensed through Most). These were huge amounts of money for 1965. The Animals were to see virtually none of it for, whatever the deficiencies in the Most contract, they were as nothing compared to the character deficiencies of Mike Jeffery.

"I don't know when the Mike Jeffries thing started to go sour," Rowberry says. "He was like one of the band really, initially. I suppose certain things started coming to light, drip drip dripping through to show that things weren't exactly going according to plan. I don't know what he was up to. It wasn't a sudden thing. It wasn't one great earth-shattering revelation. He was a great guy. He was one of the boys. But I'm not sure if he was capable of handling the American side of it. Heavy dudes over there." Most, in contrast, was reported by *Billboard* at this point to have no plans to issue further discs from unreleased Animals material in his possession "in view of The Animals' fairness to him." He stuck to his word.

In fact problems with an unauthorised Animals release came from, of all people, their new label. Decca managed to get hold of the Graphic Sound EP and issued it as *In The Beginning There Was Early Animals*...despite the band seeking an injunction to prevent the record coming out. "I don't know how they got hold of that," says Steel. "It must have come from Phil Woods. It was just something that we didn't want conflicting with what we were doing there and then. It was not much better than an amateur recording by that time." It was an astoundingly crass and high-handed approach to their new clients by the record company. However, Burdon made the best of a bad situation by supplying an amusing illustration for the cover featuring the Animals as cartoon caveman, with photographs of their faces inserted in the relevant places. Though The Animals were no strangers to the UK's Extended Play chart via compilations of their material in this format, *In The Beginning There Was Early Animals*…didn't even manage to break into its hardly ultra-competitive environs.

On November 11 1965, The Animals made history by taking rock'n'roll behind the Iron Curtain, embarking on a tour of Poland. "We actually got half the money upfront in sterling, which was unusual, and the rest in zlotys on the road," says Steel. "So we did get a good tour out of it, financially. But it was a strange experience." They went equipped with a new invention: fake fur coats manufactured out of a very lightweight man-made fibre by a London style guru. Arriving in a Poland under six feet of snow, the band were very grateful for them. "It was bloody freezing," Valentine recalls. Rowberry: "I don't think we did any business for the company that was responsible for providing these. We certainly got stares from the people." Steel says the coats made the band "look like a bunch of Disney characters. Looked like they forgot to put the joke animals head on."

"It was an experience because it was still Communist control," Valentine says of the tour as a whole. "Everything did seem sort of grey and damp and cold, but yet the audiences were really great. They were starved for a bit of rock'n'roll." Steel: "The main gig was the Palace of Culture in Warsaw. We did five concerts there and they were all packed. It went back to the blokes. We had loads of young guys in the audience — same sort of reaction as the UK or Scandinavia or Germany where it was mostly the guys who latched onto us. They were absolutely going potty. The police — big fur hats on and leather belts and great coats and big sticks — kept walking around whacking people to make them get back in their seats. They knew their stuff. They even had some Western import albums. At that time, you could get

25 quid for an album from the West. Ten quid was the wage for a blue collar worker then — in England. It wasn't a mindless following of Western fashion." While in Warsaw, the band stayed in the Bristol Hotel, an unbecoming berth of which Steel says, "It was like a big old barn. It had been grand in its hey-day. Time had just stopped there." "The concerts themselves were fantastic," Rowberry states. "The rest of it — forget it. You couldn't go to parties, you couldn't pull girls. You had police — mostly women — watching every level of the hotel. You're not sure that your room's bugged or not. I didn't care if it was. I didn't get up to anything. They didn't let us. It was boring, the food was boring, but the actual concerts themselves were frenetic. These people had never seen anything like it — rock'n'roll live on stage. Strangely enough, I did a gig about a month ago at the 100 Club in Oxford Street and this guy came up. On the tour in Poland we had a Polish band touring with us. We were barely allowed to mix. This guy introduced himself and said, 'Do you remember me?' and I said, 'Well, where from?' and he said, 'Well, from Poland. I was in the band that was touring with you. Now I can talk to you!'" Preparing to return to England, the band found themselves pointlessly still in possession of zlotys. Valentine: "We couldn't take them with us because they were all worthless outside of the country. So we stood at the airport trying to get rid of them."

In early 1966, recording sessions for the band's first Decca releases took place. Not only did the band have a new record company, they also had a new producer in the shape of Tom Wilson, best known for his work with an Animals hero, Bob Dylan. "We thought, 'It's a fresh start,'" Valentine says. "It was quite exciting, starting off in a new company." Steel says, "Eric and Chas said, 'Ooh, Tom Wilson's done Bob Dylan. Let's get a real monster, proper producer over from America.' He was more hands-on than Mickie. I don't think Mickie knew what to do with a fader. He just stood behind an engineer and said, 'Can you get a bit more of this?' I think Tom Wilson knew what all the bells and whistles were for." "I'd have liked a lot more to do with Tom Wilson," says Rowberry. "Then I thought we were getting nearer to our roots. He'd worked with a lot of my great idols in the jazz field. We had a lot more in common with him than the likes of Mickie Most. That was from a purely esoteric viewpoint, rather than making hit records. He pleaded with us to stay together because it was that point that we were breaking up. He knew his way around the desk. Very together guy." "I really enjoyed working with Tom Wilson," agrees Valentine. "He was really a likable person, very jolly. He had a knack of getting the best out of you."

The first Animals single bearing Tom Wilson's production credit was 'Inside — Looking Out', released in February 1966 in both the UK and the US. The first record of the new era of The Animals' story was an absolutely uncompromising piece of work. Whatever defence Valentine and Steel make of Most, it can't be denied that their first post-Most record was something their former producer would not even have countenanced as a single. The song bears the publishing credit "J & A Lomax/Burdon/ Chandler", reflecting the fact that Eric and Chas had custom-ised the prison song 'Rosie', which is what the track had been billed as when the band played it on BBC radio and television in late 1965. One of countless numbers gathered by blues and folk archivists John A. Lomax and Alan Lomax during journeys up and down America (including visits to state penitentiaries), the Burdon and Chandler re-write offers the bleak point of view of a man incarcerated for an unspecified crime pining for the woman he left behind. Of the source material, Valentine says, "I've got a version of us doing that. It's mainly the lyrics that were changed. The rest of the track in the recording I've got is very, very similar to 'Inside — Looking Out'. Practically exactly the same." Though The Animals had dealt with depressing sub-ject matter on 'We've Gotta Get Out of this Place', they had done so without sacrificing a commercial sheen. This record's instrumentation, however, is as brutal as the prison regime the song describes: Steel pounding away on drums that boom in the claustrophobic mix, Chandler contributing tension-building bass and Hilton Valentine producing the most ornerey, scratchy guitar sound he'd ever committed to tape. Valentine's lines are precursors, alternately, to similar ones on Ike and Tina Turner's 'Nutbush City Limits' from 1973 and ones in the instrumental break of 'I Can See For Miles', which The Who would release the following year. Meanwhile, you can almost see the spittle flying from Burdon's mouth and the muscles of his neck straining. An incredibly intense performance all round, except for Rowberry's organ, which is barely audible.

Whether it's a great record is another thing entirely. After seven consecutive great-to-classic UK singles, this feels like a slight falling away in quality. It's a good piece of work alright, and brave, but Mickie Most could have been forgiven for a feeling of justification, not only on the artistic side but on the commercial front, which would have interested him far more: 'Inside — Looking Out' was — not counting the exploitative and unpromoted US release of 'Boom Boom' — the least successful Animals single on either side of the Atlantic since 'Baby Let Me Take You Home', reaching number twelve in the band's home country and only 34 in the States.

Dave Rowberry actually rejects the idea that the record con-stituted The Animals finally being allowed free rein to play the bluesy music they wanted to. "Another song I don't care to sing," he says. "Again, it just didn't seem to be in the right groove. If you look at the Stones and The Beatles, they seemed to have some semblance of a thread. Our songs were just totally disjointed. It had an edge, yeah. I wouldn't call it bluesy. Johnny Cash sang about prison and he's about as bluesy as my cat — and I don't have a cat. I wasn't happy with it."

The English flip of 'Inside — Looking Out' was superior to the A-side. Although 'Outcast' (written by Campbell/Johnson) also has a harder edge than previous Animals material — especially the echo-drenched, vibrating guitar figures from Valentine — its pop hooks and frilly piano make it sound a more obvious choice for the A-side. Strangely, the American version of this single had a different B-side. The Burdon/Rowberry composition 'You're On My Mind' is a lovely road-weary song of heartbreak possessing lush instrumental overdubs, with both organ and some deliciously plaintive piano underlining the sad sentiment. Burdon's voice — unusually baritone even by his standards — is mixed up front for a feeling of intimacy. A very promising first outing for the Burdon/

Rowberry team: no less than the best self-generated Animals song since 'I'm Crying'.

The new record deal and the high creativity of the band weren't enough, however, to persuade John Steel to remain in The Animals. In February 1966, he gave his notice. "I just felt we were being ripped off and fucked around," he says. "We just worked continually and we were still getting the same basic retainer as we were a couple of years before. Where was the money? All this bloody work and all the records sold. I never saw a big cheque yet. I was just fed up. I got married at the height of things in July 1964 and we had a baby the next year and I was on the road all the time and when I wasn't on the road we were in the studio or at photo sessions. If we'd been getting some really nice money I could've seen the point of it but it got to the point where I thought, 'What the hell am I doing this for anyway?' I was really beginning to not enjoy it." It wasn't too much of a wrench to decide to leave the band because as Steel points out, "I'd mentally given myself a couple of years when we started off." He adds, "The band was starting to fall apart."

The beneficiary of Steel's disenchantment was Barry Jenkins, drummer with the Nashville Teens, another act discovered by Mickie Most. Then as now they were chiefly known for their 1964 UK top ten and US top twenty hit 'Tobacco Road'. Jenkins came into the world on December 22 1944. "I was born in Leicester but I was a war baby and grew up in Greenwich," he explains. Rowberry: "We were supposed to have auditions for a new drummer. Eric had picked Barry before we even heard anybody else. More because of the social aspect with Barry. He was an outgoing sort of bloke. He obviously got on well with Eric. That's what counted." "We were on the same tour with The Animals and Johnny Steel left," Jenkins recalls, inaccurately (the only time The Animals were on the road with the Teens was the Chuck Berry tour of '64). "He got fed up with it 'cause Alan Price screwed everybody with the royalties from 'House of the Rising Sun'. Johnny Steel fucked off. A couple of days went by and Eric said, 'Do you want to join The Animals?' Couldn't refuse that, could I? A massive band. They'd just come back from America.

We was all mucking about on them tours anyway. Before I got asked to go with The Animals, I got on really well with Eric and the boys. Same music — we used to like blues and that, all of us." "I would think Barry was more of a rocky drummer and my playing always had that jazzy swing in it somewhere," says Steel of the difference between the styles of the two sticksmen. "He was a good competent drummer. Neither of us were particularly brilliant but we were good enough for what we did."

In his new berth, Jenkins immediately found himself in novel terrain. "The night I met Hilton, we went to Donovan's place in Kensington 'cause Hilton was friends with Donovan," he recalls. "We was all sitting around smoking pot and I'd never had pot before. I was out of me box and we got in my car and I said to Hilton, 'I can't feel the pedals — they're like big clouds.' He said, 'Oh you'll be alright, let's head off down to Wardour Street.' So we all got down The Ship. Everybody was in that pub. Richard Green from *Melody Maker*, they were all coming up, saying, 'Congratulations Barry, you've joined The Animals' and all that. I was mashed out of me box. It was like the paranoia was setting in." Things would only get wilder for Jenkins from here.

Asked if the fact that Steel was leaving under a cloud of financial recrimination made him doubt what he was getting into, Jenkins shrugs, "Well in them days you didn't worry about the money so much. You weren't business-minded. You just got on with your music. It was all for the music really and just the thrill of it all." Perhaps this attitude is understandable for a new boy jumping ship from a less well-known group, but his colleagues evinced a similarly *sang froid* attitude to money. Valentine: "I was in such a state anyway, everything was going over the top of my head, unfortunately. Or fortunately — I don't know. Everything was supposed to be going into this account and we were drawing a weekly wage or a monthly wage. So we never actually saw the money from gigs in lump form." Of the wage, Valentine says, "I guess it was a fair sum of money in them days but in comparison to what the earnings were, the hit records that we had, it was just nothing really." "I was having a ball," Dave Rowberry says. "I didn't give a shit. I'm a drifter in life. I just go along with the flow.

He was a married man. He'd got a child. He goes home and he gets the wife nagging him about the money." Did he try to persuade Steel into staying? "He's a man who knows his own mind. There's no point, if that's what he wanted to do. Everything moves on. I was never short of money but never stacked with it. It was there. It was like an ephemeral thing." The main money-spinner in The Animals' so-far brief but lucrative career was, of course, 'The House of the Rising Sun' and inevitably the main question with regards to royalties was related to that record. Valentine says, "When we did ask about what was happening with the money, we'd get a little lump to keep us quiet. That would shut us up for a little while. But then when we started digging into it to find out what was going on, it was right, left and centre. We were getting ripped off." Interestingly, Rowberry — who didn't play on 'House' so had no financial interest in it — says that there were at least some initial steps taken to resolve the injustice of only Alan Price receiving money from it: "I remember an agreement which I don't think ever got signed. Alan actually went back to Mike Jeffries to manage him. One of the clauses in this management agreement would be that we had half of Alan's management and his royalties. That was certainly discussed and agreed on. [Price] must have known about it, although he wasn't at the meeting. I'm sure he must have been informed. I guess that was it: 'Where's our reparation?'"

John Steel played his last gig for the band on March 5 1966 at Birmingham University. "I remember going into the studio after I'd left to try and get severance money," he recalls with sadness, "and Barry Jenkins was in the drum cubicle and it was a strange feeling seeing somebody else there. You're on the road together, you know each others' ways, you know the way somebody sleeps and breathes and eats and all the rest of it and suddenly when you cut yourself off from it, this bloody great big shutter comes down between you. There was this feeling of, 'I don't belong here anymore.' I didn't know what I wanted to do. I didn't know whether I'd made the right move or the wrong move. With hindsight, it was the right move in that I got some money out of it 'cause I insisted on being paid a lump sum. It was just about that time we switched to Decca and there was supposed to be a really big advance in it and I thought, 'Well I might as well get my piece of it' because it was partly my efforts that had brought us this far. So I did get a lump of money out of it. The band stumbled on for a few more months and when the dust settled there wasn't any money there."

Jenkins played his first gig with the band on March 15 at the Paris Olympia. "I knew a lot of the songs because obviously we was on the tour," says Jenkins. "I used to stand in the wings looking at most bands. It was where you got your influences from, looking at other musicians. It was quite easy for me to fit in really. We had a couple of rehearsals and it was done." Of Chandler, his new rhythm section partner, he says, "That Animals stuff and blues stuff is not very technical. He was a good solid bass player for that stuff. Hilton Valentine, he weren't no bloody Segovia or Django Reinhardt, but all them guys together made that sound. They were all good players."

For all this financial and personal uncertainty, The Animals' product continued to sell very well. The last album to boast Steel's drumming, *Animalisms*, reached number four in the UK charts. The album (featuring an unimaginative cover shot of the band variously standing or lounging on a patch of grass) was actually released a considerable while after Steel's departure (June '66). So long, in fact, that in the meantime the first single to feature the drumming of his replacement had been recorded and had charted. The US equivalent of this album was not the similarly-titled *Animalism* (no 's') released at the end of that year but *Animalization* (August 1966), which dropped some tracks in favour of 'Inside — Looking Out', 'Don't Bring Me Down' and 'See See Rider'. It reached number 20.

After all the fuss involved in extricating themselves from Mickie Most's clutches, not that much seemed to have changed on The Animals' albums front. While the recent 'Inside — Looking Out' was undoubtedly far more rough-hewn than those singles Most had produced, *Animalisms* is not that great a departure at all from the band's previous two LPs. Rowberry's visions of adding brass to the sound came to naught. "Nothing changed because nobody made the effort to change it," says Rowberry. "You never had time to think for yourself." Because of the work load? "Well, that and the drinking, the partying. You always got up an hour before you went to bed." The guitar is certainly more to the fore on *Animalisms* than on albums hitherto, but that is for the worse: whatever Valentine's considerable merits, keyboards are what made The Animals' records transcendent where most other R&B groups' material sounded earth-bound. Take the swooping organ away and you are dealing with a deficiency in blues music that The Who's Roger Daltrey has described as "just different lyrics over the same eight bars." Also disappointing is the fact that The Animals were not developing their own songwriting in the way that their recent B-sides had suggested they were able to. With two compositional teams now in the camp, why were they resorting to mediocre covers of by-now hoary old chestnuts like 'Sweet Little Sixteen'? Dave Rowberry, while clearly not of Alan Price's twisted genius status, seems to have quickly become a dominant influence in his new band, co-writing two songs (as well as copping the publishing for the hardly musical 'Clapping'), which makes it all the more strange that he and Burdon didn't write more together and that his keyboards take such a back seat. In any event, Valentine seizes his chance, proving his mettle with some truly raucous playing. Tom Wilson's production is a bit more echoey than Most's and is bereft of the gloss that he would later bring to the New Animals, although to be fair this is probably because there is only so much lushness in which you can dress up the blues.

The first edition of this book stated that although John Steel was there for the recording of most of the album, Jenkins played on the tracks 'Gin House Blues', 'Squeeze Her, Tease Her', 'That's All I Am To You' and 'She'll Return It'. This information was based on the tracks on which Steel claims Performing Rights Society royalties, but Jenkins insists, "I'm on none of them. It's all Johnny Steel on that. But I'm on the cover."

'One Monkey Don't Stop No Show' is a strangely uncertain, mid-tempo album opener. References to Newcastle Upon Tyne, the Smoke and the Flying Scotsman would have mystified author

Joe Tex, who hailed from Texas. 'Maudie' is more of a tribute to John Lee Hooker than a cover of his love song to his eponymous wife. It sees Burdon relate in spoken-word passages how Hooker would write a new verse every time he and the missus had an argument. 'Outcast', that fine B-side of 'Inside — Looking Out', follows. The Animals' version of 'Sweet Little Sixteen' — Chuck Berry's rewrite of Arthur Troup's 'Route 66' — is strangely ramshackle, sounding suspiciously like a run-through rather than a finished take. Burdon's singing (which customises the lyric to mention The Beatles) is muffled and Steel sounds like he's banging on a biscuit tin. Things perk up a little with the lovely 'You're On My Mind', the first British outing for this track, following which we are treated to Dave Rowberry's 'Clapping', not a song as such but a percussive montage. It's quite cleverly done and its running time of less than a minute-and-a-half militates against any accusations of constituting filler. Rowberry: "It was my idea. I wanted to call it 'The Clap'. It came about from what we used to do on the road." To pass time backstage, one of The Animals would set up a rapid clapping pattern with his palms while another would clap on the off-beat. Rowberry: "There's not many people can do that. They wouldn't let us call it 'The Clap' for obvious reasons." In Troy/Henderson's 'Gin House Blues' Burdon is propped on a bar stool with the weight of the world on his hunched shoulders, staring into the bottom of a glass and snarlingly ready to take on all-comers with his fists. Its minimalist tone makes it sound longer than its actual 4:35, although there is something chord-striking for anybody who's ever nursed a grievance against the world in Burdon's declaration that he'll fight both the army and the navy if he doesn't get what he wants (i.e. gin). By 1990, Chas Chandler had no recollection of recording 'Squeeze Her, Tease Her' (Tucker/Wilson), a number dispensing advice on love *a la* 'Try A Little Tenderness'. Small wonder for what is a bag of blues clichés. In 'What Am I Living For?' Rowberry's organ swoops in the instrumental break are the most attractive feature of another lovelorn affair, this one written by the team of Jay/Harris, to which Burdon is predictably committed. A few months before the release of *Animalisms*, Alan

Price's new band, The Alan Price Set, had released a cover of Screamin' Jay Hawkins' classic 'I Put a Spell On You' and seen it climb to number nine in the British singles charts. As John Steel explains, the song's presence on *Animalisms* wasn't coincidence or even a case of Price's former colleagues taking their cue from him: "We were working on that song when he left. Again it was Eric's idea. [Price] kind of poached that away from us really and whipped it out quick before we did anything. It was basically the song we'd worked out with The Animals, just sort of lifted. The choice of songs generally came from Eric. Alan didn't have much idea." Hawkins' eerie tale of jealousy and witchcraft has also been covered by, among many others, Screaming Lord Sutch and Creedence Clearwater Revival. The Animals were wise not to pull the track from this album after the Price release for their version is one of the best recorded, mainly due to a taut, punchy rhythm, some spikey guitar and the double-whammy from Rowberry of atmospheric piano and spooky organ. In 'That's All I Am To You' Eric's got the blues yet again but the pace on this Blackwell/Scott composition is uptempo and the tone is light, almost vaudeville. Valentine experiments pleasingly with his fuzzbox while whoever's drumming never stops working the ride cymbal. Cheerful and cheering. On 'She'll Return It', Burdon and Rowberry attempt to dispense their collected wisdom in the art of seduction. "Set her soul on desire, make love your one desire" seems as valid a piece of advice in matters *d'amour* as "Squeeze her, tease her" and the music is better than on that track. However, when Burdon hands over the spotlight to Valentine with a "Look out, Hil!," the guitarist shows a hesitancy absent in his belligerent performances throughout the rest of the album.

Chas Chandler was devastated by John Steel's departure. He said, "If anything, the real sound of The Animals was the swing of John's drumming. I think that's what distinguished us from other bands at the time. And when Barry Jenkins came in, we were just another rock band and I lost interest literally overnight." Chandler seems to have been more devastated than — that melancholy final visit to the studio aside — Steel himself. "I just went back to Civvy Street," Steel recalls. "I got jobs playing clubs and little bands and got a day job. I was never star-struck. I think that's one thing that got me through. I had a drummer's mentality: 'I'm just a drummer in a band, not a proper musician', sort of thing. It wasn't a huge adjustment. It was strange that people couldn't understand. 'Christ, you've been on television. What are you doing working in a shop?' One of the first jobs I got was briefly in a department store in Newcastle called Bainbridge's, in the hardware department. I'd worked there once before. Somebody came and said, 'You're The Animals aren't you? What you doing here?' I said, 'I've bought the place.' He said, 'Bloody hell!' It was stranger for other people than it was for me."

chapter seven

In early 1966, the gruelling workload The Animals had endured for the last few years was eased. April saw them recording some of what turned out to be the last (Sixties) album of the original Animals, *Animalism,* at their leisure in no less a locale than the Bahamas.

"It was one of the greatest times of my life," says Rowberry. "Before the Bahamas, we'd been in Majorca for a month. While we were there we did one gig, which paid for our accommodation, cars laid on. Everybody had been asked before we went there, 'Do you want to stay in a hotel? Do you want to stay on a yacht?' And we'd all chosen this sailing yacht, 64-foot ketch. But after about two days nobody liked it. Everybody wanted to be ashore, so I kept it on. It was all paid for, so I had it to myself. It was French-owned, French crew. So I used to go sailing every day. Lovely bays. Used to swim ashore and have a barbecue. French food and wine. I said to them, 'Look, if you want to take people on board, charter, I don't mind, I've got my own cabin. As long as it's not swamped with people.' So they were making extra money on top. I was happy. They were happy. Then we went to the Bahamas, where this recording was supposed to take place. We were there for about two or three weeks. And then we went to Hawaii and we stayed on *another* boat. Another month or so. We did a couple of TV shows. So it was a great period."

Of the Bahamas period, Valentine says, "I enjoyed that. We were just hanging out there. We were on this yacht — apparently the Royal family used to stay on it when they were out there. It was a very relaxing time. It was a relief to not have to keep getting up and packing a suitcase and go somewhere else. We took the opportunity of recording and having a relaxing holiday."

Says Jenkins, "All I knew was Mike Jeffries had set up a holiday for us in the Bahamas and then all of a sudden we flew him out, Tom Wilson, to start recording with us out there. It was done in the ballroom in the hotel. He set all the gear up. All portable stuff. He had it all flown in." Jenkins says there were no baffle boards, let alone a control booth. However, he says the *ad hoc* situation was not a problem for the band: "If Eric didn't like it he wouldn't have done it." This insistence that Burdon could not be made to do something he didn't want to is a matter of consensus amongst the Animals personnel.

Rowberry says the Bahamas sessions saw the band making a conscious — and futile — effort to write their own material. "We actually sat there in this room," he recalls. "The five of us just couldn't come up with anything. The mind was on the golf course outside and the beach and the birds. It was so gorgeous there. We didn't want to be in there." Does it surprise him that the band failed to develop as songwriters? "It does, yeah. You've got the talent there. Why couldn't we get anything together? Today, you've got your home four-track studio. You just bung down some drums and you add this…We were trying to do it all together. It just didn't happen. Eric was a prolific lyricist but he didn't come up with anything. I think it might have developed just given a little longer."

One of the tracks recorded at these sessions was Goffin and King's 'Don't Bring Me Down', which turned out to be the next single, the third consecutive one to be dominated by guitar. Asked if he was becoming more confident as a musician during this period, Valentine says, "Yeah I was, and I was experimenting more and more with pedals, fuzztones, vibratos and tremolos." Rowberry was engaging in his own experimenting, although his wasn't voluntary. Recording the track, his organ was played through a radiogram speaker. "The equipment was very inferior," he recalls. "Pathetic, isn't it, when you think about it? There was no other amp." To the best of Jenkins' recollection, the only track recorded in the Bahamas to end up on *Animalism* was 'Hey Gyp'.

'Don't Bring Me Down' was released in May in both the UK and the US, with the Burdon/Chandler song 'Cheating' on the flip. On the A-side, Valentine achieves with his fuzzbox a roaring effect similar to that achieved by Keith Richards on The Rolling Stones single '(I Can't Get No) Satisfaction', released the previous year. "I think I was trying to emulate a sax sound," he says. "A rasping, baritone sax off old rock'n'roll records that were playing one note. With the fuzzbox you could get that sustain." This pleadingly sung complaint of a man who feels unappreciated by his lover is much easier on the ear than 'Inside — Looking Out', striking the right balance between melodiousness and the rawness the band wanted to add to their sound. This seems to be borne out by the public's reaction, especially in America where in reaching number twelve it was their most successful single since 'The House of the Rising Sun' itself. In Britain it climbed to number six. The track is no relation to the Pretty Things and ELO songs of the same title. The B-side is another fine Animals original, Eric and Chas teaming up to chide a lady who has broken her promises of fidelity. In the midst of a percussion- and-handclaps heavy arrangement, the ever more confident Valentine once again lets rip.

In June, an extraordinary film called *Animals Around the World* that could be viewed as The Animals' equivalent of The Beatles' *Let It Be* movie was screened briefly in a London cinema. It is a documentary which shows a fragmenting group bickering backstage at gigs and in hotel rooms and being pleaded with by an American woman not to give in to their instinct to throw in the towel.

July 6 saw the start of a bizarre five-week US tour supporting their old Mickie Most stablemates Herman's Hermits. "Ridiculous," says Rowberry. "It's like The Sex Pistols going on tour with Cliff Richard or something." However, he adds of The Hermits, "I got on great with the band. There was no animosity whatsoever. We used to play cards on the plane. We had a chartered plane between us. Used to take Peter Noone's money off him regularly." It was on this US visit that Chas Chandler was persuaded by journalist Linda Keith to check out a bright new talent calling himself Jimmy James but who would become better known as Jimi Hendrix at New York's Café Wha, an auspicious event in Chandler's life.

Before that tour the band had recorded some more tracks for their next album, this time in Los Angeles. These sessions were supervised by one Frank Zappa, whose Mothers of Invention released their epoch-marking debut album *Freak Out!* that very month. Zappa was there in his capacity of sidekick to Tom Wilson, although Burdon remembers things this way: "On some of those sessions Frank Zappa came in and took over as producer, just 'cause he happened to be two studios away and he wandered in and Tom Wilson went off hunting girls somewhere." The sessions yielded the track 'All Night Long'. Some have suggested that its mellifluous guitar part beyond Valentine's abilities must be Zappa, but Jenkins goes one step further by insisting, "'All Night Long' wasn't even The Animals. It was Eric Burdon singing with Frank Zappa with some band." The fact that 'The Other Side of This Life' features a throbbing bass part well beyond Chandler suggests it is also a Zappa collaboration. The aforesaid brace were both released on *Animalism*. It's said that 'See See Rider' — which transpired to be the band's last single — was also Zappa-produced. However, Valentine says, "There is no way that Zappa produced 'See See Rider'. I was on that recording and he was never at any session I was at." Burdon: "Working with Frank Zappa was a thrill. He's a great guy and I used to see a lot of him socially." How come Burdon and Zappa got on so well when Zappa was notorious for being down on acidheads? "Frank was down on vegetables and LSD rarely made a vegetable out of me," says Burdon. "I took LSD to heighten my sexual performance for one thing. I wouldn't put anything into my body that would stop me from having sex. That is one of the most important things in my life. When I stop fucking, I'm ready to roll over and die. So Frank and I hit it off on that score in the same level that I hit it off with Jimi on that score. That's how I got to know Jimi — we shared the same girlfriends. Frank and I hung out with the same girls in Hollywood, the Plaster Casters and all those guys. Who we found to be at the time revolutionary women. To me, most of the girls weren't groupies and weren't there to be abused and misused and I liked Frank's attitudes toward the GTOs and the Plaster Casters, turning them into viable rock acts and helping women get onto the stage. Somebody had to do it. It was only black women that were on the stage at that point in time. That attitude that Frank had worked. Glad it happened — glad the girls took over."

'See See Rider' could not have been a better valediction. It's a magnificent record — catchy, bluesy and passionate in the classic Animals tradition. Dave Rowberry came up with the arrangement of this blues standard, the first well-known version of which was recorded in 1924 by "Mother of the Blues" Ma Rainey, although it had been around for a while before that as 'See See Rider Blues'. "I'd heard the original one but my arrangement wasn't much different from somebody else's," Rowberry admits. "I can't remember who it was now. It was almost a theft. I'm a great inventor of riffs but I don't know if I can claim that or not." Hilton Valentine should also be given credit for his playing of that incessant, horny riff which is hypnotically maintained from start to finish. Burdon's lustful singing is packed with character. The band's collective performance is superbly tight right from the faded-in intro to the double-time finish and Burdon's "Oww!" of a sign-off. This classic single was not even released in Britain. In America it was issued in September '66 with 'She'll Return It' on the B-side. This was the month that The Animals officially ceased to exist, though it can be safely assumed that it wasn't sentimentality that saw the public going out and buying the record in sufficient quantities to give it an even better US chart placing — number ten — than 'Don't Bring Me Down'.

Dave Rowberry feels he can pinpoint when The Animals were doomed: "We'd tried to get rid of Chas. Basically we couldn't. I thought he was a bruiser, that bloke. I think that was the start of the break-up." Though that second (that we know of) attempt to dispense with the bassist may have been the start, everybody seems to be in agreement that an internal divide between drinkers and acidheads was the ultimate reason for the band splitting. It is for that reason that John Steel feels that his leaving the group made little difference to their eventual fate. "I don't think the band would have gone on much longer," he says. "Hilton got turned on to acid by Brian Jones in the back of a van in New

York City in 1965 and suddenly Eric and him were sharing an apartment. Tappy was there as well. They were going into the drug culture thing with cubes of sugar in your fridge with acid drops on them. All that was happening. They did start to change personality a bit."

LSD — first synthesised by German chemist Albert Hofmann in 1938 — is an acronym of the German equivalent of its full English title, Lysergic Acid Diethylamide, from which the slang name "acid" derives. For a substance that has no odour, taste or colour, the effects of LSD are staggeringly vivid and powerful. The common claim of users is that it heightens perception. Those undertaking an LSD 'trip' have claimed to see for a thousand miles, or through walls, or to hear the ticking of a wristwatch amplified to a deafening clang, or even to think so fast and so lucidly that they have apprehended the true meaning of life. Such perceptions are illusions caused by the drug's suspension of the 'gatekeeping' part of the human brain: the mind of an acidhead is assaulted by unfiltered information, the classic 'sensory overload'. Today such an experience — a kind of chemical equivalent of getting drunk — would be more likely embraced simply as an enjoyable experience. In the insurrectionary context of the Sixties, LSD trips almost inevitably became equated with enlightenment, the supposedly heightened consciousness of those already hip enough to reject the rules and assumptions of conventional society. Those who dismissed the effects of LSD as meaningless hallucinations could be ignored because it was plausible to suggest that they had a vested interest in doing so: they were 'straights' who felt threatened by the counter-culture. Additionally, acid genuinely did seem to alter some people's behaviour for the better. Although its harmful long-term effects can be observed in the ruined careers of talented musicians like Fleetwood Mac's Peter Green and Pink Floyd's Syd Barrett, such adverse transformations only became common knowledge at a later juncture: at the time there was a general consensus that LSD generally made people more easy-going and gentle. Many observers credit John Lennon's change from a violent firebrand to an altogether more likeable personality to his infatuation with the drug.

LSD was made illegal in America in 1965 and in Britain in 1966. By then, millions of people had been turned on to it.

"It opens up the doors of perception," Valentine says of LSD. "It's very difficult to explain. It certainly opens up your creative avenues but whether you're actually playing any better under the influence or not, I don't really think so. I took quite a lot of it but I took it quite seriously, it wasn't just for fun. It was searching. Trying to find out about myself. I'd read quite a few books and stuff on the subject. It didn't do you any good in the long run. Took me a long time to get over it. It affects your memory and your perception of reality. Acute paranoia — it makes you want to keep going inside of yourself. I don't think John Steel took LSD, I don't think Dave Rowberry took LSD but I think everybody else had a dabble." "Oh God, big-time," is Jenkins summation of how much he and his colleagues were into acid. It should be noted that the following impressionistic memories may be a merger of his experiences with the original Animals and the new variation he was soon to be part of: "We took it to play on. Walking around New York, freaking out. I bought a Polaroid camera once, thinking I could take photos of what I was looking at, the effects of LSD. Hilton [is] the guy who turned me onto it. He was [into] the psychedelic experience with Timothy Leary and all that and Alan Watts — he was quite a thing then. We had all the books. *The Tibetan Book of the Dead* and all that, we used to read all that stuff." "Hilton, Barry Jenkins, myself and Terry McVay, the road manager, we'd become psychedelic tripping buddies," says Burdon. "We were by then attempting to change the shape of our minds. We were trying to step out of ourselves, look at ourselves in a whole new light. We were trying transcendental meditation. We were trying all kinds of drugs: peony, LSD, you name it. It's impossible to explain to people today that what we were doing was, we felt, a very positive thing. It wasn't junk, it wasn't speed, it wasn't smack, it wasn't sleeping pills. We were trying to wake ourselves up, not put ourselves to sleep." Chas Chandler said, "We'd all been doing pot long before then. But acid changed it all… It just seemed to make all the people around you suddenly look crazy. I think it was more or less responsible for the demise of the band. It had an effect on all of us. All of a sudden we were different people." Steel says, "Hilton and Eric both dived in feet-first and became acidheads. I've heard Eric waffling on about how he used to smirk at me and Chas for being drinkers and how out of control of our senses we seemed. To me and Chas and Alan, it was quite the opposite: they seemed to be out of control, waffling on about peace and love and all that hippie stuff. The thing about drinking is you can talk a lot of shite, but next day you're sober. Not so with acidheads. It seems to me that, these days, Eric and Hilton are both very paranoid people, so I don't know what good it did them. I suppose they always had that in them and the acid just brought it out and made it worse. It certainly didn't bring peace and love to all mankind. I've never regretted not going that way. Zoot's about the only one I know who seems to have come out of it pretty well, but then he always had an upbeat, jolly personality anyway." Kathy Etchingham, a friend of Burdon since — she estimates — 1962, says, "Eric Burdon, although he's no schizophrenic and he didn't go mad in that kind of way, he certainly became a bit of a gibbering wreck. His memory is completely shot. He remembers things and you go, 'No, Eric.' His memory has completely gone and a lot of it is fantasy. He's just made it up."

"It certainly splits a band," says Rowberry. "You're on two different wavelengths. You must have been in a situation where somebody's on some sort of stimulant and you're not — and particularly if they're getting stupid with it: they laugh at any remark. If you don't laugh, you're not part of it." Burdon is in agreement: "There was a short period of time when we were all pulling together and we all thought we could make it. It was a very short time from the inception of the band. That quickly digressed into two camps: those who took LSD and those who kept on drinking booze. Each side hated each other for what each other was doing."

As well as the drug-drink divide, Burdon says that there was "hatred" between Chandler and the road management over the former's interference. "I couldn't blame Chas — he was the ultimate organizer," he says. "He got a lot of resentment from people for trying to kick us into shape. That made me even more pissed off 'cause years ago I told Chas he should have gone into management. He should have stepped down from the bass position and become management and let somebody else play bass. That's what he did, ultimately."

Says Valentine, "People that were handling us, supposed to be looking after [us], weren't doing too good a job and that just causes friction within the band. We just started fighting and arguing amongst ourselves. And they started playing one against the other. At that point everybody had had enough. I think Mike Jeffries might have pulled Eric to one side or Eric might have pulled Mike to one side — I think they both went to one side! — and said, 'Look, this whole situation's a mess, it would be far better for Eric to go off on his own, keep the name and he'd have total control. Start afresh.' There was a lot of bickering within The Animals and when you've got a group like that, a democratic group, you've got everybody's opinion to take into consideration. Whereas, for Eric to take the name, then he's got total control. Whichever direction he wants to go, he can do it. Which is what he did and, let's face it, he was quite successful. I was past caring, spaced out." Burdon acknowledges, "We were all being manipulated by Jeffries. That isn't to say that we didn't see it. Mike Jeffries was trained by the British army in dirty tricks tactics. He was attached to British intelligence. Chas supposedly checked out his army record and came back with the story that he was in the catering corps as a cook. Fuck, give me a break. The guy wrote his personal notes in Russian. He studied language and sociology at some southern university before he came to Newcastle. He was no idiot."

Rowberry: "There was never any sitting down, the band together, saying 'What shall we do?' It just happened. I think it was Eric's decision, basically." "The break-up of the band only happened when it became extreme pressure and it became way obvious to me that we couldn't live together, we couldn't go any further," says Burdon. "It was unfortunate that there wasn't a writing partner in the group to help me realise further new concepts and new materials. That's part of the reason why The Animals broke up. They were a blues band, they interpreted the blues, and it came to the end of its run. We were all ligging around, trying to pretend that everything was great. Trying to keep up with the Stones, with their development. Trying to think that we could keep up with bands like The Beatles. It just wasn't so."

The first the other band members — except perhaps Jenkins — knew about a formal split was when they were invited to a lawyer's office in London's Jermyn Street. "We all went along there for a meeting," Valentine says. "I didn't know what the meeting was going to be about 'til I got there. Then it was discussed and laid on us. It was a bit of shock, coming out of the blue. My feeling was, 'Oh well, if that's the way it is, that's the way it is.' You just think everything's gonna get sorted as discussed. It's in my nature to say 'Oh well' and just get on with it." The "everything" to which Valentine refers as something he trusted would be sorted was a pay-off, the prospect of which would have considerably softened the blow of losing his livelihood. "With the deal that we had signed with Decca and MGM there were advances paid over three or four years," he says. "There was an agreement drawn up that he [Burdon] would continue with the name 'The Animals' and fulfil the obligations of the recording contract. He would take fifty per cent and the other fifty would be split between us. Which to this day I've never got." "What a farce that was," Rowberry says of the Jermyn Street meeting. "The band and Mike Jeffries and the lawyer, and he had one of these speaker phones and he was in contact with a barrister [acting for the band]: it could have been his charman, could have been *anybody* on the other end. We had a break-up agreement which we all duly signed after some arguments. Nothing ever came of it. We were supposed to get something like forty grand each, which was a lot of money. The lawyer, next thing I knew, was living out in the Bahamas on money that probably we should have got. You can't fight an international case. In the Bahamas, we opened up accounts. Not a penny ever reached it." "A whole package deal was set up with a tax shelter in the Bahamas," says Burdon. "Our friends The Beatles had done the same thing and everything seemed to be fine in their camp. We all had an undying respect for Brian Epstein. We thought, 'Why not?' We weren't given a chance to think about it because it was like, 'Okay, you're starting a US tour tomorrow, if you don't sign this you're gonna get killed and the UK government's gonna take all your money.'" Burdon would seem to be spinning the factual into the apocryphal here, especially when he adds a comment that places this meeting during The Animals' first visit to the States in '64: "The meeting in New York, I just looked at the faces: they looked like waxwork figures and they were quoting figures that were going way above my head. I couldn't understand the dialogue. What I'd came for was to see the Apollo in New York and I walked out of the meeting, downstairs, got in the taxi in the snow, went up to Harlem and stood outside the Apollo underneath the façade. It was Monday night, it was closed, but I felt that I'd arrived. I was quite happy to be on that trip." John Steel says of the Bahamas account(s), "I can't remember a particular meeting. I think we just learned about it from Mike Jeffery. Anyway, it happened and it might just as well have been a burglary because the money just vanished."

Burdon further says, "Pricey, I might add, who was a tax officer himself before he joined the band, he was the only guy who had any inkling that this was illegal and impractical, which is probably one of the reasons why he took the money and run. I knew early on that we weren't going to see any money."

Jeffery would shortly become co-manager of Jimi Hendrix, another recording artist whose finances are reputed to have been looted by those supposed to be looking after him, but Kathy Etchingham, Hendrix's girlfriend from 1966-1969, finds it difficult to view Jeffery as a villain. "I think that Mike Jeffries has had a bad press, quite frankly," she says. "We used to go up to Mike Jeffries' flat in Jermyn Street, me and Jimi. He had a wife called Jill. He used to have us in stitches. We were practically falling on the floor with laughter, he was so funny. Never, ever did he talk about, 'You've got to do this, or you've got to do that.' He just used to tell amusing tales and everything. Yes, okay, he did rip them off, but then lots of people ripped off bands in those days. Just ask The Kinks, ask anybody. They all got ripped off because the business wasn't like it is now. Now it is *a* business, then it was just like ambition, and you signed up with anybody to reach your goal, even if the contract was unfair." Speaking specifically about Jeffery's handling of Hendrix's finances but therefore by implication of The Animals', Etchingham says, "I don't think he stole anything. I think it was the contract. The contract was all weighted in the manager's favour."

"It didn't surprise me when Chas went down to the Bahamas and came back and told me that the bank had disappeared," says Burdon. "It physically disappeared. It was gone. Different name-plate on the door. Different government." "He did tell me about that," says Etchingham of Chandler. "That's what they are: they're just front offices with a nameplate, and you can't investigate them or anything, tax havens. Mike Jeffries from that point of view did spirit away quite a lot of the money." Both Rowberry and Burdon suspect that Animals money was used to kick-start the career of Hendrix, whose co-manager with Jeffery was Chas Chandler. Burdon: "You cannot create an international star of the level of Hendrix without a bit of funding somewhere."

Rowberry managed to take the split philosophically: "My feet never left the ground. I missed the artistic sense of it, but not the rest of it. It's a shame. You've got talented people together. It was a great band to be in because there was no stardom in the band. Even Eric. I'd be in a limousine sailing through New York with motorcycle out-riders and I'd be going, 'I'm Dave Row-berry — what the fuck's all this about?'" The money issues ensured Valentine was more bitter. "As soon as The Animals broke up, I had a very bad taste in my mouth about the music and the music business and I stopped playing for a few years," he says. "I just couldn't pick up the guitar anymore. We were ripped off finan-cially right, left and centre."

"It was inevitable that the band would break up," says Burdon. "I've always looked at The Animals as being designed like a hand grenade. All you got to do is pull the pin and it goes off."

The Animals officially ceased to exist on September 5 1966. Their last album, of course, was already in the can. When *Animalism* was released, in the US only, in December of that year , it reached number 33, a surprisingly respectable figure for the product of a band that had been defunct for three months. *Animalism* is the great lost Animals album. Lost not only in the sense that it was only released in America but also lost in the sense that its title is so confusingly similar to the completely different British album *Animalisms* that many reference books mistakenly assume the albums are the same. This is the bitterest irony, for — despite its atrocious sleeve (Dave Rowberry doesn't even appear in the fuzzy picture) — *Animalism* was the best-ever (original) Animals album. Despite, also, the fact that it was another hodgepodge. Though the general slickness and the tough, brawny element to its sound suggests an LP recorded as a cohesive whole, Jenkins claims, "Some of the tracks I'm not even on them. This is old tracks they dragged from when Johnny was with the band." Jenkins is certain that his drumming can be heard on 'Shake', 'Hey Gyp', 'Rock Me Baby' and 'Lucille' and is less certain he is on 'Going Down Slow' and 'Louisiana Blues.' The rest of the material he claims no knowledge of.

The album's only real failure is the lack of new songs: following good collaborations between Burdon & Chandler and Burdon & Rowberry only a few months before, the absence of any self-generated material whatsoever is a real step backwards. By late 1966, this made The Animals something of an anachronism: even the most mediocre of groups were writing by now. Burdon, however, despite citing The Animals' inability to compose as a reason for him splitting the band, passionately rejects the idea that covers bands are in any way inferior. "I hate the terminology 'cover'," he says. "I don't cover other people's songs, I interpret them. Songs are written to be sung. You ask any songwriter whether he wants to have his songs sung by other artists and receive royalties for it, they'll agree that yes, it's a good thing."

'All Night Long' (Trad: arr Zappa) is a very good, uptempo, randy opener with a rather Pricey organ solo. The following 'Shake' is just as good. Sam Cooke's dance exhortation had already been done by anybody and everybody but The Animals manage to wring a few last drops of originality from the song by adopting a different approach to most who tackled it. Burdon is heard, incredibly, to employ understatement: compare his restraint to Ronnie Lane's near-hysteria in the Small Faces' version. Valentine deploys his fuzzbox again but the mix favours Rowberry's organ swoops. Burdon alters the lyric to acknowledge Otis Redding's version of the song, released earlier in the year on *Otis Blue*. Probably the album's most sophisticated song, both emotionally and musically, is Fred Neil's 'The Other Side of This Life'. The narrator is a man unsure of his destiny who is trying to convince himself that relocation will cure his unhappiness. The track boasts fine, sharp bass playing. King-Josea's 'Rock Me Baby' is another 12-bar but such is the band's newfound powerhouse style that it in no way sounds plodding or boring. Valentine's playing is particularly impressive, starting out with gnarly rhythm stuff and then moving into superb virtuoso lead work. However, it's a tight performance all-round, with a punch-packing rhythm section. Rowberry's organ contributes merely occasional and faint dashes of colour. There's an absolute world of difference between 'Lucille' and The Animals' previous cover of a song made famous by Little Richard ('The Girl Can't Help It', from their first album). Such is the development of the band that this time they can stare Little Richard down. In fact, Burdon sounds uncannily like Richard in many places. Valentine's guitar is necessarily mixed up front, as he has to compensate for the absence of the piano and the brass of the original, and the performance is generally powerful enough to overcome the song's ultra-familiarity. The Animals' version of Howlin' Wolf's 'Smoke Stack Lightning' is more of a jam session than a cover. At 5:19, it's way too long, and despite its nicely menacing atmosphere and remarkable voicebox tricks by Burdon, there were much better versions recorded. 'Hey Gyp', a composition by English Dylan clone-cum-flower child Donovan, is, on the surface, a most unlikely song for an R&B band to cover. "That was my choice," says Valentine. The Animals' translation of Donovan's spiky acoustic original to an electric treatment works wonderfully. Its chugging guitar riff and references to car models makes one wonder whether the then-nineteen-years-old Marc Bolan was taking notes. Rowberry, for once to the fore, produces sounds that make his organ sound like a flute. Even Jenkins is given the spotlight at one point and lives up to it, creating a simulation of a human pulse when Burdon sings "Can't you hear my heart beat?" and then sustaining imaginative patterns as the other instruments accommodatingly drop away. 'Hit the Road, Jack' was written by Percy Mayfield but was, of course, made famous by Burdon's idol Ray Charles. It could never live up to the more familiar rendition — not least because, with this version lacking the female chorus of the Charles record, Burdon peculiarly sings both parts of this exchange between disenchanted woman and spurned man — but it's a game and enjoyable attempt. The following 'Outcast' is a very different version of the song that appeared on the B-side of 'Inside — Looking Out' and on the UK *Animalisms* album but just as good. It's faster with a thinner, pleasantly brittle guitar sound and with a guitar rather than organ solo. 'Louisiana Blues' (uncredited, but a song made famous by Muddy Waters) is another slow blues but again sprightly and short enough to be resistant to the 12-bar tedium curse. Scratchy guitar is played in synchronisation with Rowberry's upbeat piano. Already released in Britain on *Animalisms*, 'That's All I Am to You' is included here because it had been left off the US album *Animalization*. Of 'Going Down Slow' (Oden), Rowberry remembers, "That's one of my favourite Ray Charles tracks of all time. That was on an album I had on the boat in Hawaii." The title is appropriate, the track being a stately, long album closer. With a 12- bar of 6:12, the band are once again faced with the challenge of producing enough tricks, virtuoso playing and moments of spontaneity to stave off boredom. They manage it well.

"By that time I was so pissed off with everybody I couldn't see straight," says Burdon of the album's non-release in the UK. "MGM were releasing stuff all over the place. The Americans released singles — not only for The Animals but for The Beatles — out of sequence with the way the material originated from England and it was very frustrating. I'm glad you like the album. I liked it too." Valentine says "When you hear that album, it is a shame that the band broke up."

Dave Rowberry became a successful session man following The Animals' demise. Hilton Valentine was going through the start of an aimless and unhappy period related to his LSD intake. "I hung around London for a while," he says. "I had a bit of money left over. There were still some royalties coming in." As for Chas Chandler, John Steel recalls, "I'd met Eric some time later in '66. I said, 'What's everybody doing?' He said, 'Oh, Chas has found this black guitarist guy called Jimi Hendrix and he plays guitar with his teeth.' Eric hadn't seen him then either. I just thought of one of those mohair-suited, very slick guys doing his tricks with the guitar. I put on the TV to watch *Top of the Pops* a little while later and there's Jimi Hendrix doing 'Hey Joe' and I thought, 'Wow!' This was like from a different planet. I thought, 'Chas has got that! Bloody hell!'" So started a management career that saw the least gifted of all the Animals make far more money than anyone else who was ever in the band — possibly put together.

Though he split the group up, Burdon is proud of The Animals as "a band that interpreted American blues. If I listen to the raw original tapes — in fact there are some BBC recordings that are better than the Mickie Most stuff, the Brain Matthews' *Saturday Club* stuff — when Pricey was still in the band, John Steel was still in the band, the original line-up, it was five guys who really believed collectively in what they were doing. We were at our best then and we carved our niche in the English scene and I feel quite happy about that."

Following the split, Burdon went to New York for what was a strange interlude in his career.

There he began recording his debut post-Animals album, *Eric Is Here*. This LP — whose title now sounds peculiar but would have made sense to anyone familiar with the strapline of a 1965 US TV advertisement for Erik cigars — was the first LP to be credited to "Eric Burdon & The Animals". It, however, had nothing to do with the group of that name that Burdon began assembling in the same month as *Eric Is Here* was recorded. Nor did the album possess any of the hallmarks of Burdon's taste in music expressed previously or subsequently. Instead, it was a *non sequitur* of a project whose parameters were set by MGM. Despite all the rucks he had had with Mickie Most about commercial compromises, Burdon agreed here to a situation whereby he had minimal artistic control in a scenario in which the label had decided to see what would result if his powerful voice was matched to pop tunes and set against the plush backdrop of the efforts of Big Apple session men.

Strange and even wrong-headed as this venture sounds, its first fruits was a quite wonderful single which must have left punters drooling at the mouth in anticipation of the forthcoming album. Released in October 1966 in Britain and two months later in the States, 'Help Me Girl' was a piece of work with production values higher than those attending anything The Animals had hitherto recorded and as instantly attention-catching as its writers' (Scott English and Larry Weiss) 'Hi-Ho Silver Lining' was the same year when released by Jeff Beck. The arrangement is just right: the lovely opening organ warble, the smoky horns and the tip-toeing piano all create an effect that is beautifully polished without falling into the trap of being bland. Burdon's deep burr sounds all the more impressive counterpointed by this lavishness. (An alternate version appears on the 1991 Polydor CD *The Best of Eric Burdon and the Animals 1966-1968*.) 'See See Rider' received its first British release on the B-side, rather bizarrely as the band that had recorded it were now history. In America, the B-side, more appropriately, was a song from the same sessions as 'Help Me Girl.' On 'That Ain't Where It's At' (Siegel) Burdon dispenses advice on life — and a phrase of the moment — to the backing of classy, flowing horn charts and stately drumming. The single reached number 14 in Britain and number 29 Stateside, though probably would have climbed higher were it not for a competing version by The Outsiders, which peaked at number 37.

After such an excellent taster, *Eric Is Here* was something of a disappointment. The instrumentation by the anonymous sessioners is almost always excellent but rather lacks passion, as is often the way with records made by people clocking on and off. Meanwhile, though the material is provided by a quite remarkably gifted array of songwriters from English & Weiss to Goffin & King and Mann & Weil (Brill Building) to Ritchie Cordell (collaborator with Tommy James and the Shondells) to Boyce and Hart (providers of songs for The Monkees) to Randy Newman, the result is something less than the sum of the compositional parts. Tom Wilson's glossy, widescreen production becomes as suffocating as it managed to avoid being on the taster single while the sure-footed arrangements by Benny Golson and Horace Ott ultimately feel as if they are following a grid. Meanwhile, although plentiful amounts of brass lend a soul tinge, there is so little that is gritty about the album (right down to a front cover watercolour of Burdon in a floral setting) that one is put in mind of writer/DJ Paul Gambaccini's wry observation about Wilson producing Burdon, "…the white man who had a pop producer [Most] help him make blues records now had a black producer, Tom Wilson, helping him make pop records." It's not that everything on *Eric Is Here* sounds either anodyne or the same but after the umpteenth uniformly immaculate and tasteful track decorated, as though by union quota, in horn charts and/or chamber strings, one can't help but long for a bit of dirty guitar or a more sparse arrangement.

The opening 'In The Night' was written by Tommy Boyce and Bobby Hart. Their song describes the same sad milieu as 'We've Gotta Get Out of this Place' and 'It's My Life', those other vignettes of proletarian life from The Animals' catalogue. Burdon by virtue of his gritty vocal and emotional fervour gives the song the smack of universal truth regarding the unskilled worker who has the home-time klaxon on his mind as soon as he clocks on. Randy Newman was a little-known, promising young songwriter at the time *Eric Is Here* was recorded. Despite having yet to release an LP, he was paid the compliment of having no fewer than three of his songs appear on this record. Burdon reasons, "Randy Newman's one of the best contemporary writers there is. I'd like to record every song he's ever written when you get down to it." The first Newman track, 'Mama Told Me Not to Come', is typical of his wry humour and acute observational powers. A teenage boy goes to a party and following the shocking sights he sees there decides that the maternal advice he was given beforehand was right: adulthood is not something he's quite ready for yet. The quality of the lyric is matched by a mock-spooky arrangement, making this one of the album's best tracks. (An alternate take of this song was released on a French EP called *See See Rider* in 1966. That version is closer to a Stax record than the more mainstream *Eric Is Here* track. Burdon's vocal is rather causal, though.) The following 'I Think It's Gonna Rain Today' is another Newman song, one of his more conventional creations despite the tinge of the unusual in the way he tries to capture not just unhappiness but an unhappiness that is made all the worse by the fact that the concern of others ("human kindness is overflowing but…") isn't going to help. The simple piano intro is one of the more soulful parts of an over-elaborate album. In 'This Side of Goodbye', as was usually the case with Goffin & King numbers, there's a pleasant little kick to the lyric, specifically the cleverness of the title phrase. The narrator wants to go back to the lover he abandoned because, "Things look much different now, on this side of goodbye." 'That Ain't Where It's At' is followed by 'True Love (Comes Only Once In A Lifetime)' (Halleyn/Nader), the song of a man who is watching helplessly as the woman he loves slips away. The track could have had more impact if it weren't for the saccharin decoration: a children's chorus is laying the emotion on a bit thick when, God knows, Eric's always been able to do that on his own. 'Wait Till Next Year' is another number from Newman. Burdon puts his own stamp on this drink-sodden anthem of self-loathing by singing it in his Geordie accent, before putting on his posh voice for the fade-out. 'Losin' Control', a number from 'It's My Life' authors D'errico/Atkins, ratchets up the plushness via woodwind and classical strings. The narrator is a man who's falling for a woman he is not sure is worthy of his affection. The chorus has a crisp marching feel that makes singing along almost irresistible. There's a similar stomping feel to Mann/Weil's 'It's Not Easy', a soul number which addresses that perennial problem of "Can't live with her, can't live without her." Burdon sang the Cordell/Trimachi-written title tune to the 1967 MGM Raquel Welch movie *The Biggest Bundle of Them All*. In the movie, Burdon is only heard for approximately sixty seconds before an orchestra takes over. The version of the song heard here is not the one heard in the movie, although is identical to the cut that appears on the film's soundtrack album. The composition offers the perspective of a man who one day hopes to find true love, which apparently is "the biggest bundle of them all." The album's closer 'It's Been A Long Time Comin', written by Brooks and Radcliffe, has the same theme — expressed in almost identical terms — as Sam Cooke's 'A Change Is Gonna Come'. However, the melodrama and the swinging brass make it less a yearning civil rights anthem and more a Sinatra-esque number.

All of the above might give a rather negative impression of *Eric Is Here*. There's not one track that's truly bad and its high production values, good musicianship and — naturally — fine singing make it an enjoyable album to have on in the background even if its lack of layering militates against undistracted scrutiny. Additionally, it provokes mild admiration in showing that Burdon wasn't constrained by the blues' limited horizons and was ready to open out his music. He hadn't quite found his sound here but he was on his way to it.

"*Eric Is Here* was a disaster," says Burdon. "It was MGM's attempt to mould me into an American star. There was a couple of good tracks on that album and it served as an interim, kept my face out there, but I wasn't very happy with it and I don't like to be reminded about it." He did enjoy the recording process, though: "It was quite an experience to work with New York session musicians."

Thanks should be given for the fact that the album was — for all its self-conscious commercialism — a flop. Heaven knows what MGM would have demanded Burdon record if it had actually been a success. As it was, it reached 121 in the US album charts, a poor chart performance helped in no small measure by the fact that by the time of its release Burdon wasn't interested in promoting it but in the imminent first record of the New Animals.

Alan Price, incidentally, clearly shared Burdon's regard for Randy Newman. On *A Price on His Head*, his second post-Animals album, he covered no fewer than seven of Newman's songs (duplicating none of Burdon's covers). One of said Newman songs, 'Simon Smith and His Amazing Dancing Bear', was a Top Five UK hit for him that year. Perhaps Price was — *a la* 'I Put A Spell On You — dogging Burdon's steps. *A Price on His Head*, released in the same year as *Eric Is Here*, also featured a cover of 'This Side of Goodbye'.

chapter eight

"I didn't know quite else what to do at that point in time," says Burdon of his assembling of a new band in the aftermath of The Animals' split. "Also, contracts tie you to certain things. When you're in the spotlight at that level, you just can't say, 'Fuck it, I'm not gonna do it anymore' and just stop it and walk away from it. You'd be tied up in lawsuits forever."

As had been demonstrated by the way the *Eric is Here* album had been credited to The Animals despite featuring session men and no sound associated with the band of that name, any new group formed by Burdon was destined to have a certain commercially valuable name regardless of the type of music it produced. "It was MGM that told me, 'If you want to keep recording, you've got to use the name "The Animals"'," says Burdon. "At that point in time, I wanted to walk away from everything, form a new English band or a new US band and pursue whatever was going on at the time with new people. I said, 'Well, let's call it the New Animals.' I didn't really care about it after a couple of weeks of arguments. I was looking at people like [The] Spencer Davis [Group] who had broken up and Stevie Winwood had created Traffic and it was fresh and it was new and it was different and it didn't fuck up his career. That's what I wanted to do."

Burdon retained Barry Jenkins for his next incarnation of The Animals but none of his other colleagues. From Jenkins' point of view, he and Burdon were always going to be the nucleus of a new ensemble "…because Eric said, 'Let's get another band together.'" "I've often wondered why Eric didn't ask me 'cause I thought we got on pretty well," says Dave Rowberry, "but as I say I think the [drug-drinkers] division was already there. I'm only surmising. I imagine that was a part of it." "Dave is a great player but his background is jazz for a start," explains Burdon. "I don't think he ever really loved being in The Animals. I don't think he really liked what we played. It was the old jazz brain attitude versus the rock'n'roll body attitude. It wasn't originally, but jazz became since the Sixties brain music. You go to jazz clubs and people are like potted brains." Of Valentine, Burdon says, "I love Hilton dearly. He became a roadie for the New Animals and even for War. He's my life-long friend. I couldn't turf him out but on the other level I was trying to get across to him, 'Come on Hilton — write something. Contribute.' But by that time he was happy enough just to go with the flow." As for Jenkins, Burdon says, "I loved the guy. He wasn't the greatest drummer in the world but he was great fun to be with." Chandler, meanwhile, had his sights set on a non-performing career.

Jenkins: "We were looking for a bass player and I knew Noel Redding. I went down to pick Noel Redding up from Folkestone and I brought him back." The auditions for the new band took place at the London pop celebrity watering hole The Scotch of St. James. Jenkins: "Just round where Eric lived. He had a flat up the top of Scotch of St. James. We had all the gear set up and we just went through some blues stuff with Noel, and Eric said, 'Ooh, no, I don't like him — he's shit.' He was a lead guitarist but he was a bit busy on the bass."

Jenkins also says, "I asked Albert Lee if he'd join the band," referring to the guitarist in The Thunderbirds, backing band of Chris Farlowe, a singer very much in Burdon's gritty, bluesy vein. "I knew Albert from '62 when we done Germany, playing all them GI clubs." Jenkins had also become acquainted with Farlowe's bassist Bruce Waddell in Germany and he too was the subject of an attempted poaching. A couple of meetings between Burdon and the prospective recruits were arranged. Albert Lee recalls, "I knew Eric through being with Farlowe because he was a big Chris Farlowe fan and used to come down and see us play at the Flamingo Club." Lee doesn't recall Burdon having a vision for a bold new musical direction at that time. "I just assumed that we were going to carry on the same kind of music with a slightly different line-up to what he'd had," he says. However, in the end

the talks came to nothing. "He didn't want to know," is Jenkins'
recollection of Lee's reasons. "He didn't like that sort of music. He
didn't like blues, he liked his country stuff." However, Lee recalls
his knockback as being more related to the fact that Farlowe had
just had a UK number one with Jagger/Richards' 'Out Of Time'.
"Things were really going quite well with Farlowe at that time
so we decided to stay with it," Lee explains. "I've always liked
Eric but I always thought that Chris was *the* British blues singer.
Everybody looked up to him... He'd recently had a number one
record and we were sharing the money out too so it was a good
gig to be on." Lee did leave the Thunderbirds in 1968 and went
on to become one of the top country sessioners in the US.

The new band obtained a bassist and a guitarist almost as a
job lot. Jenkins: "I got another bloke I knew, Danny McCulloch.
He was in a group called The Plebs and he was in Screaming
Lord Sutch and the Savages. And he knew Johnny Weider. That's
how we got Johnny in the band." Bassist Danny McCulloch was
born July 18 1945 in London. Also a Londoner, guitarist John
Weider was born April 21 1947. "I was picked over a lot of big
names who tried out for the gig," Weider remembers. "I guess
nice Jewish boys can play the blues. I had never met Eric before.
He was looking for a blues guitarist and ended up with a violinist
as well — two for the price of one. I was classically trained as a
violinist from the age of seven to sixteen and kept up my studies as I entered the pop world. People knew that I played violin
and guitar and hired me for that reason." Weider had previously
played in Johnny Kidd and The Pirates.

The same set of auditions that resulted in McCulloch and
Weider being picked also led to the rejected Noel Redding hook-
ing up with Jimi Hendrix. Jenkins recalls, "Chas was there and
he said, 'Here Noel, if you ain't got nothing to do, what about
coming with me with a bloke called Jimi Hendrix?'" The drumming seat in the The Jimi Hendrix Experience would ultimately
go to Mitch Mitchell, but Jenkins reveals the job could have been
his: "[Chandler] asked me to go with them and I turned him
down... they got Mitch instead." The New Animals auditions
had a further significant effect on rock history when Burdon

gave a sack containing all the rejected applications to The Moody Blues, who were currently looking for a guitarist to replace Denny Laine. The first application the Moodies picked out was from one Justin Hayward.

In addition to McCulloch and Weider, Burdon recruited keyboardist Tom Parker, although he only played in the band on a short UK tour in October. During this tour, Burdon was unable to perform at a couple of gigs and McCulloch had to take over singing duties. According to Weider, some members of the audiences thought McCulloch was Burdon and commented on how he'd gained weight.

During this period, The Animals' touring party crossed paths with that of Brian Auger, who employed a guitarist called Vic Briggs. As well as being known to all the New Animals, Briggs had once played in a band with Weider called The Laurie Jay Combo. "I was sitting in the Blue Boar Café with Brian Auger and company and the whole tour came in," recalls Briggs. "I had this blue sailor's cap that this girlfriend of mine had given to me. Eric came in — and I know he was on acid — and he looked at me with this big stupid grin on his face and he goes: 'Every one of us!' From 'Yellow Submarine'." The phrase must have stuck in Burdon's mind because the third album by the New Animals was given that title, by which time Briggs had been a member of the New Animals for nearly two years. "We used to go down The Scotch of St. James club and all the speakeasies and Brain Auger was a really shit-hot band in them days," says Jenkins. "That's how we met Vic Briggs. Eric said, 'I want him' and we just sort of headhunted Vic Briggs."

Briggs was born in Feltham, West London, on February 14 1945. "My family on my mother's side came from Tyneside," he points out. "So I had a lot of connections with Tyneside. I used to go up there when I was a kid." Although he had piano lessons as a child, his first serious instrument was a banjo ukulele he found lying around the house and which he taught himself to play. His mother bought him a guitar in the middle of the skiffle craze when he was twelve. He started playing in bands when he was fifteen. Before he'd even left school, he had performed with Jerry Lee Lewis. By the time Briggs met John Weider in The Laurie Jay Combo, a band he joined when he was nineteen, he'd already started to teach himself musical notation. In 1965, he became guitarist in Dusty Springfield's back-up band, playing live with her and performing on her records, including 'In The Middle Of Nowhere' (a UK number 8 in 1965). He then went on to play in Steampacket with Rod Stewart. He loaned Jimi Hendrix his amplifier for a performance at The Scotch of St. James on Hendrix's second day in London in September 1966. In mid-October 1966, Briggs was in Paris playing with French pop idol Johnny Halliday when he was approached by Mike Jeffery, who was there in his capacity as co-manager (with Chas Chandler) of bill-sharer Jimi Hendrix. Recalls Briggs, "A couple of hours before the show, Mike Jeffries comes up and says, 'You wanna go get a cup of coffee?' I was surprised because Mike's not the type of guy to ask you to do something unless there's a real good reason behind it. So we go and sit in this French café and he goes, 'Would you be interested in joining the New Animals?'" Briggs had actually been quite jealous when he'd heard his former colleague Weider had gotten the Animals gig. "I was very surprised when Jeffries asked me to join," he says. "Eric had never been terribly friendly towards me. I tried asking Eric what led him to have me joining the band. He never would tell me." "When I wanted to expand the sound of the band in the studio, experiment with sounds, he was capable of writing charts and all that kind of stuff," says Burdon. "I think Zoot Money had told me he was [a] capable, highly trained musician." Briggs says, "I always thought of myself as being a musician-musician, rather than being a teen idol. It was kind of a shock." There was a condition attached to Briggs' recruitment: he had to shave off his beard because Jeffery was worried it wouldn't fit in with the band's image. Six months later, Burdon was the only Animals member who was clean-shaven.

Briggs also reveals, "I did hear that they'd asked two other people to join before me. One was a young guy with the Alex Harvey Band. He was really good but apparently he was scared of flying so they said, 'We don't want another Pricey here, forget it.'"Jenkins doesn't remember this but suggests that if it is correct it might have been the suggestion of Dave Rowberry, who had played with Alex Harvey. Intriguingly, Briggs reveals, "While we were rehearsing, Mike Bloomfield showed up." The American Bloomfield had played guitar with the Paul Butterfield Blues Band and for Bob Dylan on his brilliant 1965 album *Highway 61 Revisited.* "I later heard that he was looking for the job with The Animals," explains Briggs. "He began to direct the rehearsal and that made me pissed off and insecure. He took us through a blues number called 'Same Thing'. It was actually quite a good arrangement and we used it on stage for a long time afterwards. Personally I found him to be an insufferable egomaniac, but I admit that I might have been a little prejudiced since I was quite insecure in my position at that time." Weider confirms that Bloomfield was considered by Burdon for The Animals. He says Burdon ultimately rejected the idea and that Bloomfield was "hanging around," trying to edge his way in even after Briggs' recruitment because he had a notion that the band could use three guitarists.

Of the fleetingly employed keyboardist Tom Parker, Briggs says, "I think the understanding was that he knew he was just in for this one tour and that was it." Burdon confirms that Parker was intended as a temporary addition. Briggs: "I do remember Eric saying — which I didn't agree with, but who was I to argue? — that you could do more with two guitars than with guitar and keyboards." Says Burdon, "The reason for that is not musical, it's what I can afford to travel with. If I could get away with it today, I'd have a Hammond B3 with Leslie speakers. You know how much that costs to travel [with], a rig like that?"

As John Weider was an extremely able guitarist, it meant that the New Animals would be a band with two lead guitarists, something rather novel for the time. Briggs says, "We'd trade off. I actually wound up playing lead on all the singles' A-sides that we did, 'til we get to 'Sky Pilot', then John did the lead on 'Sky Pilot'. John was a blues guy. He was into Clapton and Jeff Beck and that kind of sound and I was more jazz-oriented, 'cause I'd been with Brian [Auger]." Despite this sensible policy of apportioning lead role according to the style of the song, Briggs admits, "John and I could have explored playing together a lot more than we did. Other groups like The Allman Brothers and Spirit took the two-guitars-in-harmony thing to a whole lot of heights. Somehow we never got round to doing that. Despite the fact that we were good friends, I think there was a lot of competition: 'Who's gonna play the solo now?'" This 'problem' merely indicated the talent-oozing quality of the band. Eric Burdon & The Animals were a staggeringly able line-up of musicians. John Weider's proficiency on the violin added an exotic tinge to the band's sound. He was also able to play keyboard parts (Briggs is incorrectly given credit for keyboards on New Animals records). Danny McCulloch's rumbling playing style made him one of the most innovative bassists of the Sixties, on top of which he was a fine tunesmith. Barry Jenkins, meanwhile, blossomed, creating complicated patterns on New Animals records that he would never have thought of when working within the narrow musical horizons of the original Animals. In 1967, Jimi Hendrix — who was already on his way to becoming the most celebrated guitarist in rock history — listed for a reporter his favourite guitarists. He nominated Eric Clapton, Jeff Beck — and Vic Briggs. "Both John Weider and Vic Briggs had more musical schooling than any of the original Animals did, except for Alan Price," says Burdon.

Burdon was now the sole remaining Newcastle lad in the once quintessentially North-Eastern Animals. Says John Steel, "Knowing Eric, he was probably trying to get away from his Geordie-ness. He always fantasised about being a black American, so it's quite within his psychological make-up to completely put his Geordie-ness in a hole somewhere and forget it and be at least a Londoner rather than a North-Easterner. As soon as he was able to, he achieved his teenage dream of living in America. Now he considers himself almost to be American, I think. He just did it in stages."

The band began rehearsing in The Scotch of St. James in early November, 1966. Did Burdon have a specific vision of the sound he wanted from the New Animals? "Not from the get-go," Burdon says. "Putting a band together is like painting. You start with an empty canvas and then you put some colours on and then it develops. I did have a rough sketch of what I wanted to do. The idea became more than vague once we started playing, especially on the West Coast. I wanted it to be *the* English West Coast psychedelic band. Which is what we achieved, so I was quite happy with that period in time… It was a true psychedelic collective band of musicians, open to any kind of ideas, any kind of jams and performances. My guru then and my guru today was Rahsaan Roland Kirk. That guy lived in a world of sound and would use everything from broken glass to pre-recorded soundtracks on mini Japanese tape machines to playing three horns at once. If he was my teacher and master, you can imagine that my mind was open for anything." Briggs says, "Eric had been taking a lot of acid. He'd been on the West Coast, he'd been very influenced by what was happening there, the psychedelic bands. He was very impressed with Zappa. He wanted to do something new."

During a visit to San Francisco, Burdon had been overwhelmed by the love-and-peace philosophy of the people living in and around the Haight-Ashbury district whom the world was just learning to call 'hippies'. "The New Animals wouldn't have been formed at all hadn't I taken a telephone call from a girlfriend of mine, Judy Wong, who I'd met on our first trip to America," says Burdon. "She came over to England. She was the only American that I knew and I was very hot under the collar about the race situation — she's Japanese-American — and I used to always have a go at her about America's lack of movement forward on the race question. She always got angry at me because she felt that I never really fully understood the American political landscape. So when things started to change in San Francisco, she called me and told me, 'Look, you've got to come here and see what's happening.' The last time I was there, I remember walking the streets with John Steel and it was the end of the beatnik period. Lenny Bruce had just been working at the Hungry I. It was the San Francisco of Steve McQueen and *Bullitt*. As soon as the psychedelic bomb hit, it was a different San Francisco overnight and I wanted to be a part of it. I saw it as a real movement forward. In England, people were just like, 'Oh, for the first time in England's history in years we're not involved in any conflict anywhere, so we're just sitting around on our asses listening to Dylan and Donovan and hoping that it'll stay this way.' 'Merry Old England Swings Like a Pendulum Do' was on the charts. Meanwhile, in the United States, you were either over there on the dark side or you were over here on the bright light psychedelic side and you knew which was right and you knew what was wrong. There was very little going on in England. Couple of riots, but there was no real political agenda anymore. It was all just, 'You've never had it so good' and Christine Keeler and all that and that was about as exciting as it got. I was just bored with the whole thing. California opened my mind and that's where I wanted to be and that's where I wanted my players to be based out of. The movies and the literature that's hit the marketplace since those days attempts to give that period a bum rap. People have forgotten what a revelation it was to see open eyes and open hearts, open arms and open heads."

Despite Burdon's intention to make the finalised New Animals self-sufficient when it came to material ("He was pretty adamant about that" — Briggs), the band's repertoire as they began playing live dates was comprised of cover versions. They made their stage debut at Birmingham University on November 25 1966, with Briggs' making his first public performance of any kind with the group on the radio programme *Saturday Club* one week previously. A cover of The Rolling Stones' 'Paint It Black' (later to appear on their debut album) was in the set from day one. "I was trying to learn to play alto sax," Briggs says. "When we went out to our first gig, we started off 'Paint It Black' with me playing alto sax and John playing violin. That lasted for maybe two gigs, that alto sax part. But the violin part went on forever." Other songs performed at those early gigs included the inevitable 'The House of the Rising Sun', 'Same Thing', 'Jailhouse Rock', 'Shake, Rattle & Roll', 'Every Day I Get The Blues', the Frank Zappa composition 'How Can I Be Such A Fool?', 'All Night Long' and a couple of jazz numbers: 'My Favorite Things' and 'If Only We Knew', the latter originating with John Handy, for whom Briggs and Weider had a penchant. Frequently, the band would start the set with 'See See Rider'. Other Animals songs attempted were 'Don't Let Me Be Misunderstood' and 'We've Gotta Get Out of this Place', although the latter was quickly dropped.

As for the way the band was billed, Briggs recalls, "It varied. Sometimes we were the 'New Animals', sometimes we were just 'The Animals'." Briggs adds, "My observation of Eric is that ever since the old Animals broke up he always wanted to get away from The Animals. There was a feeling amongst [the rest of the group] that we wanted to establish ourselves as different from The Animals. It was a source of frustration to us for a long time that we were always coming up against that thing of, 'The old Animals were better', just because people were familiar with the old Animals." Despite this, Briggs says that the early gigs went well. "They liked us. I don't recall having any particular problems. The only thing that used to piss us off — we used to make a joke out of this — people used to go: 'HOUSE OF THE RISING SUN!' Eric didn't want to do 'House of the Rising Sun' but he had very little choice."

Jenkins was excited by the new band he'd help put together. "We clicked, all of us," he says. "Me and Danny got on fantastic, drum and bass. Johnny was into the Eric Clapton sort of stuff. Fantastic player he was. And Vic Briggs was into the more Wes Montgomery jazzy stuff. Great sort of influence. The two of them were different. Vic done a lot of arranging and stuff. I was still practising me arse off all day because I thought I wasn't any good all the time. It's a funny feeling, that. But The Animals gelled so good as we got to the end." He cites the group's performance of the Martha and the Vandellas B-side 'A Love Like Yours (Don't Come Knocking Everyday)' on German TV show *Beat Club* in January 1967 as some sort of high water mark: "Oh, the band was so good live. Really enjoying it, really getting on top of your thing."

For his part, Briggs remembers this period as being rather tentative and uncertain. "I just didn't feel very confident about the band just 'cause I was new and here we are coming in, following these other guys. I don't think we really picked up our confidence until probably the summer of '67, after the Monterey Pop Festival. It was a very hard time for me. I was insecure. Even though we knew each other, we were weighing each other up: 'Where's the pecking order in this band?' Perhaps feeling a little overwhelmed by a lot of responsibility. It didn't get exciting for quite a while." Was it not thrilling being attached to an already successful artist like Burdon? Briggs: "Absolutely, but that maybe added to the pressure." One thing about which Briggs wasn't unhappy was the money he was now receiving as an Animal. "We were getting fifty pounds a week in England and in the United States we'd get two hundred dollars," he reveals. "It doesn't sound like much but in 1967 it was a fair chunk of change. That was to be renegotiated after one year and then we were going to go on to some kind of percentage basis. To me, it was fair. We were under Eric's name. To us, there was no reason The Animals shouldn't go on for years and years and years."

In addition to New Animals gigs, towards the end of '66 Briggs and Burdon played a couple of concerts in the style of the Richmond Jazz Festival performance the previous year. Briggs: "One was at South-East London, the other one was at the Marquee. Eric, knowing I had a feel for jazz, had me come along and play with this big band."

The New Animals' first recordings were a session for the BBC in the first couple of weeks of the finalised line-up's existence. One of those tracks, 'Jailhouse Rock', was released on the compilation album *Roadrunners!* in 1990. Zoot Money and Georgie Fame are also on the track, playing organ and piano. Recorded at the same session was 'Same Thing', which is presumably still sitting in the BBC vaults. The band's debut recording session, meanwhile, led to them finally making the transition to writing their own material. Mike Jeffery suggested they record 'Connection'. This daringly druggie Jagger/Richards song would not see release until the January 1967 Rolling Stones album *Between The Buttons* but it had been part of the New Animals' set for a while. "Jeffries gave Eric an acetate of the song in November 1966," says Briggs. "I have no idea how he came by it… I think we did it at the first gig, and I think it lasted into the US tour, but was soon dropped." On the recording session, he continues, "So we started to rehearse it and Eric goes, 'Well, this is a Stones song. I'm not fucking recording this.'" Instead, Burdon went through one of his journals of lyrics. He chose an autobiographical piece and bolted it to a tune already devised by Weider, creating the song 'When I Was Young'. Tom Wilson flew over from New York to produce and the band recorded the song at Olympic Studio in Barnes, London in December '66 with Eddie Kramer (who would work extensively with Jimi Hendrix) acting as engineer.

Not long afterwards Jeffery rang Briggs to announce that the band needed to go back in the studio. Briggs: "He says, 'There's this movie coming out and I've landed a deal where you guys write a song for the movie. The only thing is you've got to write it in conjunction with this guy, Johnny Scott.' Patrick John Scott, the film music composer." (Scott also played the flute part on The Beatles' 'You've Got to Hide Your Love Away'.) The fact that Jeffery contacted Briggs over this indicates that from the outset it was accepted that Briggs was the New Animals' musical director, something reflected in the arranger's credit he would receive on their records. Burdon says, "Vic Briggs did contribute quite a lot with his arrangements to those rather experimental recordings that we made during that period."

"So we got together," Briggs says of Scott. "We actually never really wrote anything. He actually wound up never having any say in the composition at all but he still got a cut. Patrick John Scott came up with the title because Bobby Darin's character in the movie was always going, 'Ain't dat so, ain't dat so?' We go in the same studio, late at night, and in the space of two or three hours we come up with this song 'Ain't That So'." Though the song was credited to Briggs/Scott — the nature of its origin meaning it had to be published by Film Music rather than the New Animals' publishing company Sealark — Briggs admits that the lyric that celebrates the counter-culture was Burdon's, written after Briggs had hummed the melody he'd written at him. "He didn't get any credit for it," says Briggs. "I don't feel really good about that. He did a real good job actually. I threw it at him in about ten minutes and the same night we're in the studio and we did the whole thing. Next morning I gave the tapes to Jeffries, he takes it to the film people, they're delighted, put it in the movie. It was a

one-shot deal for *Stranger in the House* [US title: *Cop-Out*] star-
ring James Mason. If you ever get the chance to see that — don't.
It was a really bad movie. They used it a couple of times." The
New Animals, minus Burdon who declined to go, took delight
in attending the premiere of the movie in rented tuxedoes upon
the shoulders of which hung their long hippie hair.

Another recording session for a movie in January 1967 was
less successful. Jeffery rang Briggs to tell him he'd secured a deal
for The Animals to perform a song called 'Let the Love Shine
Through' written by the hot Burt Bacharach/Hal David com-
posing team for the James Bond comedy *Casino Royale*. Briggs
recalls, "I went up to see Burt Bacharach — he was in London at
the time — and he had a moviola. He shows me the thing and he
says, 'This is how it goes' and he gives me a tape. So we went back
to the same studio and we recorded. Then I bring in some horns.
We overdubbed the horns. All that's left is to get Eric to sing the
song. I give him Bacharach's demo and give him the tape of our
backing track. We get to the session. Hal David shows up. Eric
hasn't learnt the fucking song. So we go through the song, stop
and go. I'm like, sing a line to Eric, then we run the tape and he
sings a line. Eventually we get it on tape. Hal David looks at me
and he says, 'No way we're gonna put this in the movie.' So that
was the end of that."

The only other recordings the New Animals ever made in their
home country were the B-side 'Gratefully Dead' and two tracks
that would feature on their debut album, 'Winds of Change' and
'Poem By The Sea'.

The band's first tour of America started in February '67 and got
off to a rather shaky start. Burdon had appointed one Phil Robertson as tour manager. (By this time Terry McVay had replaced
his fellow Geordie Tappy Wright as road manager.) Briggs: "This
Phil character has been around the music scene for a while. He's
basically so fucked up that Eric wants to save him, so he gives
him a job as tour manager. He's been touring with us for a while
and we're all set to go to the States. All of a sudden, we find out
that Phil has gone to the States ahead of time. Probably a week
ahead of us. That Sunday, there's this big article that comes out

in the *News of the World* on pop stars and drugs. In those days it was a big deal. It turns out that the main informant for this article is Phil Robertson. So all of a sudden, in London there's a lot of people pissed off at Phil Robertson. He turned out to be an enormous liability on the tour: he was skimming money off the top and doing all kinds of weird shit."

Terry McVay, although in no way untrustworthy, created his own problems, as illustrated by an incident from the end of March '67. On that first US tour, the New Animals had to double up in rooms through lack of funds. "Terry and I used to room together," recalls Briggs. "I'm sleeping away. All of a sudden I hear the sound of running water. I look over and Terry is standing there pissing on his bed. I went back to sleep. Later on I said, 'Terry, I saw you pissing on your bed this morning.' He said, 'Oh! I was wondering why it was wet when I woke up.' Later on, in the fall of '67, we finally got to have our own rooms but Terry's room was always the party room. I was in there talking to him one day and he says, 'You know what? I'm gonna stop having everybody coming into my room. It's getting too much, it's getting out of hand.' I says, 'Why, what's the problem?' He says, 'Well, I woke up this morning, there's a big turd in the middle of my floor.' I says, 'Terry, the only person I can think of who'd do that is you.'" Nevertheless, McVay was universally considered a vital and much-loved part of the New Animals' entourage. "Terry McVay was a really, sweet loving guy," Briggs says. "We all had our nasty stuff but Terry didn't have a nasty bone in his body. I remember him once saying to me when he was really drunk, 'You guys don't understand how much I love you.' He was really sincere about it."

Briggs recalls of the first US tour, "In the aftermath of the Herman's Hermits tour, which I understand was an artistic disaster, [Burdon] wanted the band to be taken a lot more seriously. We rehearsed a lot of songs from varying degrees of obscurity. In fact, that tour was supposed to be a college tour. The idea being that more mature audiences would appreciate more mature music. The first gig of the tour was Hunter College in New York City. This was a pretty major gig in terms of the NY intelligentsia showing up. We actually played two sets with an intermission and featured the two jazz instrumentals John Coltrane's 'My Favorite Things' and John Handy's 'If Only We Knew.' I thought the gig was well-received and a great success. In fact the tour turned out to only have a few college dates. So we found that often we were going over the audiences' heads and we had to do more of the 'pop'-type material. But there were a few college dates where we did have a chance to stretch out and play our more arcane stuff. After that tour, the only place where we played our more eclectic stuff was when we played the Fillmore auditorium in San Francisco" (June and October 1967).

That American tour gave the other Animals the first glimpse of the paradise on earth that Burdon had told them existed in San Francisco. "We didn't really know what he was talking about 'til we got there," says Briggs. "We just didn't know what to expect. We did some gigs in the San Francisco bay area. Did the Oakland Coliseum, did the San Francisco Civic Auditorium. And that's where we started meeting the hippies. When I was a kid, growing up as a teenager, people were very harsh to each other, especially in London. When I went to San Francisco, here was a whole group of people who were really trying to be considerate of each other in a way that I'd never seen before. Of course, it was drug induced but there was a real attempt to be concerned about other people's feelings and other people's needs and I'd grown up with a post-war survival-of-the-fittest thing. For me, post-war England was so fucking depressing. It was heavy-duty in London. Fucking heavy. It was actually hard for us Brits to fit in because we were used to this aggressive, throw-your-weight-around, London approach. We were taken aback with all this gentleness and peace-and-love. I think it was about as sincere as you can get. In the intervening thirty years I've learned an awful lot about psychology and manipulation and people's intentions but I'd say that within the framework people were doing the best they could to be sincere. The intent was 100 per cent." He adds of the San Francisco culture, "People were trying to live on very little or nothing. There was a lot of free food being given out. The whole Back to the Land movement started then." Almost hand-in-hand with the peace-and-love philosophy was a music scene featuring bands who lived in the area and espoused the same new era politics, chief among which were The Grateful Dead, Jefferson Airplane and Quicksilver Messenger Service. Country Joe and the Fish were also considered part of the scene, although were an East Bay rather than San Francisco group. These bands were usually prone to extended and improvised playing, matching their political progressivism with aesthetic boundary-pushing. Despite this, English bands often looked down on the abilities of the San Francisco groups. "I always loved the Dead but I thought Country Joe and the Fish were really sloppy," confirms Briggs, "and I never thought much of Quicksilver." But how did a blunt, hard-drinking Geordie like Eric Burdon connect with such a gentle outlook on life? Briggs: "He was trying. It seemed to me, with that whole thing Eric was able to open up a side of himself that he could never acknowledge before and quite possibly he's never been able to acknowledge since. For me, I've spent the rest of my life pursuing that side of myself. In a lot of ways, Eric was very spiritually inspiring to me, particularly between the summer of '67 and the fall of '67. I don't really think he changed. I think he was temporarily given a reprieve from that Geordie personality and I think he went back into it."

Not all the band's experiences on tour were as happy as those in San Francisco. In Ottawa, Canada they had a hairy time — as the New Animals almost always would when they visited that country. "We got to Ottawa, checked into this hotel," says Briggs. "We got to the gig. The way we'd do it, the promoter would send half the money ahead of time to the agency and then before we'd go on stage we'd collect the other half. We went to go on stage and Phil's going, 'Where's the promoter? The promoter was going to go get the money. It was a half-hour ago and he hasn't come back. What we gonna do?' Eric says, 'I wanna make a stand. If he doesn't come back with the money, we're leaving.' We waited and we waited and the crowd were starting to stomp and whistle. Finally he says, 'Okay, we're out of here.' Terry stayed behind. The rest of us jumped in the car and dashed back to the hotel and got all our stuff out of the hotel and took off down the road. We're heading down the road, listening to the radio and all of a sudden: a newsflash about a riot in Ottawa. They'd actually trashed the stadium and Terry McVay had locked himself in the dressing room, piled a bunch of amplifiers against the door. All of our equipment was trashed. The police put out a warrant for the arrest of the promoter. We decided to go through the border very quickly."

chapter nine

That *Eric Is Here* made little impression on the record-buying
public was probably a good thing. Those who were aware of its
existence must have been bewildered by its lack of resemblance —
musical or spiritual — to the 'real' debut of Eric Burdon & The
Animals, 'When I Was Young'.

This latter record had long been ready for release by the time
of *Eric Is Here*'s March '67 emergence. When the band had got to
America in February, Tom Wilson pointed out to them that he
needed a B-side for 'When I Was Young'. The Animals offered
'A Girl Named Sandoz', a song celebrating the glories of LSD.
The recording of the track in New York occasioned some unpleasantness between Wilson and Briggs. The latter explains, "Tom
Wilson and I had a big fight because I kind of wanted to produce
it. I freely admit I was pretty obnoxious then." Briggs at least had
something of an outlet for his artistic frustrations: shortly before
this, Giorgio Gomelsky, an old name from The Animals' past and
currently manager of Brian Auger, offered Briggs a job as producer on his new label Marmalade, which was to be distributed
by Polydor. Briggs accepted and began developing a behind-the-
console career in parallel with his work with the band.

That unpleasantness aside, the recording career of the real Eric
Burdon & The Animals couldn't have gotten off to a better start.
'When I Was Young', finally released in Britain in May 1967
and a month earlier in America — on the MGM label in both
countries — is a classic single: not just a superb piece of music but
also an impressive manifesto. In his first volume of autobiography,
Eric Burdon tells of how he feels his life was lived in black and
white until he met a teacher called Bertie Brown. Brown (a very
influential figure in Burdon's formative years in that he put his

name forward for further education, which led to him going to
art college) would regale his classes with tales of his war exploits.
An awe-inspired Burdon was transported in his young mind to a
world of glorious Technicolor. Burdon did much the same for his
listeners when he formed the New Animals. The original Animals
were a great band but their product was as dark as a Newcastle
coal seam. The New Animals shared the first band's capacity for
excellent music but, courtesy of high production values, exotic
instrumentation and greater compositional ambition, opened out
and enriched Burdon's musical vision. 'When I Was Young'/'A
Girl Named Sandoz' was almost a declaration of intent: That Was
Then, This Is Now.

The A-side starts with a booming and abrasive guitar effect. "I
like to think I was the first person to put a guitar dive-bomb on
a record," says Briggs. "I thought, 'We need something to really
come in.' So I hit my E string and went 'Boooooom!' Spontaneous,
really." Following that explosive beginning, comes another first:
the premiere of electric violin on a record. John Weider's sinister-
sounding bowing propels the song into a plainly autobiographical
Burdon lyric about a childhood hedonism rooted in poverty that
flows on a fine melody. Despite the tunefulness, Jenkins' drums are
thrillingly thunderous. The instrumental break confirms the hint
of exoticism lent by the violin as Burdon chants rapidly to instrumentation that smacks of the Far East. The B-side, though not
quite as good, is enjoyable, and even more likely to blow the minds
of Animals fans who were expecting another 'We've Gotta Get
Out of this Place'. 'A Girl Named Sandoz' is Burdon's attempt to
convey the experience of a trip ("My mind has wings…"), though
such were the mores of the time he feels compelled to dress up it
up as a love song to a woman with a strange name (Sandoz was
the name of the company for which Albert Hofman was working
when he first synthesised LSD). The most prominent part of the
instrumentation is a huge, booming fuzz bass. The glockenspiel
which decorates the nursery rhyme-like chorus is a stark contrast
to that and the track's recurring Hendrix-esque guitar.

"I remember playing it to George Harrison and he thought it
was a great track," says Burdon of the A-side. "To hear him give

it the thumbs-up, I felt very enthusiastic. I felt very confident that we were going to be around for a while." Yet despite the record's brilliance, it surprisingly only reached number fifteen in America and didn't even crack the top forty in Britain. This could have been interpreted at the time as a sign that the radically new sound had alienated the old Animals audience. Was the Animals' camp concerned about this? "Maybe Jeffries was," says Briggs. "Eric didn't give a shit for sure. Eric was going to do what he wanted to do. We wanted to be recognised as something that was a distinct entity from the old Animals. If you look at press clippings, we always used to talk about the honesty of our music. It was a very important issue to us. We weren't just recording songs to make a buck. We were recording songs to express ourselves." Possibly the sales of 'When I Was Young' mattered less to Burdon than the fact that in 1984 Tina Turner — a musical idol and erotic icon of his — covered the song, featuring it on the B-side of her US top five single 'Better Be Good To Me'. Briggs was delighted: "They almost exactly lifted the same arrangement. I was very proud of that fact. It's really good. She sings the shit out of it." Burdon says, "It's a great compliment."

Both the A- and B-side of the 'When I Was Young' single gave joint writing credit to Burdon, Briggs, Weider, Jenkins and McCulloch, as did every New Animals song up until their third album except 'Ain't That So' and 'Orange and Red Beams'. It was one of the first times that all members of a group were given equal credit and (theoretically) royalties for the songs they recorded together, something prompted by Burdon's conversion from Northern man's-man to flower child. John Weider points out, "I wrote all the music and Eric wrote all the lyrics. We would get together at the house I was living in and put it all together. The songwriting credits claimed all five members as writers but in reality Eric and I wrote everything." Weider would always have the music written first before calling Burdon up to come over. Burdon would arrive with one of his journals and proceed to pluck a lyric from that to match the melody Weider had devised.

"Hmmm," is Jenkins' response to that. "Well we all partici-pated. We'd all be in the studio swinging ideas around. Vic Briggs was pretty good on the arranging." Says Briggs, "There was a definite agreement amongst all of us to share royalties. I think it was… Eric's idea. Remember, he was doing a lot of acid at the time and I think it was a kind of peace-and-love thing. I remember that we signed contracts, not only with a publisher but also for each song, with each of us getting twenty per cent." For his part, Weider says he was actually surprised when he saw that his name was sharing space on the single's label with those of four other people, rather than with just Burdon's. At the time, he was so caught up in the excitement that he didn't think much about it. Yet now, while he acknowledges Briggs' significant contribution towards arrangement, Weider regrets the fact that publishing royalties that he considers should have been fifty per cent his are shared between five people. Still, he is at pains to point out that he bears no ill-will toward the other Animals over these democratic credits, putting it down to the management's sloppiness when registering song copyrights and the surprising fact that, even with the 'House of the Rising Sun' episode fresh in his memory, Burdon didn't take much interest in publishing credits. Weider: "He wasn't business-savvy." Briggs admits, "I'm really glad that Eric was in one of his psychedelic moods of brotherly love [but] I did not have much to do with writing the songs. More it was Johnny and Danny. Eric of course would provide the words. Except for those two songs from Danny [on the second album], the lyrics were Eric."

In any event, the 20% royalties that were promised the band members turned out to be a mirage. "I found out a few years back, the Animals songwriting royalties were split 50% for Eric Burdon, 12.5% each for the other four guys," Briggs says. "So it wasn't an equal share. Not only that, but Jeffries tried to split it again by doing a dual publishing company thing. He tried to set up another publishing company whereby Eric Burdon would have taken a hundred per cent of the royalties that went to this publishing company and then fifty per cent of the royalties that went to the other one. So that would have wound up being 75% for Eric Burdon and a quarter of 25% for each of the four of us." Briggs says he doesn't know whether or not Burdon knew about this arrangement but does feel that Burdon bears responsibility for the fact that he and his colleagues receive no performance royalties from the CD reissues of New Animals records while Burdon received a healthy advance.

During March, the band had started recording their first album at TTG studios in Los Angeles, the location for all the band's US recordings except 'A Girl Named Sandoz'. The album was committed to tape over a two-week period, a remarkably short recording time considering that the group entered TTG with nothing other than Burdon's lyrics. Briggs says, "The songs came together quite well. It seemed to flow pretty good." Though this period saw Burdon truly blossom as a songwriter — transcending the generic blues rhymes that had been his stock-in-trade in this department hitherto, while also cranking up his level of productivity — Briggs feels that Burdon's continued reliance on a musical foil created a slight sense of inadequacy: "He's got a big complex about his inability to express himself in terms of what he wanted musically. He came across as a bit surly. When somebody's coming onto you in a surly way, you don't realise until later on, 'Oh maybe that guy was actually really insecure and that was just his way of covering that up.'"

Burdon cites Bob Dylan, Chuck Berry and Randy Newman as his biggest influences as a lyricist. Barry Jenkins offers a surprising additional name: Dominic Behan, the Irish playwright, novelist and songwriter. In fact, Jenkins is under the impression that it was Behan's brother Brendan, author of 'Borstal Boy', who Burdon knew but the latter was dead by 1964 and Burdon himself has said (talking about The Doors' Jim Morrison), "Part of my relationship with Jim was because I'd met Dominic Behan and he thought that I knew Brendan Behan, whom he admired. Which wasn't true." Though he seems to have the name wrong, Jenkins has vivid memories of Dominic Behan's character: "He was an old alkie. He was a fantastic writer. He was hanging around with him in London, 'cause we used to go up this club and watch films and that and that's probably how he got to writing a lot. That was early '67. [Behan] influenced Eric into writing more." Steel remembers The Animals spending a couple of riotous nights in

Dominic Behan's company in his time with the band. Though Briggs doesn't remember Behan, he instinctively finds it "very possible" that Burdon interacted with him, on the grounds that Burdon was a much more prominent media figure in the Sixties than people realise: "He used to get quite a lot of time on TV talk shows as he was always opinionated and quite articulate in defending often indefensible positions. I remember him once in a heated discussion with some folkies, with him insisting that The Beatles wrote folk music."

Tom Wilson was, naturally, retained as producer for the album. "Tom was a very relaxed guy," Briggs says. "Too relaxed for me. He'd worked with Dylan and Simon and Garfunkel. Now both Dylan and Simon and Garfunkel, their material is priceless, so Tom would just turn on the machine. He would not edit. Whatever Eric came up with, Tom would say, 'Okay, great, record it.' I think the first album, probably about a third of the tracks shouldn't have even been on there. I think it's very weak material." Briggs further avers, "Tom basically didn't use to do much of anything. He divided up his time between drawing American football plays on pieces of paper — one team is the zeros and the other teams is the x's — and calling up white women he wanted to screw. I'm not kidding. It seemed like he wanted to get the thing over with as quickly as possible. Occasionally he'd even listen to the music. Tom was pretty good with Eric. I just wish he could have said, 'Eric, this track sucks — don't put it on the album.'" Burdon agrees that Wilson could have been more hands-on. "I loved the guy and all that but he wasn't as into us in the studio as he had been with other artists," he says. "We were just drifting from one experimental gig to the next."

The "Arranged by Vic Briggs" credit that would appear on the first two New Animals albums was something on which Briggs insisted because he felt it accurately reflected his role in the studio, especially when it came to writing string and horn parts. However, he accepts that he was putting his case somewhat aggressively. "I laid a very big control trip on the band," he admits. "I was directing the music a lot. I realised right off the bat that Eric was not really competent musically so I thought, 'I'm going to put my stamp on this band.' In those days, the arranger was the one who wrote the score, and I'd written the score." Regarding *Winds of Change*, the first New Animals album, he says, "It's probably going a little overboard to say I arranged the whole thing. I did a lot more for *The Twain Shall Meet*." Incidentally, Keith Olsen played bass on some tracks (including 'Good Times') due to McCulloch breaking his wrist after being rushed at by girl fans in March. (One Pat Burke depped for McCulloch at the sole concert he was unable to play, not contrary to some reports Mothers of Invention bassist Roy Estrada.) Following completion of recording, Wilson took the tapes back to New York for mixing.

The Animals, meanwhile, resumed live work, still a matter of introducing themselves to the public prior to their first single's release. April 19-25 saw them playing an Australasian tour, including Melbourne Festival Hall on the 20th. It was a tour that Jeffery and Briggs had had to persuade Burdon to agree to after Burdon had told them, "Australia's a place you go when you're at the end of your career." Briggs would come to regret talking Burdon into it. "It was a whole hassle from start to finish," he says of the trip Down Under. Weider describes his memories of the experience as "bleak." Burdon says, "It was the worst. It was even more backward than the backwaters anywhere that you can find in Britain. It was just awful. We just stayed indoors all day and took acid." Things were never going to be ideal in Australia. The Animals were sharing the bill with Dave Dee, Dozy, Beaky, Mick and Tich, a pairing even more fatuous than the original Animals' bill-sharing with Herman's Hermits the previous year. "This is totally Jeffries," says Briggs. "I'm not even sure if [Burdon] knew that 'til we got down there."

The tour started with concerts in New Zealand: Christchurch, Wellington and Rotorua. "The next day after Rotorua," Briggs recalls, "we have a day off and I'd decided that I was gonna take LSD for the first time. When we get to Rotorua, we're in this hotel. We go on the balcony. Right below this balcony, there's boiling mud pools, there's thermal geysers going off. It's just incredible. Eric says, 'If you want to take LSD, this is the place to take LSD.' Right before we go on stage, I take this LSD. Now LSD takes about an hour to come on, so we go out on the stage, we do this absolutely wild set. The set was so wild that after the first song, Phil Robertson rushes out on the stage and gives Eric this big hug. We go into the hotel. We all go to Eric's room because that's gonna be the trip room. I'm lying there, looking at these two walls and the ceiling and all of sudden they don't meet. So we had this whole night of tripping, going out and looking at the boiling mud pools. Very profound and very powerful."

It was never going to be as good again on this continent. Following this, The Animals performed a gig in Aukland before getting on a plane to Sydney. Briggs: "When we get to Sydney, they totally take us apart at customs." "They arrested me for attempting to bring pornography into the country," says Burdon. "Pornography, Jesus Christ — I had two Henry Miller books and I think a Jack Kerouac, *On the Road*. They confiscated the books and it was headlines in the press: 'Rock'n'roll pornographer is coming to pollute your daughters' and all that shit." (Briggs' memory is that Burdon was not arrested but had his books confiscated.) Briggs: "Then we had this press conference where the Aussie journalists were really hostile. At the time Australia was a very conservative country. They were just out to nail us." Burdon says, "Australia has just managed to magically change in the wink of an eye since they started making movies. Movies inspired them to see themselves in a different light. Back then, just for having shoulder-length hair, people would spit on you and beat you up." Briggs "The next morning, I'm walking around Sydney. There's these newspaper sellers. They've got this big placard in front of them. It says, 'ANIMALS DRUG SEARCH AT AIRPORT.' We do a couple of gigs in Sydney and we go down to Melbourne. We do two nights in Melbourne. The second night after the show we go to this party at somebody's house. There's this guy there. This guy's a cop. I talked to him a little bit. He was reasonably friendly. I left the party in the company of some young lady and I went back to the hotel. I'm sharing a room with Terry McVay. Come six o'clock in the morning, there's no sign of Terry."

Jenkins explains, "Terry got all stroppy in the hotel and they come in the hotel and they arrested him. He was pissed as a newt. We got on great. I said, 'I'll go with you, Terry.' And they started being stroppy with me and then it kicked off. It got silly." Briggs: "All of a sudden the door opens and Terry comes in with these two guys. At this point, this young lady gets up and leaves really quick." Briggs had recently purchased a cowboy souvenir bullwhip in the States. Briggs: "Terry says, 'Where's that bullwhip you bought?' I says, 'It's in my black bag.' He goes and grabs my bullwhip and starts heading out the door. And these two guys grab him: 'Terry! Terry! Come back man!' I said, 'What the fuck's going on?' It turns out after I'd left the party, this cop had gone to the local police station. He'd got a bunch of cops and he bought them back and they busted the party. They were actually out to get us but we'd all left except for Terry and Barry Jenkins. They'd beaten up on Barry. Barry's a pretty sweet guy. He goes, 'What you beating up on me for man? I love ya.' Kind of hippy thing. Being a Geordie, Terry's like, 'Fuck you!' *Bom*! They hit him again. 'Fuck you!' They took him back to the station, just beat the crap out of him all night long because he wouldn't roll over and play dead. Then in all the papers, they're putting out this thing: The Animals had resisted arrest and The Animals had done this..." Jenkins: "I think we was all on trips. It was in the papers the next day, 'Drummer from The Animals tells policeman that he loves him' and all that." One suspects a certain bravado behind Jenkins' answer when asked if he was frightened during his ordeal: "No, it was a laugh."

There was further trouble in Melbourne. Briggs, an inveterate hat wearer, had bought an Australian army slouch hat (distinctive by its upturned side brim) and wore it onstage. Unbeknownst to him, the gig in question took place on the eve of ANZAC day, when Australians mourn their slain battle heroes. The following day, the band found themselves mired in newspaper controversy again as old soldiers condemned what they described as an insult. And the gigs? "They went okay," says Briggs. "The audiences were more there for Dave Dee. We got some good reviews. The psychedelic revolution had really not hit Australia at all."

Following their unhappy Australian experiences, 'When I Was Young' hit the shops and although it failed to be the big hit it deserved to be, it meant the public knew where the band were coming from, to use an expression of the time. That and their live work brought about an altered outlook amongst the band. Briggs: "After being in Australia and New Zealand and getting back to England, we'd all changed. We had a lot more confidence. We felt we *were* The Animals now. People were treating us differently in London. We were for real now, rather than just wannabes."

In June, The Animals had an experience as blissful as Australia had been miserable. "One day, I went over to see John," recalls Briggs. "He said, 'Guess what? There's gonna be a festival in Monterey!' He was really excited. 'At the Fairgrounds! Eric's trying to get us on it.'" The New Animals had actually played at the Monterey County Fairgrounds a couple of months previously and had been excited then too: one of the favourite albums of Weider and Briggs was a John Handy live album recorded there. This new gig, though, was something else altogether.

The Monterey International Pop Festival, to give it its formal title, was held on June 16, 17 and 18 1967. Chiefly organized by John Phillips of The Mamas and The Papas (but with considerable and little-known assistance from Paul Simon), it was the first time pop/rock artists had been considered worthy of the kind of organised mass gatherings that had long been a feature of the jazz and blues worlds. (Indeed, the Monterey Jazz Festival had been held for many years at the Monterey County Fairgrounds.) All the artists playing at 'Monterey Pop' were doing so for nothing and all festival profits were to go to charitable causes. Eric Burdon & The Animals were booked for the opening night as a late replacement for The Beach Boys. "The only problem was," says Briggs, "we were set to do a tour of Italy. Eric really leaned on Jeffries. Jeffries called up the promoter in Italy and basically cut the tour short. It started on a Friday and we flew over on a Thursday."

Upon arrival in LA, the band were met by Kevin Deverich, an American friend of Burdon's who had started organising The Animals' American dates the previous March. Deverich booked the band into a replacement hotel after their original hotel — seeing their 'alternative' appearance — denied they had a booking. The next day they flew on to Monterey where they booked into the same hotel as The Jimi Hendrix Experience. Vic Briggs shared a room with his old friend Mitch Mitchell. "In the evening," recalls Briggs, "we went down there early-ish, six or seven o'clock. It didn't start 'til about eight. The Monterey Fairgrounds seats six or seven thousand. There's the arena, then around the arena there's a certain amount of land. There's places for craft booths. People milling around with flowers. Just this kind of carnival, third world, surrealistic atmosphere. People with their faces painted and outrageous clothes. I'd never seen anything like it." Of the local residents, Briggs says, "There was a certain amount of tolerance, although they weren't really prepared for the hippies and the Hell's Angels." Of the actual music on the first evening, Briggs recalls, "First group on was The Association, a very slick group from southern California, and they were bad. They did this Las Vegas lounge act and people received them politely and that's as far as it went. Lou Rawls was on and he kind of did a Vegas act. So we went out [and] kicked butt. Just started rocking. We played 'Paint It Black'. We played 'San Franciscan Nights'." The latter song was a gentle number Burdon had written in celebration of San Francisco's alternative culture which would shortly be released as a single. Briggs: "We did play it a couple of times in Italy just to rehearse it but this was the first time we seriously played it on stage. It was clearly a wonderful venue to present it for the first time and people loved it." The other two numbers in The Animals' set were 'Hey Gyp' and 'Gin House Blues'. Jenkins recalls, "It was nerve-wracking to go on. I think we were all a bit uptight because we were so nervous. The thing was to go on and play good. Just get your shit together and let them have it." "We did very well considering it was the first major date that we did," remembers Burdon. "I was quite excited and nervous about the whole thing. Usually I'm not that nervous on stage but I got the feeling that we were a part of something really special then and it was time to step up to the plate and do my best. We were well received." Says Briggs, "After us was Simon and Garfunkel, basically two guys and one guitar. They did pretty good but I have a review somewhere that says, 'Friday night belonged to The Animals.' We had no competition on Friday."

Following their rapturously received performance on the Friday, The Animals could now sit back and enjoy this unprecedented event, although they did put on another performance at the festival, this one on the Free Stage on Saturday night after Burdon had expressed disquiet at the way the Festival's pleasures were denied those without money. "It was some distance away," says Briggs. "It was on this football field. There were a whole bunch of people sleeping in the rain. We got up and played a bit. I remember Jimi got up." The field-dwellers were thrilled to find these big stars performing for them, probably more so with regard to The Animals, who were then much bigger than Hendrix in America.

The performances on the main stage on Sunday are now part of rock'n'roll folklore, starting with Indian sitar player Ravi Shankar in the afternoon. Briggs: "It was cold, it was drizzling, there were planes flying overhead and it was obvious he didn't want to be there. So instead of taking his usual five, ten minutes to tune up — I looked at my watch — he took thirty minutes to tune up. When he finished tuning up, the crowd gave him a standing ovation and he says, 'Well, if you like my tuning, I think perhaps you might like my music.' And he just took off. It was incredible. That night, it was The Who, The Grateful Dead and Jimi Hendrix. That was the crux of the evening. I didn't like The Who. I know a lot of people did. Seeing them just smash up their instruments, it was just, 'Why? What are they doing this for?' When you're on LSD, which I was that night and I know Eric was, you get very sensitive. It just looked so violent, unnecessary, wasteful. But the crowd liked it. Somehow or other, when Jimi burned his guitar, it was a much more profound thing. He had this headband like a native American and I saw in my psychedelic inspired mind primitive man moving into the power of harnessing the atom and destroying himself maybe. It seemed an incredibly powerful symbolic statement. It was overwhelming. I could barely watch it." "It was a joy to see Hendrix come home," says Burdon. "He was just another struggling black face in New York before Chas picked up the story. For him to come back to the United States and have what then was powerhouse management behind him…When he and Chas were running together for the first time, it was pure magic. Chas did a great job in engineering Jimi's take-off."

The event's impact was incredible, starting with 'San Francisco (Be Sure To Wear Some Flowers In Your Hair)', the single John Phillips wrote almost as an advertisement for the event and which Scott McKenzie took into the top five on both sides of the Atlantic, through to the way it made superstars out of the previously moderately successful (The Who and The Jimi Hendrix Experience) to the way that attracting 50,000 generally peaceful souls from all over the US proved that those who were rejecting conservative values for the hippie ideal were not, contrary to much adverse propaganda, unwashed drug-addled scum. "This was really the first public national expression of a movement of consciousness," says Briggs. "The music was a metaphor for the change of consciousness. We were off on this new tack: we don't want to do things the old way anymore. We really thought we were going to change the world. Well, we did but not as much as we would have liked to have done." It's easy to pinpoint an event as history-making with hindsight but did Monterey really seem so important as it was happening? Weider: "Yes, all those great artists together at one time." Briggs agrees: "Yes, definitely. We didn't exactly know what was going on but we knew something major was happening. We hoped that we could really change things so that we could have this atmosphere at all our concerts. Of course, it didn't happen that way." However, Briggs admits that Monterey wasn't entirely the "three days of understanding" Burdon would describe it as in the eponymous song he wrote about the festival: "One of the things was the tension between the very hip LA people that actually put the thing on and the bands from San Francisco. Lot of tension at that festival, behind the scenes. When The Grateful Dead were on, they told people to throw their chairs away and dance." He also says, "The Brits weren't so much into this peace, love and understanding. I remember Noel Redding getting a bit uptight. The Who were their usual obnoxious selves."

Burdon's memories are that, "Politically it was special." He explains, "There was The Grateful Dead going around backstage, going from dressing room to dressing room telling musicians not to sign any contracts with John Phillips' production company 'cause you were gonna get fucked, that years later people would still be looking at this movie and you'd signed your rights away to it and you weren't gonna get anything for it. That was the first time that I was exposed to a political force within music. That woke me up to realising that we had to stick together and we had to fight for each other and we had to take care, wake up, look at what's going on. Get yourself in a position where you were able to work hard but receive the royalties and receive the rights and that there was no shame in making money. I remember Hendrix coming offstage one day laughing at me and saying, 'Shit, you mean I get paid for this as well?' That was our attitude then and The Grateful Dead were true American revolutionaries on the level that they were hippies but they were capitalistic hippies. They wanted to make money to expand their community and do things for the community. There's still a little bit of that feeling left in San Francisco. That's what makes it very special."

Burdon says that "as a collective spirit thing," Monterey was the greatest experience of his long career. "It still seems special," he states. "Bright memory. I still think it has a profound effect on people. I thought it was the beginning of a worldwide peace movement."

In July or possibly August 1967, the — to use the argot of the day — far-out nature of the New Animals was underlined by their incorporation of a new element into their live act. "The New Animals was a total open experimental band," says Burdon. "We shot movies to play behind us. That was part and parcel of the group. We had a guy who operated a travelling light show, which was quite an undertaking in those days. The machinery was very delicate. That was as much a part of the band as anything. We were open to anything that we felt could contribute." "Eric took on Buddy Walters, an American who had worked with Zappa, for the light show," says Briggs. Though psychedelic venues such as the Fillmore, the Avalon Ballroom in San Francisco and the

Roundhouse in London had them, at this juncture in history Pink Floyd and Dantalion's Chariot were the only bands who travelled with light shows. Says Briggs, "Film loops and clips were an integral part of light shows as well as coloured oils in petri dishes that were pressed together and moved around on an overhead projector to make blob-like shapes that moved in time to the music." The effects would wash surreally across the band's faces and bodies at a time when anything other than an unobstructed view of performers was virtual sacrilege.

In August, The Animals decided to release 'San Franciscan Nights' as their second single. Unfortunately, while MGM America agreed with their choice, MGM UK demurred, claiming British audiences wouldn't be able to understand the song. 'Good Times', the B-side of the American 'San Franciscan Nights' single, was chosen for the second British New Animals single instead, inaugurating a confusing series of discrepancies in British and American Eric Burdon & The Animals releases.

Burdon wasn't unaware of the darker side of Haight-Ashbury. "There was a lot of people living on the streets and a lot of people without any money and a lot of hungry people," he says. However, he adds, "It seemed like we were all in it together and it was a great time. I wrote 'San Franciscan Nights' to express the dream side of that period." Briggs says of its recording, "That was beautiful. That came together very quickly and very smoothly." The song is just as much a summation of the spirit of the Summer of Love as The Beatles' 'All You Need Is Love' or 'San Francisco (Be Sure to Wear Some Flowers in Your Hair)'. If anything, The Animals' record has the edge over the other two because of its complete sincerity: Scott McKenzie was actually singing the words of somebody else while The Beatles were rather self-consciously trying to produce a record that captured the zeitgeist. Of course, this genuineness would be immaterial if the recording itself was rubbish. The song is beautiful and sultry, the blissed-out lyric perfectly complemented by a gorgeous, lilting acoustic guitar figure (played by Briggs) running throughout. 'San Franciscan Nights' truly captures the happiness Burdon felt at having found what he considered heaven on earth. Some hippies would later repudiate the naïveté of their flower power youth but even they must surely wish they could recapture that naïveté when they hear the unequivocal joy evident in this song, especially the line that is, at the same time, the happiest and saddest imaginable: "I wasn't born there, perhaps I'll die there, there's no place left to go…" Briggs asserts that, though 'San Francisco (Be Sure to Wear Some Flowers in Your Hair)' was the bigger hit, The Animals won the contest where it counted: "All the people in San Francisco hated that song and they all loved ours." By sending it to number 9, the American public made this Burdon's best US chart placing since 'The House of the Rising Sun'. Briggs: "'San Franciscan Nights' probably would have made number one except that we got feedback that the East Coast DJs were down on The Animals because The Animals never played the East Coast."

Meanwhile, across the Atlantic, the alternative second exposure to the New Animals was no dud. 'Good Times', like 'When I Was Young', is both a reflective, autobiographical piece of work and a classic record. "He was talking about how it used to be in the Fifties," Briggs reveals of the song. "You'd go into a café or a dance and you'd catch somebody's eye and the guy would come over and beat the crap out of you for looking at him. Eric was saying [to me] how that had happened to him… At the time Eric was really trying to clean up his act. You can see the people you've hurt and wounded and you feel a lot of compassion for people… LSD does that to you." A Burdon interview printed in *Melody Maker* just before the single's release seems to confirm Brigg's comments, with Burdon quoted as saying, "I look back and see how stupid I was, and I can see 25 years of pain and hurt to other people. I look to a future without trying to be hurtful." The Animals are helped in no small measure on 'Good Times' by Tom Wilson's deep, rich production, which almost serves as another instrument in itself. Echoing, clicking percussion is pushed to the fore as Burdon rues his days of wasting good times by having good times and drinking when he should have been thinking. Rumbling, rolling drumming, ominously strummed acoustic guitar and Weider's tense violin all contribute to a relentlessly building drama that is only relieved by a sarcastic music hall interlude. The B-side was 'Ain't That So', a good track with clipped rhythm guitar, burbling bass and Byrds-style backing harmonies. The subject is a favourite of Burdon's at the time, namely the superiority of the hippie/freak lifestyle ("You stick to your scene, baby, 'cause we got our own"). For such an excellent record, the chart placing — twenty — was again disappointing.

Also in August, The Animals played a Love-In at the Alexandra Palace. This marked the only occasion on which they performed a version of Jefferson Airplane's 'White Rabbit', Vic Briggs contributing sitar. Because Briggs' girlfriend — a journalist — mentioned it in a review, the band subsequently often found American audiences calling for the song. An attendee of the show who was unimpressed by what he saw was John Steel. "Walking down King's Road and people were handing you flowers dressed in kaftans," he remembers with disdain. "Eric was all in kaftan and flowers and Zoot was there with Dantalion's Chariot. Where's The Big Roll Band? I thought, 'What's going on here? It's a load of bollocks, this.' Going on about the Indian culture. I used to say, 'I've never been to India but my understanding of it is everybody's living in shit.' I just didn't connect with all that at all. It was a period I didn't feel comfortable with."

On the 27th of the same month, the band played the Festival of the Flower Children at Woburn Abbey. It was a sad occasion because the news had come through that day that Beatles manager Brian Epstein had died. "I think Eric was fairly close to Brian," says Briggs. "He was kind of upset by it but we went out that night and we kicked butt. Boy, that was a hell of a gig."

September 7 1967 saw a much happier event in Burdon's life when he married his girlfriend Angie King. The event was supposed to be a secret but somehow the public found out and hundreds of people flocked to the ceremony at Caxton Hall. Zoot Money was best man for a true flower power union with bride, groom and guests dressed in psychedelic and hippie gear. It featured prominently in papers the following day. Briggs: "I don't know if it's true or not but he [Burdon] said it in his autobiography and he definitely told us all, that the night before the wedding he took a bunch of acid and he went round all the regular women that he screwed and he screwed them one last time." "That's a load of crap," laughs Kathy Etchingham, who not only has known Burdon since 1962 but was Angie's best friend. "Absolute nonsense. That is just rubbish. Angela would have killed him. Angela wouldn't have let him out of her sight. She was with him. They were down at the Speakeasy. No, there's no way. That's what Eric does. Eric's always boosted himself up as being the great Casanova."

Bridesmaid at the event was Carol Fielder. Eight days later, on September 15, Danny McCulloch married Carol at a ceremony at Paddington Register Office with John Weider acting as his best man. "It was kind of a weird one," says Briggs, "because Carol had actually been Barry's girlfriend and Danny had just decided he wanted to get married."

It was during September that The Animals played one of the Saville Theatre's legendary Sunday nights. Brian Epstein had bought the theatre in Shaftsbury Avenue, London in 1965 and had begun staging pop concerts on Sunday nights when theatres were usually left dark. By '67, it was regularly used by bands for out-of-the- ordinary performances. The Animals' concert was no exception. Briggs: "Eric had planned a number of things. He wanted to have a Harley Davidson on stage. The fire marshal wouldn't let us [start the engine]. So he played a recording of a Harley starting up. At some point in the show, he had this guy — Eddie Thornton, a black trumpet player — come down through the audience chased by Terry Slater [an employee of Mike Jeffery] and another guy dressed up in an American policeman's outfit and they were supposed to beat the crap out of Eddie Thornton. When we were singing 'San Franciscan Nights', where it goes, 'Jeans of blue/Harley Davidsons too,' we had a spotlight go on this guy with this Harley Davidson. And when we did 'Good Times', in the middle there's this kind of party. He had Zoot and his wife and a whole bunch of people up in one of the boxes so when we came to that segment of the song we had the spotlight going: they were all up there partying." The gig actually got gener-ally bad reviews but Briggs says, "Fair play to Eric, he was trying to do something. These Saville concerts were the hot thing of the time." During the show Burdon made a dedication to Epstein: "Hope you're watching, wherever you are."

Shortly afterwards, the band were back in America to promote *Winds of Change*, which was released in September (October in Britain). This time, The Animals were receiving far better treatment and money than they had on their previous two visits to America that year courtesy of the fact that Mike Jeffery was no longer handling US live work. "The first time we went, The Animals were going out for a ludicrously low amount of money, about $2,000 a night," says Briggs. "Most of the gigs were shitty too. When we got to LA, March of '67, Eric said, 'Oh, I've got this friend in LA.' That was Kevin Deverich. Kevin was very slick. All of a sudden we were getting limos…He said, 'I can't believe what kind of money you guys are going out for. It's ridiculous.' When we went back in June to do the Monterey Pop Festival, Kevin arranged for us to do Whisky A Go Go, which is a big gig in LA, and he arranged for us to do the Fillmore in San Francisco. When we did this next tour in the fall of '67, Kevin set it up and he might have been angling. He might have smelt what was going on and saw his opportunity to get in with The Animals and make a lot of money. We were happier because we were just getting better gigs. Kevin knew how to treat rock'n'roll guys."

Mike Jeffery by this time was distracted by other ventures, not just Jimi Hendrix but the clubs he was running in Spain. Briggs recalls, "At the time there were restrictions on exporting sterling. He'd get a briefcase, he'd fill it full of pound notes or five pound notes or whatever and he'd go off to Spain and stash all the money in Spain. He had these clubs in Majorca. Chas was running Jimi, it wasn't Jeffries. Jeffries was just taking all the money."

Not only Hendrix's money apparently, as demonstrated by events when The Animals went over to Jeffery's flat in St. James, London to renegotiate their contract, also in the autumn of '67. Briggs: "He served us dinner. At the end of the dinner he came out with a silver platter and on this silver platter there was a rolled joint for each one of us. Not a joint to share but one each. Eric refused to touch it. I think Eric was starting to get the idea by this time. So we all smoked these joints and we tried to renegotiate the contract. And what he asked for is fifty per cent for Eric and fifty for us. I managed to squeeze an extra five points. The thing is, I wasn't getting any support. Not that it made any fucking difference because we never got any in the end. Of a hundred thousand dollars net profit, Eric would get 45,000 dollars. That leaves 55,000 dollars. The New Animals would split that 55,000 dollars in four ways. We got all these agreements, they were typed up and signed. Sometime in 1968, Terry Slater comes to me and he says, 'Listen, you know those agreements? We need them back because we need to get them copied.' Like a fool I says, 'Okay, fine' and I give them back to him. And that was it. Any chance that I ever had to sue Burdon or Jeffries or MGM or whatever else. In theory, after about the first of December '67, we were on a percentage. In practice, we were getting advances. Dribs and drabs to keep us alive."

The Pagans, Church Assembly Rooms, 1959. COURTESY OF JOHN STEEL

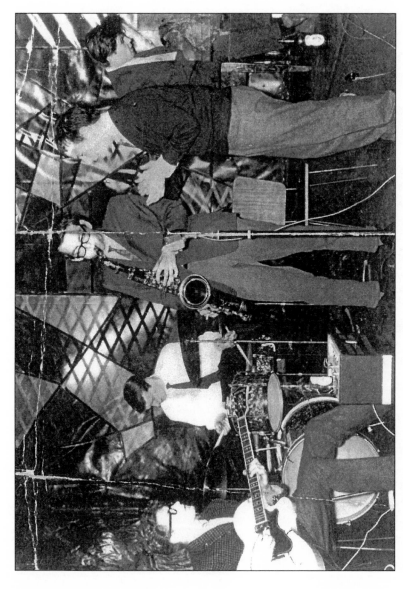

The Kansas City Five at the Downbeat Club, 1962. COURTESY OF GEORGE PEARSON

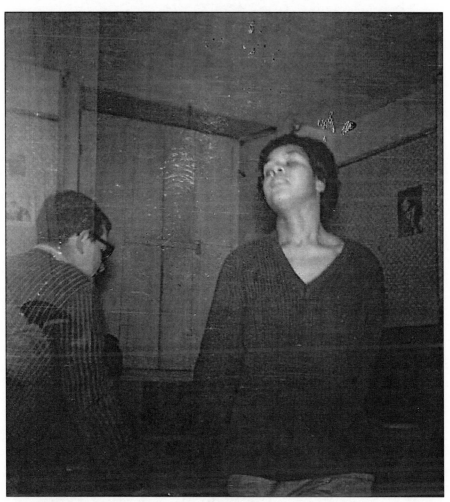

Burdon with his big love and muse Doreen Caulker.

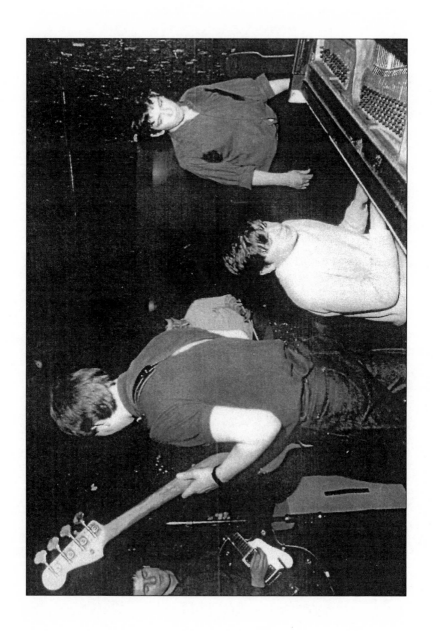

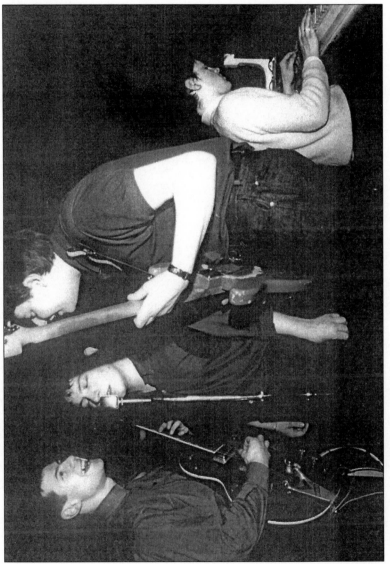

Two shots of The Animals at the Scene Club, Ham Yard, early 1964. The Scene Club was the venue for the band's first London shows. COURTESY OF JOHN STEEL

The classic line-up of the original Animals as seen on their first LP: Alan Price (left), Chas Chandler (right) and, descending, John Steel, Eric Burdon and Hilton Valentine.

Always an exciting live proposition. COURTESY OF JOHN STEEL

The mysterious Mike Jeffery. COURTESY OF JOHN STEEL

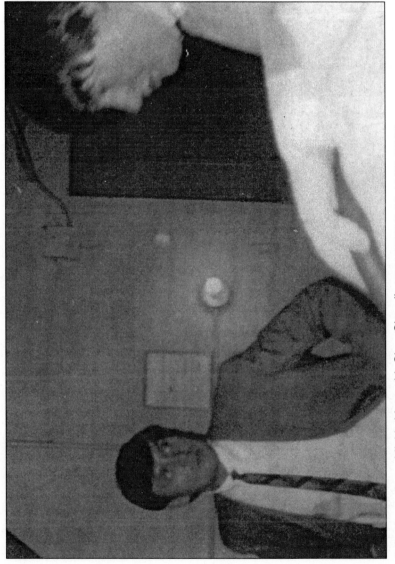

Animals producer Mickie Most with Chas Chandler. COURTESY OF JOHN STEEL

The Animals back in London after touring Japan, 1965. L-R: Chandler, Dave Rowberry, Steel, Burdon and (lying) Valentine. COURTESY OF JOHN STEEL

The 'new' Animals, 1967. L-R: Danny McCulloch, Barry Jenkins, John Welder, Vic Briggs, Eric Burdon. COURTESY OF ANTION MEREDITH

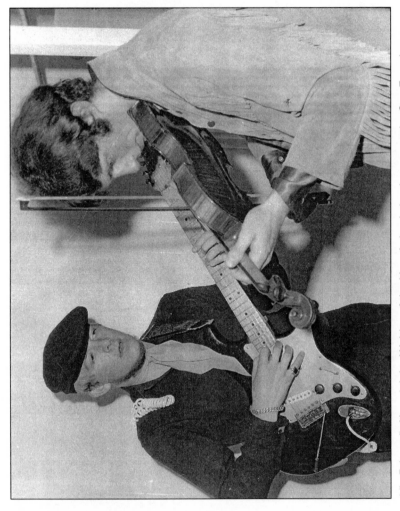

Vic Briggs (left) and John Weider of the New Animals backstage at the San Francisco Civic Auditorium, March 1967. COURTESY OF ANTION MEREDITH

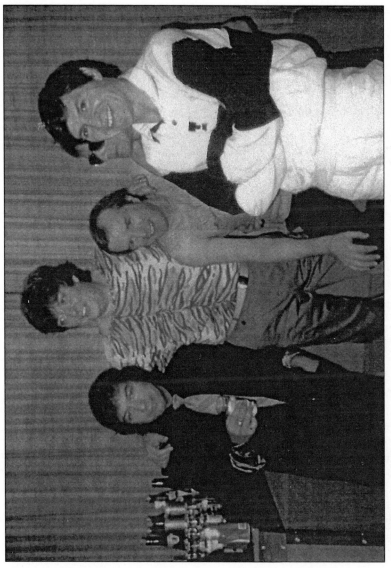

The Animals are all smiles for the camera backstage in Newcastle in December 1983 but this gig, like their reunion tour in general, was ill-tempered. COURTESY OF JOHN STEEL

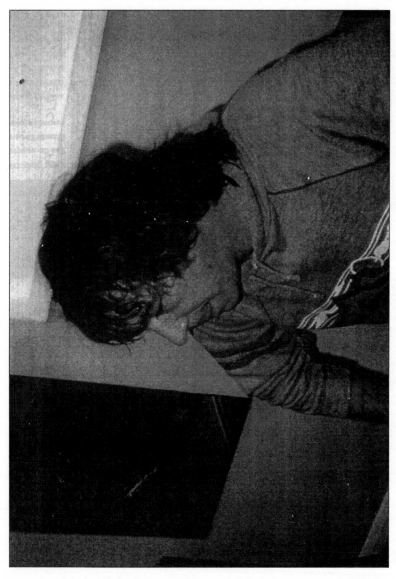

Eric Burdon following The Animals' late ever gig, Wembley Empire Pool, New Year's Eve, 1983. Is that relief on his face? COURTESY OF JOHN STEEL

chapter ten

Following no fewer than three classic and at times groundbreaking singles (spread across two countries), the record-buying public could have been forgiven for thinking that the debut album of the New Animals would be an artistics milestone almost on the same level as The Beatles' *Sgt. Pepper's Lonely Hearts Club Band*, released three months earlier. They were in for a disappointment.

Winds of Change is a work studded with tracks that smack of either laziness or else a sincere but misguided artistic vision. Material like 'Poem by the Sea' and 'The Black Plague' are not real songs at all but monologues intoned over backing tracks. Excellent musicianship and glossy production save them from complete tedium but such experimentalism is now incredibly dated and even then was rather strange coming from a band who with their first batch of releases had displayed a knack for conventional pop techniques that in no way ruled out progressivism: nobody could accuse 'Good Times', for all its whistlability, of being a run-of-the-mill chart song. Constructing a solid album wouldn't even have been a matter of finding additional material: had the experimental numbers been jettisoned and replaced by 'When I Was Young', 'A Girl Named Sandoz' and 'Ain't That So', *Winds of Change* would have been a highly respectable record.

"There wasn't any producer there to crack the whip," Burdon says in his defence. "I realise there have to be perimeters and back then we were going *way* over the perimeters. There was no real cohesive producer in control so therefore you got flashes of real musical viability in certain tracks and on the experimental stuff there wasn't anybody there to say, 'Wait a minute, you're going too far.' But that still doesn't make me ashamed of that stuff."

The opening, title track is a reference to a speech made by British prime minister Harold Macmillan in 1960 to the South African Parliament in which he told them that the winds of change were sweeping across the African continent, the constituent parts of which were no longer prepared to tolerate being part of another country's empire. Burdon appropriated the phrase for a song which discussed the development of popular music, which meant that just as the first original Animals album had begun with a history of rock'n'roll — 'Story of Bo Diddley' — so did the first Eric Burdon & The Animals LP. The story is now updated to include figures and sounds unimaginable to the world only three years previously: Jimi Hendrix, Frank Zappa and The Mamas and the Papas. Yet the lyric is nothing like as witty and well-judged as that of 'Story of Bo Diddley'. Or as Briggs somewhat more caustically says, "It was fucking stupid. 'Frank Zappa zapped'. Come on, Eric!" The funereal and spoken-word track makes for a peculiar start to the album. Even so, there are several good things about it, particularly Briggs' sitar-playing, which — far from the amateurish dabbling on the instrument then rampant in rock — is extremely professional and provides a riff as memorable as any guitar lick. 'Poem by the Sea' sees Burdon, in true hippie fashion, marvelling at how small he is in the grand scheme of things. Like the title track, it relies on atmospherics rather than a tune. It's a wisp of a recording, gone from the memory at the first gust of a new thought. Jenkins' drums were artificially slowed down after he had played fast to a speeded-up tape of the song, a typical example of the experimentalism of the period.

Ironically, considering 'When I Was Young' and 'Winds of Change', The Animals' cover of one of the first examples of raga-rock — Jagger/Richards' 'Paint It Black' — features no sitar at all. In place of the driving, insistent performance on that instrument from Brian Jones that graced The Rolling Stones' remarkable 1966 single, there is some excellent rattling guitar and a huge pounding rhythm. The band adroitly manage to maintain the original track's air of mystery as they extend the song to six minutes, twenty seconds. The absence of sitar is explained by Briggs:

"We didn't want to put it on the album. At that point everybody was very sensitive about doing their own material. Tom Wilson kind of played a trick on us. He said, 'Look, we're not going to put this on the album but you guys just play this once so we have a little recording of it.' We played it once in the studio. The next thing we know it's on the album. There was a lot more we could have done with that. Tom Wilson didn't like to overdub. He was a one-take guy. He'd do one, maybe two, takes and that was it. We're not talking Phil Spector here." 'The Black Plague' is another spoken-word track. Monk-like chanting, doomy acoustic guitar and a tolling bell make it feel like a short story read aloud in a particularly eerie monastery. The lyric is from the substantial flaky end of hippiedom, a fatuous commentary on class divisions. Though Wilson impresses for the way he gamely tries to make something weighty of the flimsy material with an evocative ambience, there is by now an uncomfortable feeling that the album still hasn't got going. "One of those things, it was a really good idea at the time," says Briggs. "Afterwards, thought, 'What the fuck did we do that for?' Eric really had this thing about wanting to be an actor. He just got the idea of doing this dramatic thing. Bear in mind, in those days, particularly on the West Coast, there was a lot of that stuff going on. At the Fillmore, the first act would be The Steve Miller Band, then after that would be Roland Kirk playing jazz, then one of the San Francisco poets would get up, recite a few poems, then it'd be back to rock'n'roll. You wouldn't dream of doing that now." Five tracks into the album and with 'Yes I Am Experienced' we finally get a 'real' song not written by outside sources. Pity it's not a very good one. If you're going to invoke in your title a great artist like Jimi Hendrix (whose group's 1967 debut LP was *Are You Experienced*), it's wise to ensure that your song is in the same bracket, quality-wise. This is a pedestrian number that not even fine propulsive bass playing can salvage. The next track is beautiful, but the public had already heard 'San Franciscan Nights'. After that comes another spoken-word non-song, 'Man-Woman'. Burdon, rather hysterically, dissects the break-up of a relationship over a sparse, bongos-dominated backing. It's conceivable that this track is as penetrating and honest in its own way about romantic love as 'Don't Let Me Be Misunderstood' but all the insight in the world doesn't compensate for the lack of a melody.

'Hotel Hell' is the album's first high-quality, previously unreleased song. It is a truly lovely track. Lonesome trumpet playing straight out of a Sergio Leone western exquisitely embellishes the lament of a traveller alone in a strange bed. The brass is not just colouring but an integral part of the creation, responding directly to Burdon's anguished vocal. The trumpet was one of the few musical, as opposed to lyrical, suggestions made by Burdon for the album. "That was written in Stockton, California," says Briggs. "Stockton is a town out in the middle of the central valley of California. We stayed at this funky hotel in the middle of the town, built in the Twenties. It was really horrible and we were all bummed out. Eric just came up with those words: hotel hell. I guess he was feeling lonely. Angie was back in England. It was Eric's idea to put the trumpet on there: there was a very Mexican feel at this place. So I talked to some of the musicians in LA and I says, 'Who's the best at this mariachi style?' They said, 'You want Tony Terran.' I brought in Tony and I brought him out a sheet and said, 'Put trumpet here and trumpet there' and we got it in maybe two takes, max."

Following 'Good Times' comes the fragile 'Anything', a ballad whose simple sentiment of devotion comes as a surprise after the profundity of the lyrics of the preceding numbers. Not quite as good as 'San Franciscan Nights' but cut from the same lovely mellow cloth with sweet string parts written by Briggs. John Weider cites the track as his favourite of all New Animals songs. 'It's All Meat' is an excellent album closer the musical intelligence of which makes the album's plethora of non-songs even more bewildering. Stabbed rhythm guitar, blistering bass and state-of-the-art sound effects make for a galvanizing concoction. Burdon's lyric is excellent, him once again name-checking figures from popular culture as he articulates his theory about what motivates everyone from Eric Clapton to Muhammad Ali in their chosen discipline: "It's all for a woman, it's all for his home." The track's hard rock sound doesn't preclude a bridge where multi-tracked

violins create an effect reminiscent of 'Eleanor Rigby'. Briggs'
guitar speaker was tearing up during the recording but this flaw
was left in because Wilson liked the sound of it.

That final flourish can't disguise the fact that much of what
has just been heard across the course of the LP is flimsy. Of the
spoken-word tracks, Briggs says, "The balance of the band had
not asserted itself. Johnny and Barry pretty much went along with
everything. Danny started to come into his own on the second
album, both as a songwriter and as a singer." Jenkins recalls no
misgivings about the spoken-word tracks. "We were all into it,"
he says. "Nobody was saying, 'This is shit' or anything like that.
We just believed in everything we was doing. It was great." "In
hindsight, yeah, sure," Burdon says of the suggestion that there
were too many spoken-word tracks. "But at the time we realised
that we were given one chance, probably, in a lifetime to really
be able to experiment in the studio where we didn't have record
company executives standing over us saying, 'That's not a song!'
You gotta take chances." But what of the argument that having
a great singer merely speak is a waste? Burdon: "That still doesn't
make me ashamed of that stuff. I understand what you're saying
and I don't take it as being a bum rap and, yeah, now that I think
about it we were a little misguided, but you've gotta understand
the feeling at the time. Never again since then have artists been
allowed to have the freedom that we had." Burdon reveals a certain pride in asserting of the spoken-word tracks, "I was doing
rap before commercial rap came along."

Of the two references to Hendrix on the album Briggs says,
"One thing that we all got really sick of was Eric always wanted
to pay homage to his heroes. We all have our heroes and we all
want to honour them but Eric would do it *ad nauseum*. He did
this tribute song to Jimi Hendrix ['Yes I Am Experienced'] before
Jimi got his first album out. Jimi was everything that Eric wasn't.
He was black, he was tall, he was a musician. Eric just idolised
Jimi. Not to say that Jimi wasn't good, but Eric, you're a fucking
star, man." Hendrix, though, was more to Burdon than a hero. The
two became close friends. What did Hendrix like about Burdon?
"Eric had a certain kind of hipness and understanding to black

people that few other musicians in England did," says Briggs. "Jimi felt very comfortable with him. He really understood where Jimi was coming from." Though Burdon and Hendrix were close, the tantalising prospect of a collaboration featuring Hendrix on guitar and Burdon on vocals never happened, at least not in the studio. "Hendrix and I jammed a lot because Jimi didn't like to sing that much," says Burdon. "He would prefer to have some-body like me sing the song for him so that he could jam his ass off onstage. We had a lot of good jams. There's one track that The Animals recorded called 'Year of the Guru' and when he heard that he expressed that he would like to have been able to play guitar on that cut. But that wasn't realised and I never, ever pushed myself in the direction of working with him as I was a raving fan of his and I saw his music far, far away beyond the New Animals. Possibly we could have fused together with War. We did play together and he did express his joy in the fact, when we were in London, that it was a chance to play with some black brothers from the United States. That possibly could have developed into something — but I doubt it."

The cover of the album featured a photograph of one of Burdon's journals. That it looked ancient and mythical in its hugeness and battered state was appropriate. These minor works of art had already become rather famous in the musical community, both because one of them had the word "BLUES" inscribed on its front cover in Burdon's own blood and because they displayed care and artistry almost on a par with a monk's scroll. "He kept them almost from art school days," says John Steel. "He would write lyrics down, write ideas down, images and all sorts of stuff. He was a compulsive jotter-journalist type thing. They would be wonderful historical pieces if he still had any. He had a nice graphic style. Black Indian ink. A nice artistic way of writing things so that nothing was like a straightforward diary. There was always little illustrations and stuff in the margins." The journals also contained the lyrics of some of Burdon's favourite songs and paragraphs from American true crime magazines, by which he was fascinated. "He always had more words than he had melo-dies," says Zoot Money. "He would write profusely. All sorts of stuff would go in as well as his drawings. He made collages and words, loads and loads of words so you would have wall-to-wall words but all the edges would be filled with stuff. He lost a few because he kept moving house and moving country and whatnot. I said to him, 'You should have been sending those to your mother or sisters or somebody.'" Of the specific *Winds of Change* journal, Burdon laments, "The book was stolen at a gig backstage in London, unfortunately."

Burdon wrote some comments for the album under the heading "The New Animals" suffused with his new peace-and-love philosophy (example: "I love you all and want you to gain something from these new sounds"). It had been the intention that the comments would be printed inside the album's gatefold sleeve but MGM placed them, in huge lettering that completely dominated the design, on the front cover. This gushing, conspicuously placed rhetoric created problems for the band. Briggs recalls, "I think it was *Rolling Stone*, when they reviewed the album, got totally indignant and started calling Eric 'Jesus Burdon'. That engendered a kind of resentment towards Eric and towards The Animals which we never really shook off. It seemed to affect the way people wrote about the band after that." Inside the gatefold sleeve, Burdon wrote out a list of people who had inspired him, many of them from the pop world but including his old teacher Bertie Brown, plus verses about the other members of the group, Tom Wilson and Terry McVay. Burdon's old pal Zoot Money is described as "second father" in the "friends" list. "In a way I brought a sort of a voice of reason to him," accepts Money. "I was still connected to the London way of life, and sanity. I wasn't all that sane, but I had a relationship — which I still have — with my wife, she keeps me very well-grounded, and in a way I suppose we were a sort of mum and dad figure on occasion, when we said, 'Now don't be so silly Eric, this is ridiculous, wait until you come down off the drugs and then we'll talk about it.' It was a question of him occasionally needing landmarks here and there. Needing ports of call to get back to reality. Because he has travelled. In the mind, I mean. He's travelled to many, many different galaxies."

Of the reviews, one of the most interesting came from journalist Mike Ledgerwood who commented on the spoken-word tracks, "Eric must undoubtedly be a frustrated actor. He obviously won't be satisfied until he can play Hamlet." Ledgerwood had just about hit the nail on the head, presumably without the benefit of knowing of the thespian and cinematic ambitions that would run like a seam through Burdon's life.

The album reached number 42 in the American album charts but, like all Eric Burdon & The Animals LPs, did not chart in Britain. Though this was the consequence of the band being perceived as American-oriented due to songs like 'San Franciscan Nights' and Burdon's excited babblings in the press about the Haight-Ashbury scene, this cool reception from the British public can't have been helped by the kind of comments Burdon made to Keith Altham in the September 30 1967 issue of *New Musical Express*. Asked why the band were more successful Stateside, he replied, "Firstly because Britain is not aware of what we are trying to communicate as the Americans. The whole world still needs a kick up the pants. The Americans are one move ahead. Secondly, in the case of 'Good Times', I never wanted to release it as a single but my management and record company were afraid that I would offend people in England if I released 'San Franciscan Nights'. I don't give a damn. I know what I'm doing is right and I can wait for them to come round." Burdon also complained, "If I wanted to I could get on a plane tomorrow and go and live in America, where I'm guaranteed good record sales. I could get a house where everything in it works. Hot and cold taps that run and a society that understands what I am trying to do. I'm here in a house where nothing works, including the taps, and people constantly misunderstand me." Britons are known and admired for their ability to simultaneously love and mock their own country. Listening to privileged celebrities knock Britain, though, tests their unusually high tolerance levels.

Burdon's frustrations over 'San Franciscan Nights' were finally alleviated in October when MGM UK consented to a British issue, backed with the previously unreleased 'Gratefully Dead'. Burdon was completely vindicated in his insistence that British audiences would understand the song. Upon its belated UK release, 'San Franciscan Nights' reached number seven (higher than its American placing) and became Burdon's biggest hit in his home country since 'Don't Bring Me Down'. 'Gratefully Dead' was recorded at London's Kingsway Studio only a few weeks before the record's release because previous UK A-side 'Good Times' could not be used for the B-side as it had been in the States. With Wilson not present, Briggs acted as producer and was credited as such. The track sees Eric espousing more of the San Franciscan philosophy, namely: "I love everybody — do you hear me?" Anybody who doesn't hear is, apparently, "stone cold dead," hence the punning reference to one of the San Francis-can bands. In fact, the track is far more Hendrix than Grateful Dead. Starting with a buzzsaw intro which merges into a barely less brutal guitar riff, it's the closest to Hendrix's style (especially 'Foxy Lady') than Burdon ever came (although Briggs claims that the riff was stolen by Weider — who plays it — from a John Mayall record). Burdon sounds like he's reading a poem in the background during the instrumental breaks but this was in fact intended to represent Burdon trying to get his hippie ideals over to a listener whose unresponsiveness is typical of what Burdon felt he was coming up against at the time, especially in Britain.

Meanwhile, the New Animals were getting better and better as a live act. "When the band got on stage, we'd fire up," boasts Briggs. "It was a hard-rocking band and we never caught that in the studio. In October of '67 we were on a concert. The White Front music festival in Hollywood Bowl. There was The Who, there was the Everly Brothers, there was The Association. We were not topping the bill, we were opening the second half or midway through. We went on and we tore the place down. We did 'Hey Gyp' — which we always used to finish with — and in front of the stage there's this pool with all these fountains and Eric jumped in the pool. I think it was ten feet deep. And I pulled him out and the crowd went berserk. Yelling and scream-ing and carrying on. Everybody got up and left. The Association came on after us and the crowd was gone… Better live than in the studio — no question about it. I tried bringing up a couple of times the idea of doing a live album but I was pooh-poohed, both by Tom Wilson and by Eric." "Oh sure, yeah," Burdon says of the proposition that the New Animals were better live than in the studio, "but I think that's true of every band that I've been a part of. I am only now beginning to grapple with the studio. It's taken me thirty years to get the point where I really feel that what I'm doing in the studio is reflecting what I want to do on stage. I really don't think I've been given a chance in the studio. Probably the closest period was with War." Weider agrees that the New Animals were better live than in the studio, especially the way that he and Briggs would trade off the guitar work, and considers it a shame more of their stage performances weren't captured for posterity. This live prowess was achieved in spite of the disadvantage of working with Vox amplifiers which the band were unhappy with but were contracted to use. Briggs gives Burdon credit for allowing the New Animals to be a band rather than just his backing musicians. "Eric was quite happy for us to play instrumentals," he says. "We used to do a couple, very jazz-oriented. He'd just go offstage." However, one of the main reasons for the New Animals' power as a live act was Burdon's voice and stage presence. "Eric sang like a musician," Briggs notes. "He improvised. He never sang the same thing twice. He was good. I didn't realise it so much when I was working with him. He was way ahead of Jagger, he was ahead of Jim Morrison." Jenkins also preferred the New Animals in a live context, although perhaps not for the same reasons. "Got a better buzz out of it," he says. "I didn't like recording much. We sort of stretched out more. Everything has to be so tight in the studio. Just fucked me head up, all that recording."

Jenkins head was fucked up a little more in October, when the Animals returned to TTG studios to record their second album, which would eventually be released under the title *The Twain Shall Meet*. The first album had only been issued the month before the new sessions but the New Animals would throughout their brief career be incredibly prolific, releasing four albums (one of them a double) in the space of a year and three months. It's difficult to assess whether such feverish activity was a good or bad thing. A slower work rate might have led to them only releasing a couple of LPs before Burdon got bored with rock, as he did, and went off to try to become a movie star and we would have been denied some great music. On the other hand, too much of the material featured on New Animals albums crossed the fine line between spontaneous inspiration and filler, an inconsistency of quality that has served to dilute the group's legacy. Weider didn't think the band were rushing into the follow-up album. "Not much else to do but record and tour," he shrugs. "That's what I thought, and still do, a musician's job is. Not like bands today: one album every four years. What do they do with their time in the interim?" Briggs: "We'd record during the week and go off and do gigs at the weekends. That was the one time we felt the group was together as a group and not just Eric and his employees. It was my favourite time with The Animals. The band was sounding great onstage. I remember feeling very fulfilled. Very close to the other guys. That was the time when I was closest to Eric too." Apart from the *Twain* sessions, Briggs' relationship with Burdon was never an easy one. "Eric never really shared a lot of stuff," he says. "Eric was a funny guy. He wouldn't be terribly close with the guys in his band but he'd go and meet some new friend at some psychedelic club in San Francisco and that person would be his best friend. He'd tell him his life story."

The first product of the *Twain* sessions was 'Monterey', a song on which Burdon had started working soon after the titular festival took place. "I'm pretty sure we did it first, 'cause Tom Wilson wanted to get it out as a single," Briggs says. "I had a few doubts because we'd done 'San Franciscan Nights' and now we're doing 'Monterey' and I'm thinking to myself, 'God, is this ever going to play in England?'" In fact, the single was initially only released in the States, appearing in November coupled with 'Ain't That So', which was mis-titled as 'Ain't It So' on some pressings and erroneously credited to all five Animals as composers. 'Monterey' shows a Burdon who seems ever more intent on asserting the superiority of the counter-culture and name-checking its heroes. His eulogy to what he describes here as "three days of understanding" could have been embarrassing. Instead, like with 'San Franciscan Nights', he manages to be messianic about his new lifestyle while side-stepping piety. Any naïveté (and there has to be more than a trace of such in a song positing a festival as the start of a change in human nature) is touching rather than cringe-making. Naturally, Burdon's lyric is helped in no small measure by the track's musical excellence, much of which is Briggs' responsibility, particularly his opening coiling electric sitar and sweeping horn charts. McCulloch's bass playing is an impressively beefy presence in the background throughout. There are pleasing sound effects for the name checks of the festival performers — distorted electric guitar for Hendrix; vibrating human lips imitating propellers for Jefferson Airplane and The Byrds; a trumpet motif for Hugh Masakela (played by a session musician because Tom Wilson nixed the idea of lifting a passage direct from one of Masakela's records in case of copyright problems). In its celebratory enthusiasm, 'Monterey' (which reached number fifteen in the US charts) seems to capture better the atmosphere of the Monterey festival than does Joni Mitchell's calm, considered 'Woodstock' that event, even despite Burdon's bewildering omission of Otis Redding in his roll call of the greatest performers.

An indication of how unfathomable the mind of Burdon could be to his colleagues came at the end of the year. With *The Twain Shall Meet* in the can by November and the group euphoric over the way they felt they were cresting on an artistic wave, The Animals had flown back to England in the first week of December '67. That month they appeared on the bill at Christmas on Earth Continued at Kensington Olympia with The Who, Pink Floyd, Traffic and The Move. "It was a very disappointing gig," Briggs says. "I remember after the gig going up to Eric and going, 'What are you doing over Christmas?' He goes, 'I'm working man, I'm *working*. After a gig like this, I'm gonna work. We gotta get our shit together.' I felt a bit hurt. He was really rude to me. So I didn't see him over the whole Christmas time. Then when I saw him, he goes, 'Hello stranger, where you been?'" The attitude Burdon had displayed after the Christmas on Earth appearance can be seen, in retrospect, as one of the seeds of destruction of the New Animals. His mystifying dissatisfaction with the band would lead to events in the New Year from which they would never recover.

As if to prove Burdon was completely wrong about the state of the group, January saw the release in Britain of a New Animals single that it was immediately obvious was a classic. 'Sky Pilot' was of such an epic scale (7:27) that it had to be spread across both sides of the record. It was daring in subject matter as well as length. Though anti-war sentiments (for which one can read anti-Vietnam sentiments) were ubiquitous in 1968, what was not so thick on the ground — for the simple reason that a still rather conservative media would not for the most part countenance it — were attacks on the hypocrisy of organised religion. Burdon chose as the focus of his pacifist's anger not the obvious and easy target of the army general but his padre — the "Sky Pilot", in soldier's vernacular — who saw no contradiction in telling cannon fodder that they had Right on their side while espousing the "Thou Shalt Not Kill" commandment. "I felt that we were in a position to make it clear to the public that we were against the war in Vietnam," Burdon explains. "I really was trying to make a statement against the hypocrisy of war and the military's collusion with the religious institutions. I abhorred and hated and was repulsed by the illegal, illicit war in Vietnam and then to have men of God back it up and actually bless bombs with holy water — that is just total perversity. It's the Nazis all over again." However, he adds, "But my character and my family, my bringing up, wouldn't allow me to slag off the soldiers — the poor guys who went for the government line and joined the army and went and fought in Vietnam. I felt sorry for those guys. I was on their side as much as I was against government policy. It was a shame and a disgrace to see them return from that conflict to the United States and get spat at and run down and pushed around and ignored by the American public. That was the big tragedy of the Vietnam War."

Vic Briggs and Tom Wilson completely went to town on this larger-than-life, effects-laden extravaganza. One of the effects was bagpipes, long an instrument associated with the military. "If

Eric was the author, I was the director or producer," says Briggs. "I said to him, 'I don't know much about bagpipes but I do know we can only play in two keys so we've got to find out what key the bagpipes are playing in. If the bagpipes are in B flat we need to play in B flat.' It just so happened that the pipes and drums of the Scots Guards was touring the United States at that time. So we got in touch with them. We got about eight guys in the studio. I said, 'Just play what you play.' So they started playing a few things and I think the tune was called 'Blue Bonnets over the Border' and I listened to that and I said, 'That's it. We'll do that one. It's the right tempo.' So we got 'Blue Bonnets over the Border' down. Then we had this solo piper playing and I said, 'Oh Jesus, that's beautiful.' We had maybe four or five bagpipe pieces down. And it didn't take that long, only about an hour, hour-and-a-half. The pipe major goes, 'Okay lads — it's Budweiser time!' So they all headed out to the bar. Nowadays you can do it all with computers but we had to build the song forward. The way we recorded the last part, we got the bagpipes on a couple of tracks on an eight-track tape and I counted the band in. We did that last two verses together, which was very quiet. And then we do the grand finale and go out to a fade. There was supposed to be an agreement signed that the Scots Guards had to hear this thing before it got put out." The Animals knew, though, that an anti-war song would not go down well with the Scots Guards. Briggs: "We never let 'em hear it, we just put it out. And they were threatening to sue us."

Burdon's vocal had been recorded at the same time as the rhythm tracks. Briggs: "In the last verse before the guitar solos, he actually makes a mistake. ["He'll *stay'll* behind…"] We just decided to let that go. Most of the time we'd just record with Eric in an isolation booth 'cause he was really good at getting good performance. We very rarely used to overdub Eric." Those impressed by the song's seamless, polished feel might be surprised to discover that the band only rehearsed it a few times before recording it. "It was a piss-easy song," Briggs claims. "When you've got good musicians and the song's really easy…We buzzed through that really quickly."

The soundscape is one of three parts. Setting the scene with effects like the soaring whoosh of the phasing-treated drums — which give the band's collective singing of the title phrase a transcendent, almost celestial quality, as though they are speaking with a Higher Authority — The Animals then take the track into a middle section of exploding shells, gunfire and a bagpipe chorus. This gives way so skilfully to mournful violin in a sudden quiet as to perfectly evoke the eerie silence of a post-battle wasteland. An acoustic guitar is sorrowfully strummed. Fluttering flutes evoke the spirits of dead soldiers ascending to heaven. Burdon's vocals have become suitably exhausted. The track contains some of Burdon's greatest ever singing, from the wonderful little rumble of contempt at the back of his throat every time he finishes enunciating the words "sky pilot" to the lovely empathy in his voice in the final verse.

Amazingly, this classic only just grazed the UK top forty, almost an insult — despite the record's admittedly ungainly division of halves — to surely the greatest thing with which Eric Burdon has ever been associated. "I think I fucked up with regard to England," Briggs says. "I went down to talk to the British head of MGM. I said, 'I think you should put out the second part of 'Sky Pilot' as the [A-side], as opposed to the first part.' I think I was wrong. They split right at the start of the guitar solo. My thinking was, in those days, sometimes in England a quirky kind of record like 'Right Said Fred' by Bernard Cribbins would get on the charts. I thought to myself, 'They ain't gonna go for this first part, so why not try at least to put the second half out as a single — maybe it's just quirky enough that the Brits will go for it.'"

Did Briggs feel at the time that the record's subject matter was daring? "Yeah, particularly since we were a British band: 'What the fuck's this gotta do with you? This is not your fight anyway.'" Almost those exact sentiments were conveyed to him by a secretary working for Ben Barrett, a contractor who brought in session musicians to play on The Animals' material. Briggs: "She says, 'Vic, you English people, do you have a presence in Vietnam?' Being a red-blooded American she expected the Brits, being on the side of the 'good guys', would have some kind of force in Vietnam. I just hummed and hawed and changed the subject very quickly."

Burdon dismisses the suggestion that 'Sky Pilot' is his greatest song. "I don't think so," he says. "I never performed it for years because I felt it didn't have any groove to it. It wasn't 'til I started working with Brian Auger that he helped me see the possibilities of using it." However, it has subsequently acquired a life of its own on stage. "'Sky Pilot' is becoming really popular with audiences over here, especially with Vietnam vets," he says. "Some of them will turn up as bag and drum-pipe marching bands and they want to come on stage and play with us at the end." Burdon also says of Vietnam, "I've heard many stories from guys who told me that in the helicopters pilots would illegally tune in to American Forces Network and listen to the music as they went into battle. It definitely was a rock'n'roll war... It was a revelation to me to find out that returning soldiers were telling me that my music got them through the war. That is the biggest compliment that I've been paid in all the time that I've been in the music business. Screw everything else. "

chapter eleven

In January 1968, the New Animals left Britain for more live work. They did not — except for gigs and promotional obligations — come back.

"Eric sort of turned his back on England," says Jenkins. "Don't know why. Maybe all the action was going on out in LA. The politics of all that, I didn't get into all that. Whatever was going on was going on. Another joint and just go along with it." Briggs has an idea: "Coming to the States, getting to Haight-Ashbury, being involved in that whole West Coast thing, then coming back to England was a big let-down. It was like, 'Forget it. They don't understand where we're at.' In England, much more than in the States, they wanted the old Animals. The psychedelic thing never really took off in England. We concentrated all our energy on the States. I thought MGM in Britain was pretty incompetent. MGM in the States was also pretty incompetent but in Britain they were worse. They didn't know what to make of us. Maybe I can't really blame them. The English music scene was still very weird. You'd have The Searchers, then Val Doonican, then you'd have Winifred Atwell. It was such a hodgepodge of stuff on the radio that it was difficult to find a niche. At that time America was much more stratified: there's a soul station, there's a country station…It was hard to get the right kind of airplay for The Animals. In England the Summer of Love came and went very quickly. It was a fashion statement. In America it was a lot more political. So when we came out with 'Sky Pilot', we went very quickly from flower power to essentially a political, anti-war statement. Of course, in England that didn't mean a whole hell of a lot. When we came back in December '67, after our third tour of the States, everything somehow or other had changed. I felt like I didn't belong there anymore. So in January of '68, we flew over to Paris, did a show at the Olympia. The very next day we flew back to London and we flew to New York. Before too long, maybe a week or so, we were in LA and that was it. We started to settle in LA. England seemed like a place I didn't want to go back to. It seemed cold, it seemed unfriendly, it seemed unaware. It seemed as though we'd moved to this new level of awareness. It felt like we were going to change the world." However, Briggs adds, "But when we came back to the States it wasn't the same as it had been. It was like the bad vibes followed us back to the States and that was when things slowly started to crumble."

An idea floated at the time was that the band should all live together in a big house as The Beatles did, fictionally, in the movie *Help!* and as The Grateful Dead did, in real life, in San Francisco. Briggs resisted the suggestion: "I had this girlfriend and I just didn't want to live with everybody else. Danny had gotten married. Eric got a house up in Lookout [Mountain] Road. Johnny and Danny were living with Kevin Deverich and his wife." Some might have assumed that The Animals, particularly Burdon, would prefer to be domiciled in San Francisco, but though Burdon suggested that he was going to die in its Haight-Ashbury district in 'San Franciscan Nights', in reality neither he nor The Animals were ever residents. This fondness for rather than familiarity with San Francisco helped explain a feature of 'San Franciscan Nights' that many inhabitants of the area had found puzzling: the song described the nights there as "warm." In fact, San Franciscan nights are notorious for their extreme coldness due to the locale being surrounded by water. "You have to understand," explains Briggs about their choice of location, "in California, LA was mostly where things happened. There were no record companies in the Bay Area at that time."

By now, the brotherly love and unity of The Animals was disintegrating at a steady pace. Not just because of Burdon's — to the others — unfathomable dissatisfaction with the way the band was going musically but because it was obvious something was very wrong on the money front. Even Burdon, who had remained with Mike Jeffery following the split with the original Animals despite the fact that it was obvious back then that things were amiss with regard to funds, was beginning to have suspicions. The disquiet on the part of the band over promised monies failing to materialise turned from quiet grumbling to full-throated defiance, exemplified by behaviour backstage at a Stockholm concert in January '68. "Chas had signed some contracts for us to do gigs so he was involved in our management too," says Briggs. "He wasn't one of The Animals' managers but he was working in the office with Jeffries… We're sitting in the dressing room. We're making up songs. Yameta was the name of an offshore corporation set up in the Bahamas. All our contracts were with Yameta. I'm going, [to the tune of Dobie Gray's 'The In Crowd'], 'I'm in with Yameta/I know where my money goes/I'm in with Yameta/I know what Mike Jeffries knows.' These cynical songs. Danny's sitting there going [to the tune of Georgie Fame's 'Ballad of Bonnie and Clyde'], 'Jeffries and Chas/They ripped off all our money/It wasn't very funny.' It was obvious that Eric wasn't getting any money. He was getting his needs taken care of but he was really concerned. I think he was probably masking a lot of his concern with drinking.

"Not long after that, we were in LA, probably sometime in February, and Eric and I went over to Kevin Deverich's house. Eric's going on about how bad things are and he doesn't know what he's gonna do. And I'm watching this whole thing and I'm going, 'I know Kevin's gonna offer to manage him.' Kevin was very calculating. Eric was just about to put his hand on the front door to walk out and Kevin goes, 'Well there is something we can do. If you wanna, we can probably break the contract with Jeffries and I can manage you.' And Eric goes, 'Let's talk about it.' Instead of walking out, we sat down and talked. That's when the split from Jeffries started."

In February, The Animals were playing in Tucson, Arizona and Briggs was making frequent calls to his girlfriend in New York. He found himself approached by a worried Deverich who enquired who he kept calling. After Briggs explained, Deverich expressed relief. He revealed that he and Burdon had told Jeffery — who was also in New York — about Burdon's intention to

pass the management reins to Deverich. Jeffery, naturally, was not
happy with this. A confrontation was inevitable and came shortly
afterwards when the band were playing in New York. "Jeffries and
Chas showed up," recalls Briggs. "Eric was stoned on mescaline or
something like that. If you're on psychedelics and something bad
happens it can really put you on a bummer. Chas was livid. Chas
was always livid anyway but he was just being nasty. It was not
nice. I was very glad to get out of New York next day. After this
night, Eric went off to Europe with Kevin and I remember Kevin
telling me later that Eric wanted to get out of the music business,
he was so affected by this ugly confrontation with Jeffries and
Chas." Was there any concern that the management contract with
Jeffery might be legally binding? "Kevin had some good lawyers
and he seemed to think that basically with misappropriation of
funds and whatever else that it wouldn't be too much trouble
to get out of it," says Briggs. "The strange thing was, there was
no action taken," says Burdon of his breaking his contract with
Jeffery. "That's what stunk to high hell. I was able to walk away
from the situation, continue using the name 'The Animals', sign
a new contract with MGM without Mike Jeffries being involved
and nobody said a dickey. So if nobody said anything, he must
have been quite happy looting from somewhere else to have not
jumped all over me and not taken me to court. I got an attorney
and instigated a movement against Mike Jeffries. In order for
that movement to take place, I needed to go up against MGM
because they had all the books of records of sales etc. I couldn't
get past that for certain reasons so I couldn't get to Jeffries. I was
quite happy to just soldier on anyway. Alright, I knew that we'd
been stung and there was tons of money missing but you can't
go on feeling bitter and sorry for yourself and throw good money
after old money. You've got to get on with your life. I didn't get
in the music business to make money. I didn't come to America
to make money. This is the land of money. A man is measured by
money here. The first thing Americans ask you is, 'How much
do you earn?' When I grew up in England, nobody ever asked
anybody what they earned. I'm still that way. I'm an old soul.
What is money? Money can be the fucking devil. It can save

your life, it can kill you." Even Chas Chandler would conclude over the course of time that Jeffery was not a man with whom one should throw in one's lot. By 1994, he was saying of him to *Record Collector* magazine, "He was a thief, a liar and a cheat. You never knew where you were with the man. He was a scoundrel, a manipulative bastard."

Asked if switching from Jeffery to Deverich was a frying-pan-to-fire scenario, Burdon says, "Yeah, sure. He was just another opportunist. What you have to grasp here — and this is why I still am so pissed off at Alan Price — once you start off on the wrong foot with a deal that goes down that becomes public knowledge in a business like the music business, you're screwed from the beginning. It follows you around like Marley's Ghost because you go from one management situation to the next and they know what happened from talk within the business. They know exactly how to entrap you, they know what the golden carrot is, they know how to use the whip. And if you don't use them, you don't get anywhere. It all has its roots in what went on in the original Animals."

There were other tensions amongst The Animals that boiled over on February 9 when the band played two shows on the same day at the Anaheim Convention Center in Southern California with The Jimi Hendrix Experience. The Animals opened one of the shows, the Experience the other. In the evening, before the show in which The Animals were due to be the main act, Hendrix, Burdon, McCulloch and Briggs were sitting in a limo outside the venue getting stoned. Burdon suddenly told Hendrix that he was embarrassed that The Animals were closing the show because he was so much better than them. "Danny and I went *ballistic*," says Briggs. "'Fuck, man! What the fuck's the matter with you? You fucking idiot!' We had a knock-down, drag out. Nobody actually hit anybody but…'For fuck's sake man, you're a star! Act like a fucking star. Stop kissing ass to Jimi.'" Briggs says that this tendency of Burdon to pay homage to his heroes — whether it be in person, in songs like 'Winds of Change' or in stage performances where he would make announcements between and even sometimes during songs about people he admired — was something that had irritated Briggs and McCulloch for some time. They felt it implied that he didn't take himself — and by extension The Animals — seriously, as did his habit of arranging gigs for the band at small London clubs like The Scotch of St. James and The Speakeasy. "The Beatles never did that, The Stones never did that," says Briggs. "Eric wanted to go and impress his friends. It was like, 'What the fuck are The Animals doing playing places like this?' As far as I'm concerned, when we went to the States for the first time, there was The Beatles, the Stones and The Animals. It seemed like The Animals were the poor cousins. Since he was the leader of the band, if he wasn't believing in himself as an artist than it was kind of putting the lid on it for us." After the Anaheim shows, the band had a 100-mile journey to their next concert during which, Briggs recalls, "Nobody said a word. Cut the atmosphere with a knife. It never quite recovered from that."

From February 17-23 1968, The Animals were in Vancouver for a week. Having embraced every other aspect of the psychedelic and flower-power age, they were naturally intrigued when some disciples of the Maharishi Mahesh Yogi came to their hotel and informed them of a day-long workshop on transcendental meditation taking place that week. "Eric and John certainly flew over to Victoria — Vancouver Island — and got initiated," says Briggs. "There may have been others but I don't think Danny. I was seriously thinking of going but flew to Seattle instead to spend the day with my cousin." Jenkins says, "We knew that The Beatles were doing Maharishi transcendental meditation, so The Animals went up — Danny didn't go 'cause Danny was a pill-freak — and we all became initiated into the transcendental meditation. We had a silent mantra and we done it for a while but it didn't last long."

In March, the follow-up to the 'Monterey' single was released in the US. It's difficult to know what was going through the minds of MGM on either side of the Atlantic at this point. After having decided not to release 'Sky Pilot', the American MGM decided that the most appropriate choice for the next Animals single was 'Anything' backed with 'It's All Meat', two tracks off *Winds of Change*, an album which the band, having long completed *Twain*, must have considered ancient history. It reached a pathetic number eighty, hardly the best way to consolidate the top twenty success of its predecessor.

That same month saw the American release of *The Twain Shall Meet* (it appeared in Britain in May). The egalitarianism of the songwriting credits on *Winds of Change* was developed to its logical conclusion on its follow-up. Eric Burdon does not appear on three of the eight tracks on the album (discounting his backing vocals on 'Just The Thought'), underlining the fact that, despite their name, Eric Burdon & The Animals were a real band rather than a vehicle for the lead vocalist. Like its predecessor, *Twain* is by no means a consistent album but it contains many fine and some classic songs.

The texture and quality of *The Twain Shall Meet* certainly gives no hint of the album's short recording process. Tom Wilson and Vic Briggs were using all the gadgetry and gimmickry newly available to producers in the age of stereo, multi-tracking (the album was recorded on eight-track, as opposed to the four-track facilities with which they'd had to make do while recording *Winds*) and sound effects (speaker-to-speaker panning and track segues abound). Combined with numerous horn charts and string sections and a sublimely judged mix, it engendered an album even richer than the plushly-soundscaped *Winds*. That the band had whole-heartedly embraced the experimentalism of the age was underlined by the fact that side two of the original vinyl album was given over to three epics, 'Sky Pilot', 'We Love You Lil' and 'All is One', all of which clock in at around the seven-minute mark and all of which are part of a concept. "It's supposed to be a war-and-peace theme," reveals Briggs. "Starts off with war. The middle song is supposed to be the suffering of war, refugees. Then the last part was peace coming out of conflict." Unfortunately the concept is undermined somewhat by the fact that two of its parts — 'We Love You Lil' and 'All is One' — are instrumentals. Moreover, they are not particularly good instrumentals, meaning that the album rather peters out in terms of quality. Nonetheless, the convention-busting, the peace-and-love mentality informing 'Sky Pilot' and 'No Self Pity', the Fred Otnes-designed sleeve artwork that depicts Burdon's face below a montage of symbols of the era (a white dove, flora, an American GI), the album's title (Briggs: "East is East and West is West and never the twain shall meet. It was like: the twain *shall* meet") and the inclusion of the paean to the Monterey festival all make *The Twain Shall Meet* the ultimate flower-power album.

Unlike *Winds of Change*, the album opens with a bang, even if one with which the public were already familiar, the excellent 'Monterey' single starting the proceedings. It features a mysterious whispered introduction ("In the beginning...") not on the single. The twain of old Animals and new meets on 'Just the Thought', Hilton Valentine getting a co-writing credit with the five current members. Valentine can now not remember what his contribution was but Briggs confirms, "Hilton was around. He was in and out of LA and hanging out a lot." 'Just the Thought' is one of only two tracks on the album not credited to Burdon/Briggs/Weider/Jenkins/McCulloch and like the other ('Orange and Red Beams', credited solely to McCulloch) is sung by the band's bassist. Although McCulloch's vocals can't hope to be any match for Burdon's mastery of the microphone, he does a respectable job on a thoughtful and reflective song about a man going through deep alterations in his perception of life. The melody is pretty (a fact initially disguised by Burdon's irritating echoing of McCulloch's vocals) and nicely decorated by flutes and mournful brass. 'Closer to the Truth' is closer to the blues than any of the other tracks, although the hippie consciousness is present and correct in the shape of the invocation of a guru figure (a man closer to the truth than ordinary mortals — perhaps the Maharishi?). The raw, electric guitar of the spare opening promises much but the song fails to take off in its meandering bridge and only Wilson's production tricks ultimately rescue it from pedestrianism. Briggs reveals, "I had one of the first stereo cassette recorders that was ever made. Bought it when I got to New York in February. What you hear at the start of that song is actually the demo tape and we played it on my little cassette recorder and then we just kicked in the band on top of the demo. That was Eric's idea. It finished with the demo as well." 'No Self Pity' is a song of relativism. The observation that no

matter how slow/low/fine/fast you are, there is always somebody
slower/lower/finer/faster is expressed in verses that alternate with
ones of wonderment at the insignificance of mankind, a humility
that is a nice contrast to the "We demand…" ethos that at times
dominated the Sixties counter-culture. The above-average lyric is
matched by out-of-the-ordinary instrumentation, including sitar-
ish guitar, harpsichord and busy, improvisational drumming that
displays just how much Barry Jenkins had developed as a consequence of the challenging melodies and unusual time signatures
the adventurism of the New Animals required him to deal with. "I
don't think we ever suggested drum patterns to Barry," says Briggs
in admiration. "He'd just come up with whatever was appropriate."
Of McCulloch's second vocal on *Twain*, 'Orange and Red Beams',
Briggs explains, "He was on acid. He saw these orange and red
lights coming from the window. He saw them go into his wife's
abdomen. I guess she was pregnant at the time. Very acid, spiritual
type thing." Brass and strings are featured on a number that is no
less intriguing for it being philosophically opaque. Though that
opaqueness is possibly deliberate, it hardly excuses those record
companies who rather render its (presumably) profound sentiments something of a waste of time by sloppy misspelling of its
title, such as One Way who on their CD release of *Twain* listed
the track as 'Oranges and Red Beans' as though the composer
is merely talking about his lunch. McCulloch can take consolation, though, from Briggs' revelation that the song had an unlikely
admirer: "Jimi Hendrix loved 'Orange and Red Beams'. He was
always on at me: 'Hey, man, that 'Orange and Red Beams', I love
that song.' He said it at least three or four times to me."

'Sky Pilot' follows and gave British ears the first opportunity
to hear the whole extravaganza without having to get up to turn
a seven-inch disc over. Though 'We Love You Lil' and 'All is
One' are instrumentals, they were Burdon's idea. "Just to prove
that music conquers all," he says of the concept. "There was two
songs during World War II that both sides sang with feeling.
The Germans and the Americans and the Brits and the Belgians
and the French, they all sang 'Lili Marlene'. That was a collective
erotic dream that the soldiers on every front were living. In the

same way in the winter of 1944 in the worst fighting in World War II the American GIs put their guns down, the Germans put their guns down and they all sang 'White Christmas' on Christmas Eve 1944. To me, this is a very important signal that music can heal anything." Briggs: "His idea was to have somebody whistling, then John had come up with this instrumental. That's all John. I wrote this choir on there. It's supposed to be a sound picture of columns of refugees moving away from the battle areas. People very distraught and devastated." 'We Love You Lil' is basically one long, undulating guitar solo. Nothing necessarily wrong with that — the endless twin guitar break by Joe Walsh and Don Felder on The Eagles' 'Hotel California' is one of the most sublime sequences in rock history — but there is nothing as hypnotic or galvanizing about these vaguely Eastern fretboard explorations. There's female cooing in the background and tolling bells but the only really arresting thing about the track is McCulloch's ever-exceptional bass. 'All is One' displays more nods to raga and Eastern philosophy. Briggs is on sitar again while McCulloch (not Jenkins) plays tablas. Burdon provides a spoken-word explanation of pantheistic belief, but there's hardly much more to it than what is articulated in the title. Like the previous track, pure head music that has dated horribly.

"Most of it was jamming," says Jenkins of New Animals music like this. "We'd go in the studio and we'd do all that stuff. A lot of it was jamming and unarranged stuff and then we'd have to learn how to play it — listen to your own music and learn how to play what you've just done to play it live on the road."

The side two suite might have had more impact had it been explained to listeners that the songs were actually inter-linked but once again there was a problem with the album's sleeve. Briggs: "Maybe MGM got scared after the reaction to the liner notes on *Winds of Change* so they put it out with nothing on. And it pissed me off because at least the musicians could have got credit. MGM was a rotten record company. Really rotten."

Though it was to be more or less expected that the album was a no-show on the British charts, it must have been disappointing for the band that this significant progression from *Winds of*

Change only got as far as number 79 even in the US. By the time it appeared, though, there were other things to think about as The Animals were in the middle of huge upheaval with the arrival of Zoot Money into their ranks. "By the end of '67, we had a balance of personalities and the band was playing tremendously," says Briggs. "When Eric wanted to have him in the band I was pretty horrified." Burdon himself now admits, "I just missed Zoot. He was a close friend. Maybe I just needed a friend out there. You're continually on the road. If the people you're around are starting to get a bit dreary, it becomes problematic. Sometimes, playability has to take a back seat." As indeed does practicality: Money's recruitment seems to fly in the face of Burdon's previously stated reason for not including a keyboardist in the New Animals' permanent line-up in the beginning. As Briggs observes, "It changed the logistics of the band because all of a sudden we had this Hammond organ. Before, we could fly everything everywhere and now there had to be somebody driving."

Zoot Money was born in Bournemouth on 17 July 1942. His given name is George but he acquired the nickname 'Zoot' after raving about a Zoot Sims concert. Contrary to a popular misconception, Money is genuinely his surname. Burdon, of course, had been trying to get his best mate into his band since back in '65 when Money had been asked to replace Alan Price. The commitments that had prevented Money joining back then no longer applied. The Big Roll Band had metamorphosed into Dantalion's Chariot — basically, much the same group but on an acid trip. It had turned out to be a bad move. Says Vic Briggs, "They were a really great band but just so out of place in the London scene of the time. And they would have been just about anywhere else except in California." Andy Summers, Money's partner in the creative axis of The Big Roll Band/Dantalion's Chariot, acknowledges that the perception was that changing The Big Roll Band into Dantalion's Chariot was self-sabotage. "That was the thought at the time," he says. "I wanted more freedom to really play and in the context of The Big Roll Band, specifically and technically we were playing R&B. I was more confined to playing rhythm guitar. I wanted to just start soaring and play soaring guitar solos. That was the wrong kind of music for it. So it was certainly promoted by self-interest and ego. But of course The Big Roll Band, which was a much more obvious commercial outfit playing those hit songs that everybody knew, people liked it and we'd sell out everywhere. When we changed to this weirder, psychedelic acid rock band, people didn't really come with us. It was great in London but once you got outside of London it got much more difficult, to the point it lasted about a year and then it finished." "Dantalion's Chariot hadn't worked," Money admits. "Hadn't brought in the millions that I had hoped and within ten months we were losing audiences and whatnot and it was obvious that I should have gone back, I should have maintained some kind of soul persona. We're talking about quite a traumatic period for me: trying to decide. Desperately trying to keep one thing together. I wanted to see America. I originally wanted to see it under my own steam. I wanted to take The Big Roll Band there actually, but we could never secure some kind of a fixed deal where we would be guaranteed the money, so I decided to join The Animals when they offered the second time." He adds, "Correction: the New New Animals."

Zoot Money and Vic Briggs have very different memories about the circumstances in which Money joined The 'New New Animals'. Briggs: "Eric was muttering about a lot of different things. Eric wasn't happy about the way the band was going. He just said, 'It ain't working out, I'm gonna bring Zoot over to be in the band.'" Money: "He [Briggs] was quite content to be relinquishing the hold on it and he welcomed the fact that I would have some musical ideas that could be utilised. He was the one that was the most musically adept in that band, with that line up, and it was, 'Well okay Zoot — you come in and be the MD' as it were. He was [involved with] an American chick so he was thinking of basing himself in America anyway and doing other things so it was a sort of a change over and he finally left and I took over." Briggs: "I didn't want to leave and I had a feeling that was going to happen and I didn't feel good about it. I've never felt anything bad towards Zoot because he's always been a friend but I was not happy about him coming in because I knew it was going to upset everything. I felt when we were recording *Twain Shall Meet* the band was just right. The right personalities, the right combination. The music was going great, the shows were going great. When we came back in January, there was something missing. Eric wasn't happy. He definitely wanted to go back to more blues-type stuff. He never explained why. Maybe he was frustrated with the album reviews, perhaps the success." Money: "I joined it because Vic Briggs wanted to write scores and be an arranger in LA. He wanted to spread out." Briggs admits, "I'd certainly indicated that was where I wanted to go. I wanted to work in the studios in Hollywood, which I eventually did." But he adds, "It's a little more complicated than that." Money: "And Eric was fed up with him or whatever. Eric moves on and likes to work with different people and likes to experiment, throws himself right into the middle of working with different people." Briggs: "It's hard for me to say exactly how Eric felt about me 'cause I never knew how Eric felt about me. I'll be straight with you: I know I was an egomaniac in those days. I must have been pretty hard to deal with. I felt very frustrated at him sometimes. It was also Danny too. Danny was champing at the bit. He was unhappy with a lot of what was going down. Eric may just have felt that I was dominating the band too much."

Zoot Money's first gig with The Animals took place in New Orleans and did not go well. Attempting to project a jolly persona for the audience the way he had always done with his own bands, United States virgin Money asked them whether they were all pissed. As Briggs points out, "In England, that would mean, 'Are you all drunk?' and in the States that meant, 'Are you all angry?'" Furthermore, such a profanity was simply not acceptable in the Bible Belt in 1968. The New Orleans police promptly shut down the concert. "So right off the bat, it was kind of like an awkwardness," says Briggs. Not only did Money's addition change the logistics of the band, it also shifted the balance of personalities and talent. Briggs recalls, "Eric was probably more friends with Barry than anybody else in the group. Then when Zoot came, Eric really started leaning on him." Money, in fact, initially moved into the basement of Burdon's house before finding his own place in

Brier Drive. "I don't recall Zoot and I talking in any depth about the whole scene," Briggs says. "We certainly stayed friends. But now there was starting to be a lot of tension. I felt very vulnerable. All of a sudden, I could have been superfluous. I'd liked my position and I knew there was going to be friction because George was a band leader. He was a damn good musician. To be honest, I was in a bit of duality anyway. I'm starting to think, 'Do I really want to do this?' Because there was so much tension. I was finding I was really enjoying working in the studios a hell of a lot more than going out on the road. And I may have made that clear to them. There's another aspect too. Danny had gotten married in September. Eric had gotten married in September. I took up in a relationship with this girlfriend and she came out to live with me, so it was like being married. The togetherness, hanging out every night and partying, wasn't there anymore. Things definitely changed because of that."

Weider, though, felt the new addition was for the good. "Great guy," he says of Money. "Kept us in line. Good for morale. It was nice to be back in boot camp." Briggs: "It became Danny and I against Eric. [Barry and John] didn't say much. They'd just go along with whatever. Danny and I started to feed each others' negativity. The last time I talked to him back in '92, Danny was in a rage against Eric." However, Briggs does admit rage was an emotion with which McCulloch was on more than nodding terms, whether the situation justified it or not: "Danny was never happy. On the sleevenotes on *Winds of Change*, it says 'Danny McCulloch never complains about anything.' Highly sarcastic."

This change in atmosphere within the ranks of The Animals was a reflection of the change in mood amongst the denizens of the counter-culture generally. The euphoria of 1967 had given way to a darker mood, particularly in America. Civil war between the anti-Vietnam/radical-types and the conservatives seemed a literal possibility. Briggs notes, "Martin Luther King was shot, Bobby Kennedy was shot. It was a very heavy year, '68." Meanwhile a snake had now entered Haight-Ashbury's Garden of Eden. "I remember being with The Grateful Dead in October '67 and I was feeling pretty good but they were not feeling good,"

Briggs recalls. "They were saying, 'Oh man, the scene up here is really bad.' The whole scene in San Francisco which had been pure at the beginning of the year, over the year it got more and more publicity. Articles in *Time* and *Newsweek*, more and more people showing up, more and more runaways, people dying from heroin overdoses, disease, young girls getting raped. It started getting really heavy in the Haight-Ashbury area. There was a general switch in the vibration of the whole hippie thing and there was a switch with The Animals too. It got back to being everyone for themselves rather than 'Here we are together, like brothers.'" On the day Martin Luther King was assassinated — April 4 — The Animals were due to play at The Fillmore, which had now switched location to Winterland, right in the middle of a black neighbourhood. The gig went ahead (as did a series of others over the next few days) but the atmosphere was extremely uncomfortable.

It was around this time that sessions for The Animals' next album, which would be titled *Every One of Us*, took place at TTG. Although odd tracks like 'Ain't That So' and 'Gratefully Dead' had been recorded without him, this was the first New Animals album not produced by Tom Wilson. Wilson was let go because, according to Briggs, "he wasn't taking his job seriously." Rather than look for a new producer, Briggs was given the role by the band. "I kind of did it by default," he says. "I was responsible for mixing the thing, getting it packaged and put together. I relegated myself to much less of a musical role, being more in the booth." And the atmosphere in the studio? "It was tense." Now though, Briggs almost felt that it was his job to defuse those tensions: "Being as how I'd assumed the role of producer, I was trying to be accommodating to Eric."

As with most of *Winds* but unlike most of *Twain*, the album was effectively written in the studio. "We didn't have anything," says Briggs. "I think the album *sounds* like it was cobbled together. This album was so far removed from what we were doing on stage. I don't know how it got like that." John Weider remembers this period as being one of "too many things going on at once. No focus. Eric was on a different path than the rest of us."

Considering that The Animals had only recently added a sixth member to the band, the public could be forgiven for expecting a rather lush product but *Every* turned out to be a rather stark, bare album. Briggs: "Eric wanted to stay away from the strings and horns. It was really Eric's album. He was back to calling the shots. He kept saying, 'I want my music to be loose and lucrative.' Kept using this word 'lucrative'. I don't know what he thought it meant. He wanted it to be less structured and less formal. More improvisation. I wanted more controlled music. I guess I'm a control freak but also I didn't really think Eric had the discipline to make that stuff work on an indefinite basis." Burdon explains his new musical vision thus: "There's a line in 'Mother Earth' with War: 'When it all is up, you've gotta go back to mother blues.' When you stop experimenting and stop playing around."

The album was striking for the fact that almost half of its length was taken up by spoken-word tracks, which, unlike the narrative pieces on *Winds*, didn't even have accompanying music. Burdon admits: "The dialogue on the album is out of frustration at the fact that I wanted to be a documentary movie maker so I was making audio documentary films." 'New York 1963-America 1968' featured a lengthy rant by a black TTG second engineer called Cliff. "After listening to his stories," says Burdon, "I just put him in the box with a microphone turned on and let him rant and rave and then we laid into the tracks afterwards. All of the dialogue was totally improvised. This could actually be perceived as one of the first rap records. That's the way I look at it. To just take the black engineer and put *him* in the box and have *him* rant and rave about the way *he* felt, I thought was a giant leap forward in terms of making records. It was me taking all the elements that were around me at the time and putting them down on wax." Money feels the spoken word sections to be a development of Burdon's penchant for spoken — or hollered — word delivery on stage. "He was not averse to doing portions of songs in a live situation where he would rhyme it, rhyming slang, or just get a thing going, a rhythm going," he says. "Ad lib and expanding on a subject." Money agrees with Burdon's view that he was making audio documentaries: "It wasn't rap as such but it was a documentation

of the times. Eric's like a journalistic poet in a way, because all
the things that he wrote about, particularly at that time, were the
state of the world, the way people were thinking, and he still does
that to a degree today." "Cliff was a real nice guy," says Briggs.
"He was a fighter pilot in World War II and he started talking
about racism in World War II. Fine, but what the fuck's this got
to do with it? But Eric wanted it on the album. I didn't feel like I
could say anything 'cause Eric wanted what he wanted and there
was no talking to him. He used to listen to Tom Wilson, at least
in the beginning, but I knew that he wouldn't listen to me. And
we'd had so many knock-down, drag-outs already about this, that
and the other, I just was like, 'Oh well, let's just make this album,
get it done.' A sense of futility or hopelessness: 'It's not gonna
get any better than this.'" Cliff's accent would at least have been
something familiar to American ears. 'The Immigrant Lad', the
other lengthy talking track, features a heated dialogue conducted
in Cockney and Geordie that would have been somewhat less
easy for the average United States resident to negotiate. Burdon
does now acknowledge, "Obviously the talking tracks are way too
long. Probably unintelligible to most Americans."

Briggs points out, "It wasn't that it was filler. If we'd have
wanted to, if we'd been in the mood, we could have written a lot of
good songs to put on that album." However, things on the songwriting front had become slightly complicated. When asked why
there were no Danny McCulloch songs on *Every*, Briggs says,
"I'm not sure if he was prevented or if he deliberately held back."
The bassist's two compositions on *Twain* had impressed Capitol
Records. Briggs: "Danny was putting his own album together."

Sessions for the album lasted for three or four weeks, after
which Briggs set about mixing it. Following the album's completion, the band flew to Britain. There, 'Monterey' was being
released as the latest British single (B-side: 'Anything'), the same
month that *Twain* was released in the UK for the first time.
The release of 'Monterey' seemed designed to prove that British
MGM could match the American wing of the label for crass stu-
pidity. In not even charting, it fared even worse in Britain than the
belated release of 'Anything' had in America, hardly surprisingly

considering it was released almost a full year after the festival it celebrated. However, it wasn't quite as crassly stupid as the band being booked that month to perform this counter-culture anthem on *The Golden Shot*, a tacky TV contest show hosted by the unctuous Bob Monkhouse. Of this experience, The Animals dressed in full hippie gear, Briggs says, "It was bizarre."

It was yet further proof that Britain did not really 'get' the new version of The Animals. "It didn't mean diddley shit in England," laments Burdon. "We did really well on the concert tours in the States but people in England couldn't swallow it. I came to England and we did a working man's club tour with the fucking light show. People just couldn't deal with it, they couldn't grasp it at all."

chapter twelve

May 30 and 31 1968 saw The Animals play two concerts billed as
The Beat Monster Concert in Zurich, Switzerland on the same
bill as The Jimi Hendrix Experience, Traffic, The Move and John
Mayall.

"They chartered a plane to take us over there," recalls Briggs.
"The stewardess comes on the intercom. She goes, 'Please, if you
heff any pot or LSD, please smoke zem now because we cannot
go through the customs at Zurich with zis stuff.' So next thing
you know, the whole plane's full of everybody smoking dope and
getting stoned." Money says of the gigs, "It was good, and actually there was some genuine jamming did actually occur on that.
That was probably one of the last times where you got that. Stevie
Winwood sat in and Jimi and Eric got up and sang something.
They actually wanted to sit in on each other's sets, but you had to
do your hits or whatever. Quite honestly, the things happening
in the hotel were far more interesting than what was going on
onstage. They were all in this hotel. One bomb and that would
have been history. It was seething." Briggs: "The Swiss have this
big national guard, territorials. To keep security at this concert
they brought in the territorials rather than the police. Next thing
you know, there's fights all over this arena. In the middle of 'Sky
Pilot' when we had the battle scene — which we had on tape —
we had a film clip of different shots and one of the film clips was
a brief clip of Hitler. When the Swiss saw this clip of Hitler, half
of them started booing and the other half started cheering and
another riot would start. It was pretty insane."

Following the second gig in Zurich, The Animals had to make
a dash for Winnipeg, Canada where they were, ludicrously, due
to play the next night. They made it but the gig was predictably

atrocious. Contrary to some reports, The Animals were not in riot-torn Paris that May — but that was about the only place they didn't play. Briggs feels the onerous live schedule was adding to the problems in the band. "There was this compulsion to work," he recalls. "After splitting with Jeffries, we've got to make some money. It would have been nice to just stop for a month, take a month off, not see each other."

In July, *Every One of Us* was released, but in America only. For once, MGM's reasoning seems understandable. *The Twain Shall Meet* had only been issued in Britain two months previously: a new Animals LP so soon after that would surely detract from sales of *Twain* and confuse the public. As it was, even the American release of *Every One of Us* was coming a mere four months after its predecessor. *Every One of Us* carries strange publishing credits. Most of the songs are attributed to Burdon alone, somewhat implausibly considering he has never been able to play a musical instrument of any description. Ironically in light of this, the work has a democratic production credit: "Every one of us". Vic Briggs is credited only as "Re-mix engineer".

The unexpected starkness and bleakness of the six-man Animals went right down to the monochrome photography and proletarian ambience (working men's flat caps) of the sleeve. (Money, being legally contracted elsewhere, was credited as "George Bruno", the latter being his middle name.) With regard to the title phrase, Money feels that it had, coincidentally, come into Burdon's life through a source additional to the presumed 'Yellow Submarine': "It's the literal translation from some Indian phrase. It's like 'karma': you can't translate 'karma' very well."

In some ways, the album seems to represent Burdon's comedown from hippiedom. Gone are the sitar and pseudo-sitars, the paeans to the alternative lifestyle and the colourful artwork from the previous two albums. Also gone is the musical ornamentation that was a hallmark of music rooted in flower-power. The violin is no longer a part of The Animals' sound (Weider: "The songs didn't need violin"). Instead we have basic rock. There is even a song that tears into the type of guru figure so beloved of the flower children. This is not to say, though, that the political radicalism has disappeared from the music. *Every One of Us* explores the issues of race, class, national identity and poverty in greater depth than anything with which Burdon had previously been associated.

The music might be spartan but is generally excellent, although this fact is disguised by the presence of too much fatuous filler, whether it be a pointless snippet of the nursery rhyme 'The Grand Old Duke of York' or the lengthy dialogue sections which bloat a couple of songs to unjustified lengths. On the original vinyl edition of the album, there were a mere two tracks on side two, nineteen minutes of that side being taken up by 'New York 1963-America 1968' — a good and concise song with a sprawling monologue grafted onto its back end. Those songs which were not disfigured in this way were of a quality that indicated this could have been the very best Eric Burdon & The Animals album, boasting fine melodies, disciplined instrumentation and — a real development for Burdon — focused and calmly observed lyrics.

'White Houses' provides a superb opener to the album. By coming up with a song that is like a cross between The Kinks' jeering put-down of straight society 'A Well Respected Man' and Elvis Presley's throbbingly compassionate 'In The Ghetto' (written by Mac Davis), Burdon attempts to highlight the contrast between the lifestyles of the bourgeoisie (inhabitants of the structures of the title) and slum-dwellers. Impressively he manages to do so without recourse to his usual histrionics and inchoate denunciations. Complementing the considered, tidy, well-observed lyric is mostly gentle music dominated by acoustic guitar and bongos, although blazing hard rock guitar is employed in the instrumental break. Zoot Money contributes piano and organ layers to an altogether very smooth-flowing and impressive piece of work. As with 'White Houses', Burdon cops the publishing credit on 'Uppers and Downers'. As it's a rendition of centuries-old nursery rhyme 'The Grand Old Duke of York', this is about as cheeky — if nowhere near as immoral or indeed lucrative — as Alan Price being solely credited for the similarly "Trad" 'The House of the Rising Sun'. Though this new, 24-second-long version of the ditty has nice massed harmonies, it is nothing more than a musical doodle which seems to exist purely to make the hilarious punning drug references ("when they were up, they were up…") of the title. Following the two Danny McCulloch showcases of *The Twain Shall Meet*, John Weider gets his turn in the spotlight with 'Serenade To A Sweet Lady', credited solely to him. It's a lengthy (six minutes-plus) instrumental in which a lilting acoustic guitar figure played by Briggs dominates. It's slightly jazzy in nature, something underlined by Jenkins' continual cymbal tinkling. Like *Twain*'s 'We Love You Lil', it's effectively a long guitar solo, but this time the solo is played with sufficient imagination to sustain interest over the running time. The ambience is exclusively acoustic almost right to the fade, at which point some tasteful electric guitar is introduced. "It was dedicated to my wife," reveals Weider. "[Burdon] was fine about it. I was very creative at that point in my life. When he heard the piece, he said 'Let's record it.'" Briggs says, "That's my favourite track on the album, without a doubt." That 'The Immigrant Lad' — another Burdon 'composition' — sounds suspiciously as though it has been adapted from an old folk melody is appropriate. The muddy waters of the Tyne (the river that runs through Burdon's home town) are used as a (rather confused) metaphor for separation from a woman and from prosperity. That and references to coal (mining of which was then one of the main sources of unskilled employment in the region) is completely within folk's People Music traditions. A good minor song then segues into a pub conversation between (keeping with the Newcastle flavour) a Geordie who has moved to the capital in search of work and a native Londoner. The Tynesider — played by Terry McVay — is shocked at the racial melting pot he finds in the city. The Londoner — John Weider — tries to explain that living and working with "wogs" doesn't seem so bad after a while. Impressively, this is all the result of improvisation, McVay and Weider having been given a vague outline by Burdon and taking it from there. You'd believe it was for real if you didn't know otherwise. Ultimately though, one is not awed enough by the extemporisation to be fooled into believing that it's not filler. The best track on the album is the Burdon-penned 'Year of the Guru', a hard rock number with a fine, clipped tune and a genuinely funny lyric. Its composition possibly marked the turning point for Burdon's belief in flower power, it being essentially a piss-take of the kind of fraudulent cult leader by which the counter-culture had been taken in *en masse*. This is almost Burdon's equivalent of The Beatles' 'Sexy Sadie', which was originally entitled 'Maharishi' and which detailed John Lennon's disenchantment with Mahesh Yogi, who he felt had convinced the 'beautiful people' of a non-existent uncommon insight. "I thought it was quite witty and quite clever," says Briggs, who has continued on the spiritual path Burdon repudiates here, "but I thought it was a bit cynical 'cause just three or four months earlier Eric was into all this [spiritual] stuff. There's always a few charlatans around." 'St. James Infirmary' — the original album publishing credits for which read "Arranged by Burdon-Weider-Jenkins- McCulloch-Briggs" — is a return to Burdon's blues roots, though thankfully not to 12-bar tedium. It has a good doomy production, eerie backing vocals and an above-average lyric and halfway through turns into a rock number with frenetic percussion and more of the blazing guitar heard on 'Year of the Guru' and 'White Houses'. Its sprightliness is all the more remarkable for a subject matter which puts one in mind of the stand-up comedian who, mocking the blues' depressing nature, posited a quintessentially downbeat blues song title: 'Woke Up This Mornin', My Woman Was Dead'. Briggs actually thought the song was single material and tried to persuade MGM of that: "I thought it was a throwback to 'House of the Rising Sun' — obviously not as compelling — an old song also about New Orleans. House of the Rising Sun' made it so why not try that?" His logic seems a little fatuous, and his reasoning — "We didn't have anything else" — wrong-headed in light of the album's better tracks.

Though closer 'New York 1963-America 1968' is a songwriting collaboration between Burdon and Zoot Money, it is Burdon's story being recounted. Burdon has always had a love-hate affair with the US ever since his first visit on the back of the success of 'The House of the Rising Sun' (in 1964, not '63 as the title erroneously states). The song explores the fact that his residency in a country whose materialism and militarism are anathema to him creates a daily conflict that makes him a perpetual stranger in a strange land. The track boasts another lovely, undulating guitar figure, as well as a pleasantly gloomy tune. This, though, is just the beginning of the track. Cliff's observations on poverty as well as race from first-hand experience create with the opening track, whether intentionally or not, a thematic circle. However, this is material destined never to be listened to again after the first hearing. The same applies to the closing musical segment which sees Burdon singing improvised words about being stoned. Money: "'New York '63' was probably a good example of him being narrator of the times. Poet-newsman or whatever. He wasn't afraid to have it stuck in time. He wasn't afraid to say something that was happening now, to comment on it and how it affected him with a view to later on listening and saying, 'God, that's dated.' It didn't necessarily bother him whereas it would have bothered me, so I was a bit reluctant to write words that really were of the time. My involvement was music. Musical ideas which I wasn't using which I thought, 'I wonder if this will do?', and he went 'Yeah, yeah right' and he would sing over it."

Intriguingly, Briggs reveals that there was at least one other song laid down at these sessions: "We recorded 'River Deep, Mountain High' but it never got put on the album. They did it again for the next album."

Burdon cites *Every One of Us* as his favourite New Animals album "for the spirit of the thing" and "its outright insanity," but adds, "maybe not musically." He accepts that the long spoken-word tracks will not have been revisited by many, but argues, "You don't learn that until you do it." For Briggs, the album marked the abandonment of any pretence of egalitarianism about the New Animals. Weider, too, accepts that the determination of Burdon in the early days to not simply use his new colleagues as a backing group had dissipated: "As we moved to LA, things changed." Briggs: "You look at *Winds of Change* and it was basically Eric doing his thing and us supporting him because we didn't have any confidence to do more. You get an album that's spotty, a lot of talking. Then you come to *The Twain Shall Meet*. We're in our power, feeling confident, and there's almost equal say from everybody and you get what I think is the best album. Then Eric

SEAN EGAN   233

comes back to being the leader and decided he wants things to be a certain way and you get *Every One of Us* — back to the talking and a very spotty album." Though not necessarily referring to this specific LP, Jenkins was also dismayed in this period by the fragmentation of the original democratic spirit of The Animals. "We were one," says Jenkins. "All of a sudden Eric wouldn't turn up and he'd have his own dressing room and stuff and we felt like it was Eric and us. It weren't The Animals anymore."

As for the new, non-egalitarian writing credits, Briggs reveals, "We didn't find out about it 'til it came out. By that time it was, 'Well, what the fuck. Let it go.'" And his credit as "Re-mix engineer"? "I guess that was Eric's way of putting me in my place." Part of the reason for the credits change may have been Zoot Money's modesty. He says, "When I came in, I didn't particularly want that [credit] unless I had actually arranged it. I did say to Eric, 'If I write them, great, if we write them together, great, but I'm not going to start claiming for anything I didn't do.' Because I'm promoting the album that doesn't mean to say that I get writing credits. If I'm not on the record I don't want the money. I was more aware of that because I had run my own band and I was aware of how that can cause aggravation in a band before you even start. I was asked to become part of the, what you might call, Animals Corporation, become part of the set-up, and I'm probably one of the only ones that refused. I didn't want to actually be embroiled in stuff that people might be coming at me from five years before and saying, 'That's my money — you shouldn't be having that.' Like, it's not just The Animals, you have to do it through some kind of a company. Did I actually want to be part of the thing and start being a member, director of the company, as I joined? I don't want to be part of a company that could go defunct within whatever."

The album only reached number 152, probably partly due to it following so soon after *Twain* and partly due to the fact that MGM released 'Sky Pilot' as a single in the same month instead of a track from the new album. It wasn't until the issue of 'White Houses' on single four months after the album's release date that there was anything in that medium to advertise its existence.

Surprisingly for such a relatively old record, 'Sky Pilot' did well, climbing as high as fourteen. It wasn't quite the same record as had been released in Britain, having been re-mixed by Briggs in April. "As usual, Tom took all that back to New York and he mixed it," says Briggs. "When it came out as a single [in Britain], Eric didn't like the mix. It took me two days to mix it. That was unheard of in those days. Mostly it was that Eric's voice wasn't what he wanted. The other thing, Tom Wilson would always put the bass in the centre 'cause in those days you had to consider the way you'd cut the record — you had this groove with this needle in. You'd put the bass in the centre so you'd be able to put more bass on the record. He would often pop the drums off to one side. I put the drums in the middle and spread the sound out a little bit more."

These chart positions were probably becoming increasingly irrelevant to Briggs and McCulloch, who were on the way out of the band. "I was feeling like I wanted to do something different," says Briggs. "It's one of these deals where you feel you're onto something good and you don't want to let go because you wonder where the money's going to come from if you get out." Something that finally helped sway him was the fact that he was beginning to wonder where the money was going to come from *within* The Animals. Although Deverich had arranged for the group to acquire houses and cars, he seemed to be making little headway into unravelling the financial mess bequeathed by Jeffery. Not only that, but Briggs and McCulloch felt that Deverich wasn't keeping the band members properly informed about the money that *was* readily available to them. "Nobody told us to do a performing rights thing," says Briggs. "Danny came to me in maybe April or May '68 and he said, 'There's this thing called BMI. We can go down and join it and get money just for having our songs on the radio.' I says, 'We can?' So we went down to BMI and signed up and they said, 'We're sorry but we can only give you money from the time you sign up.' Danny was furious. I was pretty indignant too. We should have been getting airplay money from as soon as 'When I Was Young' went on the air. We didn't get anything for a year. That year was the most potent in terms of the airplay money. You would think that somebody would have had the sense to tell us about this."

The simmering resentments and bad atmosphere within The Animals' ranks finally came to a head when, Briggs recalls, "Kevin came to us and said, 'Eric thinks probably it's time for you and Danny to leave.' It came from Eric rather than from us but I wouldn't exactly say we were fired because we were on the brink anyway. It wasn't a shock." Says Jenkins, "Vic got in a big ego trip with his producing other bands. Danny was smashed out of his head all day on bloody speed. It just started disintegrating. You can't blame the guy for splitting it up." Briggs and McCulloch then gave notice of the date they would be leaving. "I was glad to be out of it," Briggs says. "I think that I lost my focus to some degree. I forgot about being a musician and I concentrated on being a personality." Was Weider surprised at the departure of two of his colleagues? "Not really," Weider says. "They had chosen a different pathway before they left." Money offers, "No, because Danny wanted to do his own thing, and that turned out to be an album. I don't think Eric was ever surprised about what Danny did. If there was anyone who was more volatile than Eric in a way it was Danny. During that period Danny was up one minute, down the next. Mostly up. Some would say psychotic. He probably thought he was more of a contributor than Eric would deem and it was obvious that he was never going to take away the thing from Eric. Eric was always going to be the singer, was going to be the kingpin member because he was the original member."

Briggs does admit, "I remember Danny telling me, 'I was always unhappy when I was with The Animals. It was really awful for me.'" Briggs also admits that McCulloch was going "full tilt" into a solo career by this point. This solo career would be masterminded, artistically, by Briggs, who was acting as McCulloch's producer. A McCulloch track left off the *Twain* album — 'Mirror of the Sky' — because its gentle, acoustic feel didn't fit in with the rest of the tracks was later lifted by the pair who — without telling MGM or even the other Animals — put it on McCulloch's (Capitol-released) 1969 solo album *Wings of a Man* (which opened with a new recording of 'Orange and Red Beams').

As to his own feelings about events, Briggs says, "It didn't upset me being out of The Animals." He avers he was more upset by the fact that discussions he'd had about being the producer for The Animals after his departure did not bear fruit. "It's a good feather in your cap saying you're producer for The Animals," he notes. "I talked to Kevin Deverich about it and he came to me and said, 'Eric's decided he doesn't want to use you as producer.'"

Burdon maintains, vis a vis Briggs and McCulloch, "We didn't have any differences. I can't remember any differences. It just seemed a natural thing to let people go their own way." However, he admits that may be down to his faulty memory: "I was too stoned. I'll be the first to admit I was out there on cloud nine."

Money: "Eric sort of thought, 'Well, okay then, if you've got to go, you've got to go' and he came to me and said, 'Right who shall we get in?' and asked me about Andy Summers." Which puts one in mind of Money's comment that he had joined the New New Animals. Could The Animals' credibility withstand yet another change in their line-up? Money had few doubts. "America will take you forever," he insists. "They'll let you play until you die as long as there is at least one original member and the concept was the same." "There were no auditions to replace Vic and Danny," says Weider. "Andy had played with Zoot before and knew Eric. It seemed natural to bring him in."

Andy Summers was born in Poulton-le-Flyde near Blackpool on December 31 1942. A diminutive man (even shorter than Burdon) with a giant-sized guitar-playing talent, he grew up, like Money, in Bournemouth and, in fact, had played with Zoot Money in The Don Robb Band before replacing Graham Bond in Blues Incorporated in late 1963. He and Money set up The Big Roll Band in 1964 (Summers: "It was the first real band I was in") and the two remained the backbone of the group through its transformation into Dantalion's Chariot. Money's defection to The Animals had necessitated Summers joining Soft Machine. Now Money was able to offer his old mucker a berth on his ship. Money: "I phoned Andy, who was living in the Chelsea Hotel and had just come out of the Soft Machine. He had been sort of stranded in New York. And he said, 'Yeah, all right, that

sounds like fun.'" Summers was in no way an unknown quantity
to Burdon, either professionally or personally. "We all knew each
other," Summers says. "Back in those days. Zoot and I had these
two adjoining flats in West Kensington. Zoot's flat became notorious for all-night drug and booze parties that went on forever
and certainly The Animals were part of that. Eric used to be
round a lot, used to come and see us play." Of the invitation to join
The Animals, Summers says, "It was an exciting moment for me.
It felt like I was in something really great. And of course moving
to LA…I lived in Laurel Canyon with Eric. It was, as you can
imagine, for a young English lad very glamorous and exciting."

Summers was employed in what we might term the New
New New Animals as both guitarist and bassist. "Either Andy
played bass or John Weider," explains Money, "and the other one
played either violin or guitar and when Andy played guitar and
[Weider] played violin I'd take over the bass lines. I could play
bass lines on the piano because by that time I had a mountain of
amplification behind me so a bass note on there was just as good
as any bass. Andy was playing it a little bit weird, because the bass
drove Andy into the ground because he was only small and the
bass was incredibly heavy. Somehow we just worked it around
so that two songs in a row were done or we'd start off a tune on
a different instrument, so that somebody's got time to change
over." Didn't the band think of drafting in an extra member?
"That wasn't on the cards," Money says. "It was at a time when
you had to have the people on the stage that were pulling their
weight. You couldn't have somebody just in to fill in this, that and
the other because it was on the record. We didn't believe in that
either. There is a certain amount of pride involved with the bands
of the Sixties in that we didn't believe you should have a backing
singer and a tambourine shaker just because you've done it on the
record. It's not so much paying them, it's transporting them." "It
was slightly strange," admits Summers of the arrangement. "Me
and Johnny Weider traded off between bass and guitar. Probably
we both really would prefer to have played the guitar but we
were pretty fair about swapping over: 'You play bass on this one,
I'll play guitar.' I don't remember any acrimony about that." The

addition of Summers meant the new line-up had one thing in common with the previous one: two lead guitarists of contrasting styles. "I was all for them both playing guitar and me playing the bass line because I liked the idea of two different characters playing guitar," says Money. "From a country or blues point of view Johnny was great but Andy had jazzy things, or if you needed to have something that was like a classical picking-type thing then Andy would know how to do that." Summers notes, "When I first got to grips with the instrument, I was fourteen years old, a total jazz fanatic. I was playing much more complex stuff. Got over that eventually. Johnny was more straightahead rock."

Summers also fitted in because like most of his new colleagues he was an acidhead. "Everybody was," he shrugs. He adds, "They're the ones who brought it to England. That's where it first happened to me, was Hilton Valentine. My primary contact with that scene was definitely through The Animals." Money demurs slightly. "We'd actually come past that initial phase," he says. "By that time we were concentrating on the job really and I was so knocked out to be in America and so would only take stuff if we were going to do extensive travelling, the occasional perk-up here and there. We were quite sensible drug takers by then, really 'cause it had been a year of lunacy. I can't say the same for Eric 'cause I just can't comment on how Eric takes drugs or did take drugs. Believe me, that's another book. For the most part in recordings he was very, I shan't say straight, but very *compos*. Gigs was another thing, because you had to find some energy from somewhere if you'd been on a plane flight or whatever and you wanted help with the ambience of the gig. Different kind of stimulants. In some cases not drugs, just a couple of drinks or whatever."

Of the financial remuneration, Summers says, "I was getting a *per diem* of about two hundred dollars a week. It was enough to live. I suppose it seemed like decent money to me at the time."

The new line-up made its stage debut on August 4 1968 at the Newport Pop Festival, California. A three-day event, it featured another star-studded bill: The Jimi Hendrix Experience, Janis Joplin, Ike & Tina Turner, Spirit, Steppenwolf and Creedence Clearwater Revival.

It would seem Money was now joint Musical Director with the newcomer. "It was an interesting situation because Zoot and I had played together for years so we'd worked out all kinds of really tight arrangements," says Summers. "We were great together, we always had been. Zoot and I really led The Big Roll Band and wrote songs: it was always really me and him and anyone else we got in. Of course when we came in to play in The Animals, we were sort of a force 'cause we played together so much. We went on and started putting this all together, it started to get really good." Summers doesn't feel that his and Money's dominance created any difficulty with longer-standing members. "Johnny and I got on really well," he insists. "It was a pretty happy outfit actually."

More live work followed, including one particularly bizarre gig. "When Zoot joined the band, it became guerrilla theatre," says Burdon. "He would play the dark forces and I would play the light forces. We'd have film going off in the background of American soldiers crucifying Christ with smoke bombs going off and oil machines and all kinds of demonic signals going across while the music ripped into their ears." Money says, "I was doing fights with Eric. I was the bad guy in 'Sky Pilot'. We would do a slow motion fight when the smoke went up and the guitar was going crazy. A guy came to me and did a drop kick on me as I was leaving the stage one night. It was incredible. This young guy took a flying leap. I was just trying to get across from the stage to where the dressing rooms were. I think it was because he was a devout Eric Burdon fan and he genuinely thought I was the bad guy. I just realised we shouldn't be doing this." What made the incident even more bizarre was the location of the gig: "It was actually at a Catholic school with nuns present." Why were The Animals playing a Catholic girls school? "My hands go up in disbelief," says Money. "Who knows? Maybe Eric thought it was a funny idea."

chapter thirteen

By October, The Animals were recording again in TTG.

Summers says of the recording span, "I don't think it was very long. We probably knocked out three or four tracks a day. Probably about a week." The material recorded would be issued as *Love Is* before the year was out: no less than The Animals' third album of 1968. This was too much even for the work-ethic oriented John Weider: he thought the album to be rushed and lays the blame for this on Kevin Deverich. Money feels impending live work booked by Deverich may have led to an album being recorded quicker than was preferable: "I can't say I was aware of a rush but I was aware that he had booked some stuff because that's where you can make cash and he was up for proving that he could sell us worldwide. Eric was a gigging person. He made money in the recordings but only as an afterthought." Summers offers another reason the new line-up went into the studio so quickly: "'We're a new band, let's get in and record.'"

The Spector/Barry/Greenwich song 'River Deep, Mountain High' was the first released from the latest Animals sessions. Issued in the States (backed with 'White Houses') in November 1968, it only reached number 67. (It wouldn't be released as a single in Britain until the following May.) The taster for The Animals' new album gave a misleading impression. Those who heard this sparkling and hard-rocking 3:52 version of the Ike and Tina Turner classic would be forgiven for thinking that they could look forward to an album of similar discipline and quality. Alas, this was an edited version of a track that would appear on album the following month in dismayingly bloated form. The same self-indulgence which characterised the album version afflicted every other track.

However, the first Eric Burdon & The Animals single not to be written by the band (discounting 'Help Me Girl') did prompt an inference that was more accurate, namely that Burdon had gone back to how he had started his singing career: interpretation. Despite the presence of three songwriters in the band and despite the album being a double-set, it featured only one new song. "I'd helped them with [*Every One of Us*] and then we were on the road straight away," says Money. "No time to set aside to writing or whatever, although Eric wrote in his room quite a lot. But once you're on the road it's not all that easy: your mind is full of, 'Great — we're in Cincinnati.'" "Everybody has dry spots," Burdon says. "And we were still allowed to run rampant in the studio. And once again, no real producer to crack the whip." Burdon reiterates, though, "I love to sing other people's songs. Songs are there to be sung. I don't regard songs as covers, I regard them as interpretations, so I record what I feel suits my voice at the time." Money feels that the inclusion of two rare Dantalion's Chariot songs and covers of songs by artists whose audience had little crossover with The Animals' cancelled out the fact of the lack of self-generated material: "He went 'Right, I'd like to do a couple of the songs that you've been doing.' 'Gemini' had not been recorded by anyone, so it was an original, so he did have the drop on it. 'Madman' — I'd only had a single out with it and that didn't go anywhere so he basically had an original. And 'Coloured Rain', 'To Love Somebody' and the other ones were ways of doing, not original music, but music that might well be appreciated by somebody who might have bought those people's [records]. Or not in the case of 'Ring of Fire' — people that buy Johnny Cash records wouldn't necessarily be buying an Animals record." But when Money accepted the offer to join The Animals, surely he was thinking of something more than putting out an album of cover jobs? "Initially, I wasn't too bothered about that," he says. "At that point I wanted to actually see America and I didn't want to do it having to lead a band. I wanted to be in a unit that was doing it anyway, with basically guaranteed sales, guaranteed audiences. He was obviously thinking in terms of his future, which you can't blame anybody. Eric was a good graphic artist but he had no pretensions to give up the music business and get a graphic artist business going. By this time he'd invested quite a lot in terms of creation, and writing songs and it being appreciated by a large amount of people. At that point he didn't feel as though he had to come up with yet another totally original concept. He felt that he had actually contributed quite a lot and he was indulging himself in things he enjoyed. He wanted to open it up to me as being part of it. We'd have got into writing and all the rest of it, but this was curtailed by the culmination of the relationship between Eric and Kevin Deverich." Summers didn't raise an eyebrow at the unexpected selection of material. "I was so happy to be in that band and go along with it all," he reasons. "It's very loose-living but I didn't have a lot to say about it. I just wanted to play them all. I wasn't trying to take over the band or anything at that point. Clearly, it was Eric's band and I was the new boy."

Yet there is a difference between the type of reinvigoration of songs from outside sources in which the original Animals had specialised and lack of inspiration. *Love Is* shows a band without any real musical vision. There is no cohesion to the material and no common thread. It is simply a collection of songs Burdon happened to like. Due to the quality of the musicians and the ability of the singer, it is inevitably very good in places but this could really be the product of any random band.

The production is another issue. The sleevenotes state that *Love Is* was "Produced and arranged by The Animals (Re-mix: Zoot Money, Andy Summers)." By now it is becoming obvious that Tom Wilson cannot have been anything like as bad a producer as Briggs and to a lesser extent Burdon claim he was. A professional producer's guiding hand is missed here even more than on the *longueurs* of *Every One of Us*. The production on *Love Is* is ridiculous. All the songs, without exception, are far too long and usually feature effects which gild the lily. Many of them contain rather purposeless lulls during which Burdon ad-libs — either by singing or speaking — whose effect is to destroy musical momentum. They also distract from the song's mood, making the listener aware of the artifice of recording, as do the many examples of buffoonish vocal effects. Whether it was the record label or the band who had the idea of dumping several minutes from the 'River Deep, Mountain High' single, it was the right one. If all the songs on *Love Is* had had at least two minutes unceremoniously chopped, Eric Burdon & The Animals would have been left with a far more worthy closer to their career.

Money defends the length of the songs, claiming that The Animals were just moving with the times. "That wasn't filling in time," he says. "That was the beginning of what was to become a thing *de rigueur* of the Seventies — extended playing. If you think that record was long, look at any Grateful Dead track. You organically let it go for as long as you could bear. You didn't think in terms of editing it. Doing an album didn't mean you had to do loads and loads of three-minute singles anymore."

The album opens with the unedited 'River Deep, Mountain High.' The Animals' version is less ornate than Phil Spector's Wall of Sound original but at 7:23 it's also twice as long. Gutsy rhythm guitar propels a very nimble reading of the song, with Burdon singing with great gusto. But then along comes a musical respite in which Burdon customises the lyric to letch over Mrs Turner, with speaker-panning of her lustily gasped name. This is the point at which a fine version of the song threatens to turn into an embarrassment. The same can be said for the way the band adopt werewolf howls when Burdon subsequently returns to the part of the lyric dealing with memories of childhood puppies. This stuff had not appeared on the single, which had ended abruptly with a vocal effect that had left Burdon's voice yodelling into infinity. Money helps prevent that embarrassment eventuality with superb electric piano work, alternately mellifluous and stabbed, but the alarm bells are ringing in the listener's head.

Money's extensive use of the electric piano, a feature of the entire album, was the result of him exploring the possibilities of what was then a new instrument. "I had a Fender Stage," he explains. "It's a Fender Rhodes, but I didn't use the dumpy two speakers that you get with it underneath. You put it through proper amplifiers. I had two monstrous ampegs: two ampeg, one slave ampeg, so I was like 200 watts and two stacks so I was like a guitar player. There was a lot of exploration there. I was using it like a rhythm guitar really and occasionally taking solos that had fuzz and sustain on it." It was Burdon's choice to cover 'River Deep'. Money: "He was a bit of a Tina fan. Completely besotted by Tina." Money describes the song as, "…a love letter to Tina: I'm waiting for you darling, sort of thing." And Tina's reaction? "He got feedback but not what he expected. Eric wasn't particularly what Tina had in mind. She enjoyed him as a singer. Rejection is the kind of thing that Eric didn't ever accept really. His suggestion of wearing certain kinds of clothes didn't go down too well. He was a bit of a fetishist at that time and I don't think at that time — or any time — Tina has needed any kind of extra clothes to do what she needs to do. She does it with what she's got."

'I'm An Animal' was written by Sylvester McCoy, main man of Sly and the Family Stone. "It's like an eulogy," Money says, "because we worked with them a couple of times." Was it intended as a signature song, a la 'The Monkees Theme'? "Yeah, it all seemed to tie in and it went with something you could do on stage. That would be a strong identification point." Summers: "Stupid idea, but there you go. We thought it was a real wheeze to do a song called 'I'm An Animal' at the time." The track has a hard-pumping rhythm appropriate to its theme of predatory sexual behaviour. The band provide massed backing vocals. There are surreal lulls featuring dreamy washes of electric piano and Burdon apparently reading the definition of "animal" from a dictionary written by someone in an inebriated state. Burdon's 'I'm Dying, Or Am I?' is the album's only original song. It boasts a fine coiling tune which makes one wonder whether the leader got a good deal of help with it from his colleagues. It also has a touching sentiment. Unfortunately the song is rather swamped in effects, including sickly harmonies, backing vocal repetitions of Burdon's vocal lines and more surreal Fender Stage washes. Both Burdon and Money acknowledge the song is an acid number. Money says "It's as a result of *The Tibetan Book of the Dead* and did I have a heart attack last night? I don't know whether it was taken out of an initial quote from the *Book of the Dead*: 'To live you have to die first.'" And the line, "Even when you're dying, there's such sweet joy in giving"? "Well that's probably to do with the fact that he's trying to find an ejaculation from somewhere, one more ejaculation. I'm afraid quite a lot of Eric's revelations were as a result of pushing himself to some kind of new sexual encounter, new height — or new low, in some cases."

The June Carter/Merle Kilgore composition 'Ring Of Fire' marks a first: Burdon's inaugural journey into what was then called country & western. The Animals' version of a song made famous by Johnny Cash turns a sombre and relatively sedate number into a pleasantly bombastic epic. Burdon is in top, lung-busting form while Jenkins executes circular patterns behind a celestial choir. Money describes the track as the result of "one of our private jokes. Rather like Buddy Rich on his deathbed: 'What's wrong Buddy?' 'Country & western.' We didn't like country & western but you couldn't deny Johnny Cash. Eric is a fan of anybody who is larger-than-life and I think he actually liked the concept of the song even though Johnny Cash had had the hit with it. He liked the idea of, 'Well, let's do it properly,' as it were. Still maintaining some kind of British integrity, but humour at the same time. Eric was big at, 'Let's knock the shit out of that, let's get rid of that!' We were up for it really. Who knows, we may have to play a lot of redneck states. We were playing places where they weren't all peace, love and brown rice. We got off the plane in a couple of places and it was a case of, 'What the hell is that?' We had long hair, for a start and of course we were dressed in a mixture of Carnaby Street-cum-something else."

'Coloured Rain' (Winwood/Capaldi/Wood) — originally a track on Traffic's 1967 album *Mr. Fantasy* — is the first indication that this album in part constitutes a melding of The Animals' identity with that of Money's previous group. Money recalls, "'Coloured Rain' we'd been doing with Dantalion's Chariot. That was another thing that was great on stage but [Dantalion's Chariot] never got to record it. We'd extended the Traffic thing and given it as an excuse to do that wonderful, extended solo for Andy and Eric had heard that and gone, 'Yeah, we'll do that.'" "That extra-long guitar solo [has] sort of become legendary over the years," says Summers of his central contribution to The Animals' 9½-minute recording. "So many journalists have asked me about that one. Going into a sort of trance-state, almost like Coltrane. Not that I'm comparing myself with Coltrane, but Coltrane had extended solos into half-an-hour, forty-five minutes. You reached a sort of state of ecstasy. Beyond the typical two-and-a-half minute pop song. This was the Sixties and the drugs were flowing and that sort of thing was going on and also the influences of Indian music and all the rest of it." Summers points out, though, that he wasn't on drugs during recording: "I would have been unable to play it." He says the solo is "completely improvised. It ended up being something like 189 bars which was counted, like, [clicks fingers], 'One, two, three, four...' It's a long time to play a solo and then come back in the right spot so we worked it out so that Zoot was counting every single bar and then we all came back in together. There's no cutting, pasting, Pro-Tool — that's just live playing. It wasn't terrifying, but we did have to take care so that I can climax at the right point and the band all comes back in." But what if he had made a mistake? "I don't make mistakes, do I?" Summers says, possibly humorously. "That's why I am who I am." Vic Briggs was in the studio for the recording of this track. "They called me in to write some horn charts," Briggs reveals. "It was all very cordial. I got the feeling that Zoot was running everything. I didn't have a problem with that."

In The Animals' hands, 'Coloured Rain' is in some ways an improvement on Traffic's rather hysterical original but again is far too long and ornate. While the lengthy guitar solo impressively mixes gentleness with distortion, behind it there gradually emerges a brass section, which is then joined by a female chorus. Pretty soon the kitchen sink can be discerned appearing over the horizon.

Another apparently out-of-character choice for a cover is The Bee Gees' passionate 'To Love Somebody'. Written by Barry and Robin Gibb, it had reached number seventeen in the US singles charts and 41 in the UK in the summer of '67. Money: "He liked the song, and, of course, we weren't in direct competition with The Bee Gees at that stage — thank Christ we weren't, 'cause we'd have lost! — and there were a couple of things that Eric and Andy had liked. Andy had like their first single actually, the 'Mining Disaster'. I was mates with Maurice and I thought, 'Of all the songs they've done, I wouldn't mind doing that', but it was Eric's choice. Obviously we were slightly overshadowed by the original at that stage because it was a little near to the thing." The Animals' provide a superb interpretation. Burdon repeatedly switches from quivering hurt to bellowed outrage in the space of a single line, occasionally accompanied by lovely female harmonies. From, apparently, female lovelies. "We brought some girls in," says Money. "Three girls from LA. Two black girls and one white girl. They looked pretty good too, otherwise they wouldn't have got through the door with Eric." Yet despite its quality, the track is almost ruined right at the end by Burdon ejaculating "Good God!" in amazement at the lung power required by the material — another reminder of artifice.

Deadric Malone's 'As The Years Go Passing By' is a 12-bar blues but the thin, wah-wah guitar is more Haight-Ashbury than Mississippi Delta. Its twilight ambience is a relief considering the histrionics present everywhere else. A galvanizing guitar duel develops in the instrumental break. At five minutes — instead of 10:13 — the track would have been wonderful. It is impressive for the way it strives to do something different with the 12-bar format. Money: "By that time we had that instilled into us, having played in bands where they started off as 12-bar blues. Quite honestly playing 12-bars all night you go nuts because your brain gets into a rut and you find it impossible to do a different lick. By that time we had developed to a point, 'Well we can't just do that. I know other bands are still doing it, Eric, but we don't.' I won't go into that because I'll be putting down too many very famous people who did quite good jobs and had great followings and stuff, but it didn't get my rocks off and didn't get Andy's rocks off." Would it be fair to say that Money and Summers were pushing Eric a little? "Yeah. He enjoyed that, because invariably if he worked with people who would just give him one form of very basic blues you could tell he would be bored because he would actually start trying to extend the blues into a free-form section or something else."

The album closes with a 17½-minute medley resurrecting two songs played by Dantalion's Chariot: 'Gemini' and the Summers/Money composition 'The Madman (Running Through The Fields)'. Money explains of 'Gemini', "That was written by a Canadian guy who was living above me, Steve Hammond. Great guitar player and singer, wrote some really good songs. I think he went to LA or back to Canada and did some writing for TV and stuff. At least he got the royalties from that. I actually recorded it with a view to putting it on the Dantalion's album, so there is somewhere a recording of us doing 'Gemini' on a demo tape. That was the arrangement, and as it wasn't out anyway on record there was no need [for The Animals] to change it." 'Gemini' has a good melody carried briskly along by neat electric piano from Money. Singing of alternate lines by Burdon and Money works well, both conceptually (two sides of a personality) and sonically (joining excitingly together on the chorus). Unfortunately another pointless lull — this one with aquatic special effects and a silly spoken word section — makes the track sag. 'The Madman' is a collaboration between Money and Summers that depicts a man whose consciousness has undergone a sudden change, the implication being through acid. Summers: "Is that on that album? That was the Dantalion's Chariot hit. I didn't know we did it with The Animals. That was available material and Zoot and I obviously knew it inside out." Money: "Autobiographical? Yes it is. Suddenly realising that there was a oneness and all the rest of it. That was my revelation really and Andy and I wrote it. Suddenly we have seen it all, seen the light and they all think a kind of fool on the hill, if you like. The person in the song is taken to be a madman but in fact he's just someone who is very elated through realising that he was on the wrong path. It was autobiographical in that I had been going down one path and in fact it was something else that I really wanted, some kind of reassurance of an inner spirituality which I probably lost through being in the music business basically." Is he saying that his Damascene

conversion was entirely due to LSD? "That was one of the contributing factors, probably the main one. I had pictured myself as
being quite false, but it was a falseness that was sort of acceptable
at one stage in my career. In showbusiness it still goes on. There
is a falseness that is acceptable as long as you realise what the real
values are, but there is a danger of you becoming false and staying
false to everybody and that was revealed to me. It was an insight
I would have had, I presume, at some other stage. Everything
that happens to you on [LSD], as far as I'm concerned, is likely
to happen to you, but without it it might happen in years' time.
It just accelerates things, that's all. You aren't actually thinking
any clearer, you just imagine you are, but imagination is part of
your make-up anyway."

Summers agrees with the suggestion that *Love Is* is an album
without any real vision or direction. He says, "We were all sitting
around in a drug haze, basically. It was more about the party that
never stops." However, he also asserts that this does not mean
that Burdon's (and by implication the band's) heart was not in it:
"We all thought it was really great at the time."

The album sleeve credits "Eric Burdon and the Animals" —
no ampersand on a New Animals record for the first time. Said
sleeve features the band's heads floating in a rain-cloud. As for
the album's title, Money explains, "If you have to ask what love
is, you haven't experienced it — that kind of thing. Love is actually a continuing state. It was an expression to the effect that life
itself is love, the whole of creation is love. Love is: everything.
The whole reason we are here."

In keeping with the suspicion with which British MGM
seemed now to be viewing Animals product, the UK version of
Love Is was a single album that omitted the tracks 'As The Years
Go Passing By' and 'Gemini/The Madman'. Money explains the
record company's attitude: "Oh sorry, financially you're joking. As
far as selling that in England is concerned, nobody buys double
albums. They do in America but not here." As his sole songwriting contribution to the LP was one of those dropped, this was
particularly painful from Money's point of view. The double-set
would finally be released in Britain in 1971. Before The Animals

had even released *Love Is* for the first time, though, their leader had announced that he was quitting the music business.

Burdon's disbandment of The Animals resulted from a catastrophic tour of Japan which started on November 13 1968. At first, there seemed nothing not to love. "There were some really good positive points and some hilarious things that went on during it," says Money. Summers recalls, "It was very peculiar in those days with the absolutely dead silent audiences. Japan was not as Westernised at that point as it is now, obviously. But of course it was exotic. I was thrilled to be there." Money: "We're talking about a stay in Japan of less than two weeks during which time I think we were contracted to play what we had thought was 35 separate things." However, the bad portents came quickly. Summers: "The minute we arrived at the airport there was a big hassle. The promoters or agents or whoever they were turned up and there was a big argument at the airport. It was probably about the money and the amount of shows we were doing."

The tour involved both TV shows and gigs. Some of the latter were very strange. Money: "Afternoon gigs at what looked like an appreciation society thing. They all sat there in suits. We're not talking about a young people gig here. Not even corporate. I think it was an educational thing. They'd sold it on the fact that people wanted to see bands from the West and they'd got The Animals and the concession had been brought by an agency which, unbeknown to us, was connected to the — dare I say the word on tape — Yakuza." The involvement of the Japanese mafia meant that those organising the tour were not playing by the rules. "So what we had was two or three weeks, where we were expected to do up to 35 different separate things, for I presume a set fee," Money recalls. "As we went through this experience it was obvious that somebody had made an agreement and signed for 45 appearances and not told us. Consequently we were constantly going from one thing to another. Which we didn't mind, we were used to it, we were English boys who'd done all the clubs and done back-to-back gigs, one in the afternoon, one in the evening, one in the night time. So that wasn't the problem. In fact, it was quite exciting in a place like Japan and we were being treated well." However, sinister events were occurring, the significance of which only became obvious as the tour unfolded. Money: "The little fella who was supposed to be our promoter had been turning up with grazes on his knuckles and limping slightly, which meant he had obviously been told get this in line: 'You've got to tell them that they've got to do this, that and the other.' Maybe the gigs were being added as he was going along. His honour was at stake and fingers were going to be cut off — you know all the usual things to frighten this little guy — and he was saying, 'You don't understand' so Eric's manager had finally to go to this meeting to say to this guy, 'Look, what's happening here? This is a different amount of gigs.'" "We were doing gigs in big theatres but suddenly we had a special request from the promoter to play in a small club," recalls Burdon. "It was obviously for him and his wife and his cronies and his girlfriend. I asked to see a contract in English, which they couldn't provide." The Animals were due to play a venue in Tokyo which Money describes as "not like a club you would go to, but like a disco club." Summers: "We ended up playing this really shitty club in Shinjuku. Obviously there was something dodgy going on. We're The Animals — what the fuck we doing in a place like this? It just didn't make sense."

Money explains, "[Deverich] said, 'Look, don't let the lads go on the stage unless I phone you and say it's alright', because he was having a meeting with this person who he was dealing with who was going to introduce him to the bloke who had done the original deal. We were actually at the club, waiting to go on. The manager was having a meeting with not just the bloke who was supposedly the promoter. He was in fact saying 'Yes, no sir, no sir, yes sir' to somebody who was Mr Big, as it were. Eric's manager had to have a meeting with that person… I got a message through — not to Eric because Eric wasn't to be bothered with this, to me as MD — and it was, 'Yes do the gig, but afterwards…'" Referring to a Japanese symbol of warning involving a deadly pseudo-tipple delivered to the band before the Shinjuku gig, Burdon says, "The 9mm bullets in the glass definitely was the signal that we had to get out of there quick." "Kevin, who was with us pretty much all the time, just did not appear that night," says Summers. "He just did not make it to the club. So we did our show, I went off with this girl and the band went back to the hotel. Kevin turned up much later that night and told everybody that they'd kidnapped him, taken him into a room somewhere. They were trying to make him write out these promissory notes for, like, quarter of a million dollars. Then they threatened to cut his finger off. Kevin apparently wrote something in English threatening to take them to court if he ever got out of this alive. He completely faced them down." Burdon says, "They actually used a knife on Kevin Deverich and made a laceration mark around his throat." Summers adds, "Eventually they bought him back to the hotel and they stayed at the hotel that night and said that everybody had to get on the next plane out." Money: "Late night the phone calls came round: 'We're leaving in the morning at 7.30. Be ready, packed to go.' So obviously an agreement hadn't really been struck, he'd [Deverich] been threatened and he'd said whatever he had to say to get through that evening so that he wouldn't be harmed. The next day we all jumped in cabs and had to try and get a message to Andy. Somebody stayed behind for Andy and he was driven in a separate taxi. I was taking it as a joke. I was very drunk on sake and was thinking, 'Get out of it, this is ridiculous', but it wasn't — it was very serious. And you don't take chances in a country that you don't know."

The Animals' party was followed to the airport by mafia men, one of whom approached Burdon and was reduced to tears when Burdon indicated that he would not listen to his pleas to remain. Burdon was under the impression that this person was the dreaded 'Mr Big' but Money says, "I don't think he was Mr Big quite honestly. The guy that talked to Eric was frightening enough in himself but I don't think to this day that that was him. I think that Mr Big is one of those people that didn't need to come to the thing to try to appeal to Eric. I think the guy that came to Eric was actually yet another minion saying, 'It's my lot, my honour is at stake, please stay' and I was the one who was standing sort of gingerly away but saying, 'No we can't talk about this anymore, this is past talking. You've talked to the manager, the manager deals with this. This isn't right you know, you've done this wrong.' For all I know I might have been jeopardising my career. The guy was in tears because he realised he would have to go back and face Mr Bigger-Than-Big. The hilarious thing about it in retrospect is that during all this, Andy was arriving in another cab saying, 'Hey, what's all this about, what's all the story?' and signing autographs with all these hundreds of little girls." Summers recalls it slightly differently. "I got back to the hotel in the morning and everybody had disappeared," he says. "I'm, Christ, just a little English kid and those are the days where you didn't have anything: no passport, ID, credit card, nothing. I felt kind of lost. Then this roadie came in and found me and said, 'We've got to leave the country immediately.' Told me the story on the way to the airport. The guys were there, the gangster types. I guess they were the Yakuza. They were sitting opposite, waiting for us to get on the plane 'cause their shit had gone down. There was three of them, all in suits."

The Animals escaped the country with their limbs intact but without their equipment. Money: "I lost my Fender, I lost my amps. Guitars we managed to grab, they went on the plane, but all the amplification, PA and everything was left there. As a part-payment for gigs we didn't do, that we hadn't agreed to do." "What I learned from it is that with my voice I could face anybody," says Burdon. "If I get angry enough, I don't need to use any other form of violence except my voice. Due to myself going head to head with the local Yakuza we possibly escaped with our lives. We were under definite physical threat from some very heavy people. I felt that if we stayed around, first of all we wouldn't get paid, and I just resented being treat[ed] like a slave." Money: "There were a lot of other little incidents we didn't think to be quite much at the time but in retrospect we realised, 'Good gracious — we were quite close there.'" Summers reveals, "When I went back ten years later with The Police, everybody remembered it. There were, like, jokes about it. It was a very well-known incident. It was in the *Herald Tribune International* or whatever it is."

Money: "We were on the plane and as a consolation prize the manager said, 'We're all going to Hawaii for a couple of days', which actually softened the blow." For Money maybe, but for Burdon things were beyond repair. Though Burdon says he doesn't blame Deverich for what happened in Japan, he also notes, "It certainly brought home the fact that Kevin Deverich had no business managing." Summers, asked if Deverich was responsible for what happened in Japan or whether he was a victim like the band, says, "I think he was a victim." However, he also has a caveat: "One of the things that they were pissed off about was that — and I don't really know why this happened — this tour to Japan had been put on again, off again several times and these promoters claimed that they lost so much money because they cancelled it so many times — Kevin — for whatever reasons." Burdon: "Right after that I broke into his office, myself and a girl-friend of mine, and went through various contracts. That was the end of that." He says he discovered, "Deals that were not strictly kosher. I can't remember the details now but promises that were made and deals that were set up but never materialised, monies that had gone missing." In his sleevenotes to *Winds of Change*, Burdon had described Deverich as "Friend" (even though he misspelled his name as 'Deverage'). His view of him was clearly now completely different. He must have felt at some level that escaping Mike Jeffery's clutches — which effort according to Briggs' recollection had made him contemplate quitting the music business — had been futile. He was tired of it all. Burdon: "Not just Kevin. All of them — the whole fucking business. The cabal of lawyers in LA and the on-going agency deals." "It was a bit devastating, quite honestly," says Money. "It was likely to be going to bankruptcy or that kind of thing because Kevin was making promises. His mouth was doing the talking but he couldn't come up with it unless he had Eric. He utilised the name of Eric and The Animals to bring himself into the music business. Kevin was actually bullshitting a little and using Eric's name rather than getting a new audience for him or doing better than before. He just promised that he could do it and it turned out later that he wasn't all that trustworthy in the personal department." Burdon came to a drastic conclusion. Recalls Money, "He thought, 'It's someone else who's ripping me off' or whatever and decided to change his manager, agent and lawyer almost all in one day. He decided all this and let me know on the phone. Said, 'Look, I don't know what you're going to do, but this is what I'm going to do…' So I sat facing this in a foreign country with my wife in London and two young stepsons to think about. He was saying, 'I'm changing it all. I'm disbanding this. The Animals is no more. I'm going to be off and doing something else.'"

Summers stayed over in Hawaii for three weeks. There was bad news awaiting him on his return. The Animals had withstood many changes but with Burdon no longer a willing party, the franchise had reached the end of its life. "I don't remember actually seeing Eric ever again," says Summers. "I must have felt at that age some sort of bitterness that he just fucked off, didn't say goodbye… that was the end of that and we're all left on our own to cope with whatever." Of Burdon's reasons, Summers says, "I've never really sat down and talked to Eric about it. Zoot told me. At least he hinted: 'I think he's going to break up the band.' Eric was very disillusioned because of the Japanese thing. I just think maybe he'd reached a point. He'd tried the New Animals and gave up on it. What I remembered is that he wanted to be a film director. He wrote all his own lyrics and he'd written something and he wanted to direct a film. At that point he felt that he had the power to do it. Of course, it all came to nothing." However, Summers has an additional theory as to why Burdon took the course he did. "By the time we played in Japan, the band was almost too overpowering," he says. "The reason Eric broke that up was that it was getting too strong for him. It was getting a bit virtuoso on stage." As though he was becoming part of the background? Summers: "Yeah. The playing was getting so good. Zoot and I were pretty well-honed at that point, we really had it together." John Weider feels that Burdon wanted to escape the frustrations caused by the way The Animals' business was being handled — of which the Japan debacle was an extreme example — and that the only way to do that was to disband the group.

"I think Kevin was more incompetent than a crook," says Vic Briggs. "I don't think he was out-and-out trying to rip everybody off. I think he was a bit in over his head. I actually was in a process of forming a partnership with Kevin and Eric for a record production company. We put it together and then it went very wrong because Kevin couldn't hold it together financially. He was putting up the money for the company and he got way in over his head. This whole production company fell to pieces. My girlfriend had given him two thousand dollars of mine to invest in stocks and he bought stocks in his name with our money and when the whole thing fell apart he just took that money. Yeah, it was his fault but I can't totally blame him because if I'd been a bit shrewder I'd have never gotten into the thing anyway. I had other opportunities, I had two other people wanting to manage me, and out of a certain sense of loyalty I stayed with Kevin. I was a kid. Had I been a little bit shrewder, I could have seen what was going on. With Jeffries it was black-and-white: he was just ripping off everybody. With Kevin it was business deals going bad, there was mistrust. It wasn't just that he was taking every-body's money and stashing it. He had money of his own before he got involved with The Animals — he was a wheeler-dealer stock investor." Says Summers of Deverich, "I actually got on okay with him but there was a whole sort of shadow side to him." Though Summers thinks that — unlike most people's memories of Jeffery — Deverich enjoyed rock music, he also feels he was a dilettante: "Kevin was some sort of wealthy guy that thought it would be fun to manage a rock band and The Animals came into his world. He was sort of into it while it was happening, because it was so easy obviously to sell The Animals. He was a soft guy from a well-heeled family. Those types don't really make good managers of bands. I don't know if he really knew what he was doing. He didn't have that drive." Summers says he found this out to his own cost when Deverich managed him after The Animals split: "I started making a solo album at Sunset Sound but the truth was that was more of a different challenge than having a band that was really world famous and having to actually work someone's career up and make something out of it. He failed at the task and it all came to an end."

However, it would seem there was a greater turmoil in Burdon's mind than simply his dissatisfaction with the music business. "Everything was starting to change," says Burdon. "Everything was starting to turn nasty. The drugs were startng to change. The Vietnam War should have ended a long time ago but it kept on going. The political figures in the country got nasty. Generally the vibe just turned sour and the vibe that had put the New Animals together soured with it, I guess. We realised the hippie movement was definitely dead and buried. It was rammed home to me in no uncertain terms when we moved into Beverly Hills in very close proximity to where the Manson murders took place." (Summers says that Kevin Deverich was a close friend of Jay Sebring, one of the people murdered at Sharon Tate's home in August 1969.) Burdon: "Everything in LA turned sour. You couldn't find pot anywhere for love nor money but you could buy coke on the street corner and Quaaludes became the drug of choice. Heroin appeared. It just became very dark. I wanted to get out of it. There was a lot of stuff going on that was really affecting me at the time. The US Army in effect went to war against its own people. Everything was crumbling apart, like the fall of Rome. I thought it was my duty to hang around. I'd signed up for the trip and I wasn't going to walk away from it but I remember trying to go to Wounded Knee when the Indians were face to face with the FBI and I got as close as the state line and I got turned around by the Feds, so I just turned around and drove south and kept on going. Picked up a friend of mine on the way and we went to Mexico for a year... I drove to Mexico. I spent a year in Mexico tooling around trying to realign myself.... When you cross the line from the US border and you step into Mexico, you are stepping into another world and I left America and all the bullshit behind and I was firmly convinced that when I returned there wouldn't be an America. I thought it would be over. I really did. When I saw army tanks chasing Indian warriors, it was quite a visual experience. It hit me really hard, and the whole Nixon thing — it just became dreadful. But I didn't feel like I was welcome back in England so south of the border came calling like it does in all the classic fucking Hollywood movies. It just put me in touch with myself. Made me realise how lucky I was to be alive."

Burdon claims, "Unlike the first Animals, the New Animals broke up amicably." Certainly, Money managed to remain philosophical about the bad news. "As I was only still marking time, saying, 'Let's see how this goes shall we', my arrangement was, 'Well okay, I'll go along with it. It's Eric's decision, that's alright if he wants to bring this to a halt.' At which time he said, 'Look, I can't get on with him but that doesn't mean to say that he can't get you a deal at Capitol for your own album' — which the guy did, the manager actually did secure a deal for me to do an album. You had to be adult about the whole thing if he didn't want to carry on doing what he was doing. Andy and I were as philosophical as we could possibly be because we were well aware that the music business works along certain lines and there are certain guiding lights, people that you form friendships with who are destined to be great and you have a great association for a certain time, but eventually the music stops and you have to think about how else you are going to perpetuate your life. There was no way I was going to retire on the amount of money I was actually earning from The Animals' gigs. It had been a mutual arrangement that had been beneficial to both, for as long as it lasted." Weider was frustrated by what he feels to be a waste of the band's potential. He considers the line-up with Money and Summers to have had the ability to last and to produce great music because both Money and Summers were able to compose. As for the direction the New Animals would have taken had they continued, Weider thinks they might have ended up as an "extended version of Dantalion's Chariot" with Burdon as the lead vocalist. This, he feels, would have been a good thing because of Money's abundance of good musical ideas. Interestingly, Money is of the opinion that although Burdon gave the impression at the time that he was leaving the music business to get into films (which many felt had always been his real dream), he might already have been toying with the idea of the band that would, just over a year later, become War. Money: "He found it easier to run into the arms of War 'cause they were already set up and he had a relationship with their lawyer, the lawyer that he used to get out of the Deverich thing. He knew the lawyer guy before we left."

The declaration that The Animals had split and the release of *Love Is* came in the same month. Despite what would appear to be a commercially catastrophic synchronisation — how could the general public be expected to buy the record when Burdon would seem to have no confidence in it or in his music generally? — the LP actually did better in the US album charts than *Every One of Us*, reaching 123. In the UK, the doctored version did not chart. Though MGM America were to release no more Animals singles, Burdon's home country saw a further two, both from *Love Is*. 'Ring of Fire' was coupled with 'I'm An Animal' in January 1969 and the impressive way Burdon wrapped his tonsils round the A-side actually gave his band a minor hit (number 35) despite them no longer being around to promote it. In May, six months after its US release, 'River Deep, Mountain High' was put out in Britain. With the band now ancient history and a B-side ('Help Me Girl') that had already been a UK hit, it was a predictable flop and a sad finale for a great group.

Eric Burdon & The Animals are remembered a lot less fondly by the public and critics than are the original Animals. This seems something of an injustice for a group who were profoundly more gifted on a technical level, who mostly wrote their own material and whose records sum up a time — the Summer of Love and its aftermath — as well as any other artists' and better than most. Part of the scepticism toward the band stems from the perception of their counter-culture anthems as being dated but it seems to be more the case that their very name inspired a certain resentment, now as well as then: many cannot shake off a view of them as imposters.

Burdon feels that they are a band neglected by history. "Whether people remember this or not, the New Animals became one of the California psychedelic bands," he says. "We were at the cutting edge of that movement at the time. We had several hit records. We played every rocked-out psychedelic venue that you can think of, all the way from the UFO club in London to Bill Graham's gigs in New York and nearly every festival." He summarises: "We fell in between the cracks."

chapter fourteen

Before Eric Burdon left the music business behind supposedly forever, there was one last matter to which to attend: a one-off reunion of the original Animals.

John Steel explains of the event at Newcastle City Hall on December 22 '68, "There was a guy in Newcastle who had been a manager for Mike Jeffries' clubs called Ray Grehen. After Mike moved everything to London, he ran things for him up there. He got in touch with Alan initially and tempted him to do this promotion supposedly on behalf of some charity. I haven't got paid for it yet. I don't know what happened to any of the money." By this time, it had begun to dawn on Steel, Burdon, Valentine and Chandler just what they had missed out on when Price had copped the publishing for 'The House of the Rising Sun'. Why, then, were they prepared to work with him again? "It's a peculiar thing being in a band," Steel says in an attempt to explain. "Being with people that you've been through things with. It doesn't add up to some people." However, he does append, "I don't think we realised even then what a big rip-off it was and how much was really involved."

Valentine says of the day, "It just seemed as though nothing had changed." Steel concurs: "It was a bit of a bumpy night. Fucking hell, the rows! It was just like we'd never been separated. Deciding what material we were gonna do and how we were gonna do it virtually on the day. Rehearsing in the afternoon and performing two shows that night. That was how immediate it was. We just met in the day, kicked a few numbers around and performed that night, and we'd [not] been together for more than two years by that time. Chas had not played at all. He walked straight from The Animals into Jimi Hendrix and become a producer and manager. He'd never picked up a bloody bass in the two years. Straight into rows about what we were gonna do and how we were gonna do it and could we do it anyway. And suddenly there was a big roar from Chas. 'Look!' he said. 'I've been manager of bloody Jimi Hendrix for the past two years. I'm the only fucker here who knows how to do anything about anything. I'm gonna tell you what to do. Alan, you shut up! And Eric you shut up!' And everybody went, 'Oh, well somebody's taking charge anyway.'" Also there, to fill out the sound, was Zoot Money, who says the event was "Strange in lots of ways. I got up and played the organ at the back, like the Phantom of the Opera." Money says that Burdon alienated many of his old Newcastle acquaintances with his 'star' behaviour backstage: "I think Eric underestimated the feelings. There was an element in Eric's mind that he could sort of cock a snook. He was a little reluctant to come back and try and see it in the same light and I think he took the wrong kind of drug and as a result of that wasn't as communicative on the right kind of level with local people that he could have been."

Following this less-than-spectacular reunion, the band members resumed their individual lives. Valentine continued his unhappy drifting. Chandler went back to his management duties and subsequently set up his own Barn label. Before long, John Steel would be joining him. "That came from the City Hall concert, actually," says Steel. "He said, 'What you doing?' I said, 'Well fuck-all really.' He said, 'Well why don't you come work for me?' I started working for his production company/management company back end of 1969. I was kind of his Man Friday. He drove the thing and made all the big decisions but I picked up the loose ends and tidied all the details and did whatever he wanted me to do."

As for Burdon, Money says, "His whole thing was he wanted to become a director and he went to the CBS school... He had always wanted to make films but the problem with Eric was he was very good visually — he could see a good photograph, a good painting — but you need a certain amount of historical and artistic study to become a director... It didn't last very long because he realised that they actually tell you to go home, study this and come back with a thirteen-page prepared homework. They weren't going to just give him the camera and say, 'There's something, go film.' He found that even when he was at school and college: as long as they let him be free in amongst his real capabilities he was great but he found the academic part of that quite hard."

Alan Price continued with what was an unexpectedly interesting post-Animals career. Though not quite in Burdon's class, he had proven to be a competent singer. His band The Alan Price Set — which made one album — was an interesting experiment in brass and keyboards at a juncture in history when guitars were predominant. He racked up six Top 40 UK hits between 1966 and the next time The Animals coalesced in the mid-Seventies: 'I Put A Spell On You', 'Hi Lili Hi Lo', 'Simon Smith and his Amazing Dancing Bear', 'The House That Jack Built', 'Don't Stop The Carnival' and 'Jarrow Song.' Because he made that switch to self-reliance the original Animals had never been able to, those singles are evenly divided between covers and his own material. The list doesn't even include the jaunty 'Rosetta', a UK #11 he secured with his keyboardist friend Georgie Fame. The pair also recorded an album and became a fixture on British television via both their own show and guest appearances.

As well as becoming a TV star, Price also made some headway in movies. He supplied a well-regarded soundtrack to Lindsay Anderson's 1973 movie *O Lucky Man!* He also appeared in a supporting acting role in Anderson's picture. Come 1975, he was taking the lead role in *Alfie, Darling,* the sequel to the Michael Caine picture *Alfie.* His film career, though, didn't progress following this auspicious start. Perhaps not surprisingly, Burdon — who it would seem safe to assume would have loved to have been in Price's cinematic shoes — is venomous on the issue. Says Burdon, "The thing that pisses me off about Alan Price more than anything is that he was given the world on a platter. After he scarpered from the band, he was then handed *O Lucky Man!* via Lindsay Anderson, who was one of Britain's greatest movie directors, thinkers and rebels. Via him bringing Alan into the fold for *O Lucky Man!* he was then handed a feature film, *Alfie 2*, [sic] where he was taking over from one of Britain's greatest actors. And he fucked *that* up!" As to his own movie world escapades, Burdon says, "I went to the actors' studio for a year. Instead of choosing a psychiatrist I used the actors' studio as a psychological realignment of myself. Then I ran into Gold and Goldstein who convinced me, 'Look, if you want to get into film production or acting, you can't do it from a position of weakness so why don't you get involved again musically with something?'"

Not too far into 1969, impresarios Steve Gold and Jerry Goldstein were the impetus for Burdon teaming up with a band who some might posit as his fantasy group: apart from their harmonica player Lee Oskar, the seven-strong War were all black. Eric Burdon and War would release their debut single, 'Spill the Wine' — a funky groove shot through with what we would now call rapping — in 1970. Its success was an amazing comeback for a man who had renounced the music industry, going top three in America. The group released two albums before War decided — it turned out correctly — that they could be successful without Burdon, who then continued his black-white musical fusion by recording an album with Jimmy Witherspoon, one of his blues heroes, which was released under the title *Guilty!* in 1971. It was artistically negligible. Curiously, it was also somehow disappointing for the fact that it was sometimes difficult to tell which man was singing, which almost suggested that Burdon wasn't as great a singer as we had always imagined. Following this, Burdon released two rather pedestrian hard rock records, *Sun Secrets* and *Stop*, the first of which rather desperately revisited Animals hits. By August 1975, Burdon was in London, hoping to form a new band. He couldn't offer any prospective new colleagues a huge amount of money: he didn't have any. As with The Animals and the New Animals, he had emerged from the War experience with nothing to show for it, plus legal headaches. "He was going to be around for a while," remembers John Steel. "He was basically at a bit of a loose end. No record deal. Chas and me went to see him at a bar."

Burdon's situation was a stark contrast to the fortunes enjoyed by Chandler and, by association, Steel. Chandler had walked out on his management deal with Jimi Hendrix (who died in September 1970). Says Burdon, "Chas had learnt and remembered all the mistakes that Jeffries had perpetrated in The Animals' early days. He'd learned by that time how not to do it and how to do it. Unfortunately Jeffries was still shadowing him and watching his every move, just waiting for the opportunity. I'm sure that Jeffries, being the student of psychology as he was and his military experiences, knew that the team of Hendrix and Chandler would eventually run aground. That Chas would eventually just blow his top. Because [Jimi] wasn't easy to handle. I was offered part of his management when they first started out. Chas offered me part of the management and there was no way that I wanted to get involved with Jimi on managerial level." However, Chandler's transformation of Hendrix from a nobody to a superstar had sealed his reputation in the business and ensured a lucrative management career. Chandler subsequently steered Slade to massive success in the early Seventies, the glam-imaged but hard rock-oriented Black Country band scoring thirteen top ten UK hits between 1971 and 1975.

"We'd been working intensely on Slade from the day I joined and we'd had a fantastic run of success with them," says Steel. "Then it sort of ran out of steam. Chas was starting to feel as though he'd have to look around for something else as well. We were just sitting in the office chewing things over one day and a little light bulb went off in my head and I said, 'What about getting together with Eric and maybe doing a record? Not touring or anything like that, just doing an album.' Chas' immediate reaction was, 'Nah, bugger off.' He wasn't into playing. And I said, 'Yeah but what if it's on the Barn label?' And that's when the light bulb went off in *Chas'* head.'Cause the potential, if it had been the right album, was a big seller." Part of that potential stemmed from the fact that in 1972 'The House of the Rising Sun' had been re-released and reached number 25 in the British charts. Steel: "An A&R man told Chas later that it was a routine thing where he thought, 'Oh that hasn't been out for a while' and stuck it out as a re-release and it took off." The record's second coming illustrated that, to quote Steel, "There was obviously still something there."

Additionally, a hard rock version of The Animals' arrangement of the song had been a Transatlantic top ten for Frijid Pink in 1970.

Steel recalls, "So I phoned up Pricey and he came round with his wife. He wasn't doing a hell of a lot at the time. I floated the idea and he didn't laugh and he didn't chuck it out. He got up and went off to the toilet and his wife said, 'You couldn't have picked a better time.' 'Cause he was just looking for something to revitalise his name at that point." This might be true, but Price needed to revitalise his name less than any of his ex-colleagues. Not only had he just finished filming *Alfie, Darling* but his rousing, socially conscious 'Jarrow Song' had been a UK top ten the previous year. The latter was part of a project that many must have doubted Price had in him: *Between Today and Yesterday,* an ambitious concept album that explored his journey from humble Newcastle lad to adult city sophisticate across two sides divided evenly between Northern brass band music and modern rock.

"Hilton was living in California scratching a living so I didn't think that would be too much of a problem," says Steel. "Basically it was just a matter of a phone call to Hilton and a free ticket provided by Barn Productions to bring him over because he hadn't a pot to piss in." Valentine says, "I went over to the States, late '69 or early '70 to do an album through Eric and Kevin Deverich, which Vic Briggs produced: *All in Your Head*." The latter record was Valentine's one and only solo shot at a big time that was by no means unobtainable for a man who was not only a talented guitarist but the closest thing The Animals had had to a sex symbol. *All in Your Head* also revealed him to be a songwriter. "Some were written before The Animals," he says, though he admits, he never offered them to The Animals to record: "Well, it was a different genre. The songs that I had written were more in the folk-type vein." Valentine isn't too happy with the record. "The instrumentation on it wasn't really right," he says. "They sweetened it up too much. When it was happening, I thought it was good 'cause it was a new thing for me, first time in the studio by meself, but on reflection and listening back, it wasn't quite right." The album made few waves. "I got an advance off that album so I was living off that for a year or so," says Valentine. Following this, Valentine ended up working for John Bloom, an English businessman who became famous in the Sixties by making previously luxurious washing machines affordable to working class housewives but who had relocated to America. "Over here, he had two or three restaurants," explains Valentine. "I ended up working for him as a day manager." Valentine says he found it "pretty easy" to return to a humdrum life, partly because it was good to have a bit of discipline. "It was getting meself back together again from being spaced out for so long," he reasons. Was he surprised at the idea of a reunion? "Yeah, but I thought, 'Why not?' I wasn't doing anything. It was an opportunity to maybe earn a few bucks and also get to play again. I'd started playing again two years before then."

Of course, there were a couple of potentially quite emphatic responses to that posited question "Why not?" The first was the disastrousness of the last reunion of the original Animals in '68. The second was how anybody in the band could be prepared to work with Alan Price now that more than a decade on they fully apprehended just how much they had lost out on through the publishing on 'The House of the Rising Sun' being credited to him alone. "When you get really down to the nitty gritty, it was all about money," admits Steel of the reunion. Of the 'Rising Sun' issue, he says, "It was just a sort of niggling thing that we'd learned to live with. We didn't like it but basically we couldn't do a lot about it. By now, Pricey had convinced himself that he had done the arrangement and it was perfectly right that he should have it. To make it a really good shot, we thought it had to be the original five members. You had to think of it in commercial terms. Plus, he was always the strongest keyboard player. It just seemed logical to us." Was the subject of the 'Rising Sun' royalties brought up at the album sessions? Burdon says, "No, because we're stupid fucking thick-headed Geordies and not one of us ever thought in our minds that we should question Alan about what happened to the royalties. We were too loyal to each other to do that. There was still an attempt at an element of good feeling and let bygones be bygones. But shit, enough is enough. The guy's had a great living out of it when we could have all shared the money. The guy's a fucking cunt, what can I tell you?" Valentine says the issue was voluntarily swept under the carpet in the interests of harmonious relations during recording: "It was brought up a couple of times, but it was sort of hushed up. Not to be mentioned." As usual, Steel has the most detailed recollection. "We — Chas, Hilton, Eric and myself — raised the issue at the beginning. We were having dinner at Chas' home where the recording took place. Alan just flatly refused to discuss it and that was the end of it."

Recording started in December 1975 in Lingfield. "Chas was living in a place called Gould's Farm in Surrey," says Steel. "A big old place that he'd bought on the proceeds of the Hendrix success. He'd been making pots of money with Slade for three or four years by that time and Barn was pretty flush. There was very little on it but Slade and a couple of bits and pieces but Slade had generated a hell of a lot of money. We hired The Rolling Stones' mobile and we all moved into Chas' place and lived there for a week or two. Chas had a live-in girlfriend of the time: Jackie just catered for us and Chas ordered crates and crates of Beaujolais for after the recording sessions. He had a big lounge, the mobile parked outside and all the catering came through the window. Ian Stewart, the Rolling Stones guy who we knew from way back, when he walked into this room and saw all of us sat round the table, his eyes popped out."

"It started off quite slow," remembers Valentine. "We weren't doing that much work until Chas said, 'Look, we've got to get ourselves out of bed in the morning.' Once we started getting up and knuckled down to it, I quite enjoyed the experience." Lack of material was as much an issue as work-rate. Says Steel, "Typically Animals, we had no real idea what the hell we were gonna record 'til we all got together. The expectation was that Eric in particular would have had a raft of songs that he wanted to do and he turned up more or less empty-handed." Even more surprising was the lack of proffered songs from Alan Price, who had proven himself far and away the best composer of the band's ex-personnel over the last decade. Steel: "We had to start scrabbling around in record collections and memories and say, 'How about trying this?' [Eric] pulled out that 'Last Clean Shirt' thing from an album that Chas had in a corner of his collection. It was a

T-Bone Walker song. We just kicked a few numbers in and more or less rehearsed them and recorded them there and then. We didn't go into a rehearsal room for a couple of weeks like any sensible person would. We just knocked numbers out and turned the tape on." For Valentine, though, this hand-to-mouth approach was the right one. "It wasn't like an overproduced album," he says. "It was very spacey. I like things like 'It's All Over Now, Baby Blue' and 'Many Rivers to Cross'. There was some good stuff on there." Recording was complicated by the fact that Chandler didn't find returning to the bass as easy as he'd imagined. Some tracks were initially recorded without any bass and later given overdubs while others saw Chandler simply filling up the space with lines he would later replace.

Of the general atmosphere, Valentine says, "There were still the underlying things. More between Eric and Chas and Alan. Maybe Chas being a bit more business-oriented — having the success with Slade and Hendrix — and Eric being an off-the-wall creative genius. There was always this thing of Eric going off on a tangent and Chas and Alan trying to pull him in, saying, 'No, you can't do it that way.'" Nonetheless, Steel says, "It was fairly relaxed. We ate well and drank a lot of red wine and chewed the rag. Eric was reasonable. Alan was on a bit of a bender when we started and then he just went on the wagon after the first night or two."

Of the product that emerged from these sessions, Steel says, "Chas thought it might be an earner for all of us and a good little album to have in his catalogue on his label. It was just simply: make an album, chuck it into the market and see what happens. If it had been a better album, it might have sold better and we might have started thinking about where to go after that but it didn't create a big fuss." One of the reasons the album — which would be released under the title *Before We Were So Rudely Interrupted* and credited to "The Original Animals" — failed to create a big fuss is that it only saw release almost two years after it had been recorded. This was due to the fact that Burdon couldn't legally issue a record without the permission of his former managers. An injunction was obtained by Far Out Productions — run by Jerry Goldstein and Steve Gold — preventing the album's appearance.

It finally saw the light of day in August 1977. "This is typical Animals," laments Steel, "and particularly typical of Eric, where you've got something waiting to go out and then all of a sudden some frigging lawyer from America's got his locks onto it 'cause Eric's got some deal that he didn't tell anybody about. That's always the way when you're working with Eric. You suddenly find this kind of complication comes into the picture. It's a very untidy life."

The album's delightful title immediately created a warm feeling amongst its purchasers and a resulting sense of expectation and excitement. The purchasers were to be disappointed. Whenever a band reunites after a long hiatus, an inevitable dilemma arises as to how to approach their new recordings. The examples of the reunions of the original Byrds in 1973 and the Small Faces (minus Ronnie Lane) in 1977 provide perfect illustrations: McGuinn and Co. seemed to be almost self-consciously avoiding the twelve-string jingle-jangle of their classic recordings yet in their attempt to avoid self-parody ended up making an album so un-Byrdsy that it begged the question as to the point of the reunion. Much the same could be said about the absence of the classic soul-pop-psychedelia stylings on the two Small Faces reunion LPs. The Animals' comeback record suffered from a similar problem. Such was the *ad hoc* nature of the recording process that the band would not seem to have had the time to actually think through what they were doing and realise that people who would be interested in buying Animals product would expect certain things: an R&B style and plenty of Alan Price's distinctive Vox Continental. The last thing the public would be expecting is what they got: a contemporary-sounding Adult Oriented Rock record with nothing but a few nods to the classic sound of their golden years. Alan Price favoured the piano over the electric organ. Were it not for Burdon's unmistakable voice, this could be any old band. Valentine, though, defends this approach, saying, "It was, 'This is what we are now.' I never heard any discussion about, 'Will we try to make it sound more closely to what we used to sound like?' The Animals just weren't like that. We just took numbers and we played them and whatever came out, that was it." Burdon concurs. "If it was a surprising choice of material, that was the point in recording the material," he says. "You can't stay in one place forever. You have to move on. You've got to do different things."

However, the album has a problem in addition to its meaninglessness/anonymousness: it's very slightly boring. *Before We Were So Rudely Interrupted* never breaks out of its mid-tempo pace. For all its professionalism, its laid-back, rather earth-bound groove makes it very much like so many other records of the mid-Seventies, possessing little of the energy and urgency that musicians of The Animals' generation had taken such pride in a decade previously. This type of well-fed and comfortable ambience was something that helped to create the punk movement and, indeed, by the time the album made its belated appearance, the ascendancy of the punks probably robbed it of any commercial chances it might otherwise have had. In early 1976 (the initial projected release period), "The Original Animals" might have sold to the kind of people who were buying Little Feat records. By 1977, "old farts" of any description were not selling to much of anybody. The album failed to chart in Britain, although the propensity of Americans to, in Zoot Money's words, "take you forever" ensured it reached a not totally disreputable number 70 Stateside.

The Animals start their reunion record as they mean to continue it with a relaxed, smoothly rolling pace and slightly old fashioned instrumentation. The Leiber/Stoller/Otis composition 'Brother Bill (The Last Clean Shirt)' is a song about the death of an old reprobate. Valentine produces a nice but rather antediluvian guitar break. Price's almost comedic honky-tonk piano solo is similarly out-dated but pleasant. 'It's All Over Now, Baby Blue' was one of the four acoustic epics on side two of Bob Dylan's 1965 album *Bringing It All Back Home*. By the time The Animals got round to covering it here, it was a song already wrung dry by every two-bit bar and cabaret singer the world over. Burdon, of course, manages to wring a few last drops of interest out of even this chestnut simply by dint of his 100% commitment. Price's piano chords resound like ton weights, while the echo on Steel's drums adds to the slightly overdone poignancy. Castanets are a puzzling touch. 'Fire on the Sun' (Shaky Jake) is a song of defiance directed at an estranged lover. Burdon is again effortlessly passionate while Price contributes an adroit double-time piano solo. On 'As The Crow Flies' (Stauley) an electric piano provides the tone of transcendence requisite to stave off tedium on a 12-bar blues, though not enough to make it a great performance. Importunate compositions always give Burdon something to really wrap his lungs around and he certainly does that on the cover of the Percy Mayfield number 'Please Send Me Someone to Love'. Price's keyboards, however, are rather reminiscent of lounge music. Jimmy Cliff contributed three songs detailing the yearning of the underclass to the soundtrack of the 1973 Jamaican movie *The Harder They Come*. 'Many Rivers To Cross', the least reggae-like of the trio, was Burdon's suggestion for inclusion on *Before*. Again, it has the combination of epic tune and stirring sentiment in which Burdon revels. We also finally get some organ from Price. The Animals had almost covered 'Just A Little Bit' (Thornton/Bass/Washington/Brown) in their first incarnation: 'Don't Want Much', which was recorded in the Mickie Most era but unreleased until *The Complete Animals* CD, was essentially the same song, re-written. 'Just A Little Bit' is the album's best track, an imaginatively dark and brooding slant on this tale of attempted seduction that boasts — just like almost all the great performances by the original Animals — an organ solo that sees Price's fingers working in overdrive. 'Riverside County' is the album's only original song. Credited to all five band members, it's — inevitably with an album recorded in just a week-and-a-half — a blues, the easiest style in which to write. Like many blues, it's a song of braggadocio and seduction. Old hands at the format, The Animals do a professional job — especially Price — but it's to be doubted whether the world needed another 12-bar blues in 1965, let alone 1975. Another 12-bar, 'Lonely Avenue' (Pomus), is not even sequenced separately from 'Riverside County', the comments on which can be assumed to apply to this. There is a rockabilly rather than R&B ambience on the album's closer 'The Fool' (Ford), especially in galloping bass lines from Chandler that could have come straight off a record cut by Sam Phillips. Valentine produces a riff that is a cross of those on 'See See Rider' and Howlin' Wolf's 'Smokestack Lightning'.

Two British singles were released from *Before*: 'Please Send Me Someone To Love' b/w 'Riverside County' came out in the same month as its parent album while 'Many Rivers To Cross' b/w 'Brother Bill (The Last Clean Shirt)' was released in October '77. Neither bothered the chart compilers. What with the damaging delay in the release of the album, its underwhelming aesthetic qualities and its lack of commercial success, it would seem that the story of the band — whether it be known as "The Animals," "Eric Burdon & The Animals" or "The Original Animals" — was over.

chapter fifteen

After The Animals went their separate ways again, much changed on the music scene.

While punk came and went, it wrought significant changes in the attitudes of record companies towards nurturing new talent playing hard-hitting material (i.e., they were now prepared to do it). Meanwhile, in the early Eighties it truly did seem at times as though a new variant of popular music — synth pop — was going to make conventional rock obsolete.

Little changed, though, with the solo careers of the ex-Animals, which continued in the downward trajectory toward obscurity that then seemed the only possible fate for former members of second rank Sixties acts. Eric Burdon was now free of Gold and Goldstein, although he had had to forfeit his royalties from War recordings. As part of the settlement, a collection of Eric Burdon and War outtakes was released as *Love Is All Around* in 1976.

Burdon was fairly productive with his newfound freedom. He released two star-studded albums that exhibited more ambition than his recent work, *Survivor* (1977) and *Darkness—Darkness* (1980), the first supervised by Zoot Money, the second by The Shadows' Tony Meehan. By 1980, he had a new band, Eric Burdon's Fire Department, and another new album, *The Last Drive*, though this was originally only released in Germany, where he worked a lot during the early Eighties. The latter fact finally led to the fulfilment of Burdon's acting ambitions, at least to a certain extent. By now the veteran of two TV movies — one British, one American — Burdon was asked to take the lead role in a German-backed feature film called *Comeback*. The plot required him to play a fading rock star and to sing a lot of blues (there was a soundtrack album and a further album of recordings generated by the project), so was hardly a huge stretch. Nevertheless Burdon must have got some satisfaction that, after all this time, his image had finally been ingrained on significant lengths of celluloid, even if the movie was badly received and its spin-off albums went nowhere.

Alan Price, meanwhile, had drifted from the artistic high water mark of *Between Yesterday and Today* into slightly soporific MOR, exemplified by his double A-sided 1979 single 'Baby Of Mine'/'Just For You'. The latter was his last UK top forty hit, although of course he had the cushion of the 'Rising Sun' royalties. Chas Chandler, meanwhile, had changed his lifestyle. He later explained, "I had five recording studios and a staff of eighteen but I found I was becoming an administrator rather than a record maker. So when I got an offer for the business, I accepted and retired to do what I've always wanted — write a book. It's something I've always wanted to do. I've been a fanatical reader ever since I can remember and I fancy I could write a book myself." John Steel had fallen out with Chandler over what he felt was the latter's obsession with trying to break Slade in America and had taken a job in his native North-East. "I was working in the pharmaceutical industry as a control room operator," he says. "With a daughter going through higher education I needed a steady income. Still gigging at weekends though." This was a period in which he was, he told author Andy Blackford, "warm, well-fed and happy." Music-wise, Hilton Valentine continued to be missing in action, him never finding the wherewithal to put together a substantial project on his own or with other musicians after his one solo album. "I came back to England in '77," Valentine explains. "I lived in London for a few years off the advance of *Before We Were So Rudely Interrupted...* I was working at Chas' office for about a year. And then I came back up to the North-East to live, about '80... I did a bit of management and producing. I was taking local bands into the studio and trying to get recording deals for them. I didn't really have much success."

On December 12 1982, Eric Burdon appeared as a guest star at an Alan Price concert at Newcastle City Hall, a gig that was regionally televised. Superficially, this augured well for another Animals reunion but those with an inside knowledge of the real nature of the relationship between the band's scattered component parts would probably have laughed at the idea. For instance, Steel recalls of an incident from the late Seventies, "Chas gave Eric some help with setting up a recording. I played on the demo work. He also helped Eric to put a band together which had a brief life under the name Barrel, and gave him the run of the office. In typical Eric style, he suddenly hit Chas with a solicitor's letter warning Chas not to go around claiming to be Eric's management. Chas went absolutely ballistic and told his secretary to get everything remotely connected with Eric — papers, tapes etc. — into a cab and round to that solicitor's office immediately and that was the end of that little collaboration."

Yet despite this — to use Burdon's metaphor — hand grenade-like quality of the congregated Animals personnel, come 1983 a third reunion of the original Animals did indeed come to pass. The catalyst was a Londoner named Rod Weinberg. "He was an agent and an Animals fan," Steel explains. Weinberg had worked with Chandler in the late Seventies and managed Burdon from 1981 to 1984. He says the idea of an Animals reunion began fermenting in his mind in the autumn of 1982. "By the end of November I had them signed up to a contract, all five of them," he says. Some skulduggery was involved in his achievement. Weinberg was good friends with both Burdon and Chandler. "At the time, Eric and Chas weren't talking," Weinberg says. "They hadn't seen each other for years. They'd fallen out time and time again. There was an occasion when Eric had a problem with his throat and I walked him round to Harley Street or Wimpole Street to go with him to the doctors to have his throat checked out and on the walk he said to me, 'Do you see Chas much?' I said, 'Funnily enough I was speaking to him very recently and he was asking after you. He'd really like to meet you and just have a reminiscence about old times.' Eric said, 'Really?' Then I did the same thing to Chas Chandler. And then finally got them together with Alan Price and we went to Langan's Brasserie for a meal and they were just talking like old times. That's when I hit them with the idea of doing another tour. I'd already been speaking to agents in America. I spoke to Ed Rubin who had Magna Artists in New York. I said, 'What do you think — do you think we could do a tour with the boys if I got them to re-form?' and he went quite wild about it. At the time it was one of the only bands of the Sixties where all the artists were alive that could actually re-form." It was decided that the reunion would encompass a new studio album, a world tour and a live album resulting from that tour. There was also talk of making a filmed documentary of the whole process.

Steel: "He'd gradually got Eric, Chas and Alan to talk in the same room about the idea and then contacted Hilton and me when they already had the thing more or less agreed." Steel admits, "Hilton and me were kind of treated as the junior partners." Weinberg says that this was "the only way the three of them would include Johnny and Hilton." He explains, "They formed a company called Triad Ltd: Eric with one share, Chas with one share, Alan with one share and then Hilton and Johnny shared a share. That was Chas' doing 'cause Chas said, 'Us three have kept our careers alive and kept the name of The Animals alive because of what we've done whereas you two haven't so you don't deserve equal shares.' I think Eric went along with things just for a quiet life sometimes. Chas was a bully. He tried to bully everybody." Regardless of whether Burdon was pressurised, his signing up to such a non-egalitarian arrangement predicated on such a dubious rationale (Chandler wasn't even a working musician) does rather provide a different context to his continuing grievance about what Alan Price did to his colleagues regarding 'Rising Sun'.

Says Steel, "I was quite happy to go along with it. It sounded like for once we might do something properly thought-through. So I thought, 'I'll go along for the ride — let's hope I make a lot of money and have fun.' Hilton was of the same mind." What made the reunion viable was that another of the big changes in the music scene since The Animals' last reunion had been — against all the expectations created by the anti-oldie punk agenda — a massive expansion in the market for nostalgia. The notion of the 'has-been' was starting its journey to obsolete status as the baby boomers who were now adults with a disposable income greater than their parents had ever enjoyed displayed an increasing penchant to see their childhood heroes in the flesh again. There seemed every reason that an Animals tour could be amongst the most viable of all nostalgia jaunts: in late 1982, their recording of 'The House of the Rising Sun' was a hit yet again, climbing to number eleven in the UK charts. The new album, meanwhile, would be released by IRS, the label run by Miles Copeland, the man who had masterminded the career of The Police from New Wave runt status to superstardom. Weinberg: "I was quite good friends with Miles Copeland and Miles offered us a pretty good price to do the album, for The Animals anyway. It was $150,000 we got from him, and then it went up in increments of a hundred grand for each further album." The involvement of Copeland itself brought a bonus in the shape of three gigs supporting Sting & Co. Weinberg: "That was all part of the deal." As if all that wasn't enough, there was another revenue stream that back in the Sixties had only been open to the really big acts. "The merchandising we got fifty thousand quid for as an advance," reveals Weinberg. "The usual: t-shirts, caps, American stuff."

"Yeah, it was a surprise," admits Valentine of another Animals reunion, "but I thought maybe it's gonna be different this time." Although Weinberg was a pivotal figure, Valentine gives much of the credit for the 1983 reunion to Chandler: "He certainly had the money to put up to get it going. 'Cause it takes a bit of money to organise something like that, put the money up for the recording sessions."

This reunion was to constitute something more than five musicians from the Sixties replicating their old sound. An Animals for the modern age required, it was decided, augmentation. "Eric insisted the original five wouldn't be a strong enough thing on today's concert stage, so he wanted extra musicians in," says Steel. "Another guitarist because he reckoned Hilton wouldn't be strong enough. A percussionist because he didn't think I would be strong enough. Another keyboard player just to have his own mates along for the ride."The additional guitarist was one Steve Grant, a songwriter, guitarist and synthesiser player who was known to both Chandler and Price and whose band Top Secret had been managed by Weinberg. Grant would actually end up contributing two songs on the ensuing album. Zoot Money opines, "It was a way of Chas presenting him to the world because actually Chas wanted to produce him and he wanted him to do his own albums. He was handling him at the time and he wanted people to see him… Very good player, very fast brain, writes well, sings okay." Money himself was partly responsible for putting the 'augmentation' — of which he was part — together. "I got a phone call from Chas," he recalls. "You must understand up until 1983 whereas they hadn't been talking to each other for twenty years or whatever, I was still probably the only person who could actually speak to them all in one day without committing suicide. They all had their own characters. He said, 'We'd like you to come along, we want to augment this band to make it bigger and heavier-sounding. We're thinking of putting an extra guitar player' — which was Steve Grant — 'and we need a saxophone.' I was friendly with Steve Gregory so I recommended him and he passed the test." Gregory in fact was a former member of The Alan Price Set, so had a head-start. "'And we need a percussionist.' Well that was down to Eric. He wanted Nippy Noya, who was very well-known in Scandinavia." Weinberg is more brutal: "Chas couldn't play the bass for toffee. That's why Zoot Money was brought in, to underwrite his bass playing on the organ. We brought Nippy Noya in to keep Johnny on time. And Hilton was useless with the guitar. That's why Steve Grant was brought in. It was Steve that was playing most of the riffs, the ones that made them famous."

Steel says that the impetus for a documentary film of the whole project also came from Burdon. "He was like James Dean and Marlon Brando from the day I met him," he says in bemusement. "He had these images in his head and that's what he wanted to be. And he's still got that. You can't sort of say, 'Eric, don't give up your day job.'" The documentary was intended to be produced by no less a figure than Lindsay Anderson, which contact presumably came through Alan Price. "He was devastated when we didn't get Lindsay Anderson because Lindsay was really interested in producing an Animals film on the road," says Weinberg. "I wasn't there that day but they decided to meet the director who Lindsay was going to appoint to direct the film. I couldn't believe it but the three of them went for a drink with this director and they fell out with him in the pub. The guy turned round and said, 'You're just a lot of old farts, I don't went to work with you guys' and he walked out. The whole thing fell to pieces." Though some material was shot, Weinberg says, "That was done with Eric finding a little crew to do some stuff." "He wanted someone to travel and there just wasn't enough money to," says Money of Burdon's crew. "Somebody tried to keep up with us for the first couple of weeks but it was obvious that this was not going to be because Eric wanted warts-and-all. Why it fell down was because he wanted to edit it and direct it and of course the others wouldn't agree."

Some of Burdon's ambitions for the project, though, don't seem unreasonable. For instance, for the first time, an album made by the original Animals was not going to be comprised of mainly cover versions. Steel: "That was mostly from Eric. 'If I'm gonna come into it, it's got to be original songs by me' and his collaborators. And of course Alan had to have one or two tracks of his own."

Steel admits, "The first time we got together, it was pretty awful." He explains, "It was in an upstairs room in a pub in Newcastle. I can remember going there and being introduced to Steve [Grant] and waiting for Alan to turn up. I set me kit up and we banged through a couple of things. Then Alan came in absolutely stinking drunk, behaving like a total idiot, real drama queen. He gets very melodramatic when he's pissed. He starts throwing orders out and banging away at the piano and conducting the band when the band didn't need conducting. Eventually he just staggered over to a bench seat and more or less passed out. I told Chas, 'If that's the way that bastard's gonna behave I'm not going to be in this at all.' I was ready to wash my hands of it there and then. The next day, Pricey was on the wagon and I think he stayed on the wagon right through that whole year."

Chandler's ambitions for this project were less aesthetic than commercial. "Chas was thinking of himself as 'business-heading' the whole thing," says Steel. "What you tended to end up with was a situation where Chas and Alan were trying to make it as business-like as possible. Alan's elder brother, who's a very suity-type bloke who runs Alan's business for him, got heavily involved with it as well. You've got that on one side and you've got Eric, the loose cannon, on the other. And me and Hilton standing to one side watching them bounce off each other. It was pretty soon into the thing you thought, 'Oh my God, it's gonna be the same old bloody mess.'" Though Price had quickly ceased to be a problem, he was replaced by another. For all his ambitiousness about the project, it was Burdon. Says Valentine of the reunion, "I think it was a bit more well-organised, but the album came out late because of Eric — again. That's what I heard." Steel: "There was an attempt at planning and organisation but again Eric was the spanner in the works there… You can't do it in a business-like way with Eric. It just never happens. In theory, it could have been a really good, well-done project but Eric was forever screwing it up with demands and complicating things, not turning up. This is not a criticism of Eric. It's just the way Eric is… It was a good live band and it doesn't come off as well as it should on the record. We were going into these big rehearsal rooms. Every day was like a job of work. We had to go in there and we'd work on these numbers. Steve Grant was a very good MD sort of bloke and Zoot Money and Alan worked on these arrangements of Eric's demos that he'd done with some guy in the States, plus a couple by Alan. We'd bang away at these things but Eric never turned up for the rehearsals. The only time you could be sure of Eric turning up at a rehearsal was if there was gonna be a movie camera there. We would do the arrangements with Steve Grant singing and the band was *steaming*. When Eric did come along he didn't know his own bloody lyrics. So the whole thing got arse-first because Eric dillied and dallied and he still wouldn't commit himself to being fully ready so the rehearsals and then the recordings took so long to complete that we started to overlap into the touring time. So instead of having a completed album in the shops ready to promote and then go on the road, we actually started off on the road before the album was in the shops. Everything arse-first." "There were certain things that Eric wanted that some people would consider to be unreasonable or diva-esque," says Zoot Money of Burdon's attitude to rehearsals. "He wasn't into it. He did like it to be all organic, but then when we were rehearsing people should do a good job. Well you can't do that unless you're here Eric, and tell people what's going wrong. And when you've got nine people on the stage it's all the more poignant. For the most part he did that right at the beginning — he did rehearse it right for an amount of time — but he was expecting at certain points for it to be more free-form than it was because he'd got used to having his own set-up where he could be free-form. Yet you can't do that, certainly not with players that have not played for seventeen years, or in the case of Alan who knows how much free-form is boring because he'd led his own band." That Chandler had had to put his novel-writing ambitions aside for the reunion must have made Burdon's eccentricity and obstinacy difficult for him to swallow. In addition, Chandler was once again having problems familiarising himself with the bass. "When we got back together again and started rehearsing, it was very difficult for me at first," he said. "Actually, I really thought it wasn't there anymore and I went through a period of wanting to give up before we'd begun. But then it gradually started coming back and I began to enjoy myself."

Of the actual recording of the new album, Valentine says, "We did some of the stuff at Dave Edmunds' studio and we did some of the stuff in Germany. I didn't know what the hell was going on." John Steel's diary entries reveal that the sessions for the album started at Rockfield Studio in Monmouth, Wales on June 7 1983 and went through to June 13. The band continued work at Country Lane Studios in Germering just outside Munich ("I think it was something to do with tax avoidance" — Steel) on June 18, where it was mainly solos and Burdon's vocals that were recorded. The sessions finished five or six days later. Weinberg recalls some work also being done in Denmark. Valentine, for one, was happy about the idea of using new material and employing modern production techniques. "I think it's important that a band progresses and moves forward," he says. "I don't think it should stick in any rut and try to be like they were in the Sixties. I think if things progress naturally, what's wrong with using modern techniques? As long as it's not computerised drum machines and things like that. It's got to be live. It's got to be a band playing, and if you can do overdubs and add other instruments, why not, if it enhances what's happening?"

With the album in the can, Zoot Money was packing his suitcases to experience life on the road with Burdon again. "We came to an agreement about doing it," he says. "I said, 'Are you sure you need me in amongst all this?' and Chas said, 'Look, you wouldn't like to think you'd missed a crack would you?' I hadn't been to America since before and I thought, 'This all ties in really and I'd love to go back.' By this time my brother was living in St. Louis, my sister was living in Canada and I thought, 'This is perfect.' We even played near Hull, so I could go and see my other sister."

The tour was a massive affair but started modestly with an unadvertised gig at The Venue in London on July 9 1983. Money: "The sound was appalling in there, which it was when I played it in my band and it was appalling every other band I saw. No revelations there. It was just to get a feel for playing on a stage again which you must remember Chas hadn't done for seventeen years. To his credit he got his sound right. He did it, he did the job." A few weeks later, the tour began in earnest, kicking off in Canada, and going through the USA (forty dates). "America went crazy," says Weinberg. "Let me tell you what the secret to it all was. At the time, MTV was a fledgling company. They'd been in business maybe for six months but they had a tremendous motivation to make it work and I became extremely good friends with one of the senior producers there. When he came over to London, I took him out to meet The Animals, and before you knew it MTV were behind us like a bullet in promoting the tour. We did very well. We did a summer tour, all the big summer venues. We sold out everywhere we went. There were gigs when I felt unbelievably elated and the goose pimples were coming. I remember Philadelphia — it was the most amazing gig. Seventeen thousand people, it was just heaving. Walking around the building seeing the scalpers getting three times the price for the tickets. Funny enough, you get pretty chuffed when that happens."

When it came to deciding the set, Valentine says, "I never really had any say in what the songs were. I just learnt the songs and somebody made up a running order. We did keep swapping the songs round a bit when we found out certain songs didn't work in certain places. We moved stuff around, dropped stuff, put new stuff in, until we found a set that we were happy with. I thought it was important to have included new stuff. I wouldn't have been that happy just going out and doing the same songs that we did in the Sixties."

The extra musicians on the live dates proved to be controversial. Some spectators were left with the feeling that the spirit of The Animals, whatever that might be, was swamped in walls of saxophone, virtuoso guitar and — astonishingly, for many — synthesiser. Other people were left wondering why Alan Price — a man with a, probably deserved, ego — could tolerate his keyboard skills being subjected to the indignity of augmentation. "Well I had still been friends with Alan for all those years, so he wasn't against that," says Money. "He would say to me what he wanted, which was perfect as far as I was concerned because I didn't want to be going there and saying, 'Hey, I'm the new keyboardist.' I played the Prophet. He wanted certain sounds that were on the Prophet and the organ so he took care of the piano. I took care of all the 'extra-terrestrial' sounds. The only specification I had for the whole thing was 'I'm not playing "House of the Rising Sun." It's you, Alan, that's your thing.' It was to do with presenting something that is now a little bit more affluent. It sounds a bit bare thirty years later. With a string section or a brass section or a percussionist and a saxophone, it gives you a show, as opposed to just five guys trying to entertain you." And what of the danger of ending up with a troupe which doesn't sound like The Animals? Money: "That is a danger. However what we concentrated on was merely strengthening certain lines. 'Get Out of this Place': I would play that with the bass on organ so it actually was a lot bigger and stronger than just Chas playing. He would start it off."

And the synth? "I didn't use the synth sound as such. I only had one solo which was synth sound. The rest of the time I used it as a brass section." Valentine feels the whole augmentation exercise was a mistake: "At the time I thought the band sounded good and it was cooking but looking back on it — and I've seen videos of the line-up like that — it makes me think, 'Well maybe we should have just went out and done what we did.'"

Generally speaking, however, the tour was well-received both by critics and audiences. The biggest acclaim, naturally, came in America, where rock consumers seem to possess a genuine loyalty to their favourite acts. "In terms of interest in the States when we did the tour, great interest everywhere and for the most part the gigs were an event," says Money. "The great part about it — which was the first time I've ever experienced this — is that we were experiencing four generations of people at a gig. That's quite freaky. You had the older members, people who were our age, in some cases with their older brothers or in some cases with their parents, plus their children, then *their* children, kids — babes in arms, holding them up in front of the audience. America is like that. Any age can go to a rock gig."

Yet the tour was already heading towards a disaster on the personal relations front. Money: "We got to the end without killing each other but there were just loads of skirmishes, disagreements. For the most part they were centered around the fact of getting forty-plus year old men back together after they first knew each other when they were seventeen. Yes, we've all grown older and wiser but when you get together you've got the same antagonisms but with seventeen years of being able to put it into a different way. Which means the same hotbeds of aggravation were there. But if you actually attacked any one of them, they're like a pack of wolves. You weren't allowed to actually have the same argument alongside one of the others. You couldn't back one of them up because the others would turn on you. They were united if you attempted to intervene, which I found was reassuring in a way." Part of the problem was that different Animals were represented by different managers or agents. Burdon was being looked after by Mim Scala and original Animals roadie Tappy Wright while Alan

Price's manager was his elder brother John. Chas Chandler, of course, didn't need management from anybody. Money: "For the most part Chas did actually know how to book the gigs and make sure everything was guaranteed and did most of that." While backstage warring is part and parcel of many rock tours, what made The Animals' '83 tour so remarkable was the fact that the bickering was often conducted through the press. Of Mim Scala, Chandler publicly opined, "I don't like associating with scum." Scala accused the other Animals of being "menopausal married men" who were jealous of the fact that Burdon had managed to make a living out of being a rock'n'roll star while they hadn't. Valentine says of Burdon, "He wanted to have his own manager on the road and I remember arguments about he would have to pay for his own expenses and this and that. I kept out of the way most of the time." Chandler later said of Burdon, "I thought he behaved like a total prat, as if he were a solo star and we was only around to support him and to follow any whim he had... I found him totally unpleasant. The only good thing that came out of it was that Johnny and I had a whirl around the world together. We enjoyed each other's company, and it also repaired all the fences between me and Hilton as well."

Money recalls Steel and Valentine being bemused by the disputes among the Triad: "Hilton particularly because he had become a Buddhist over this time, so aggravation and tension is just something that you learn to float above, so it actually didn't affect him all that much. When we'd parted company originally, Hilton was in the middle of the acid thing and had turned to Buddhism and from being a very manic and very troubled young man had become very placid and of course seventeen years had gone by and he had become even more placid. Johnny Steel was hoping that it would be less traumatic but in fact found himself attempting to appease the disagreements. Basically it was the main three protagonists all made worse by the fact that Alan became tee-total from the beginning of the tour until the end. He could remember things, which is what you don't really need. You've got to be able to have a certain amount of, 'Well I was pissed last night and sorry what I said' — but in fact he wasn't prepared to just say, 'Well let's just forget it', he was prepared to say, 'No, let's talk about it.'"

"It wasn't a happy experience for anybody very much," says Steel, "but I'm afraid a lot of the blame has to be Eric's. Chas and Alan were doing their best to keep it on a business-like level but Eric hates the authority thing. He hates being told what has to be done." In August, Burdon failed to appear at a gig in Sacramento, ostensibly due to a sore throat, and Price had to handle vocal duties. "Allegedly his voice ran out," says Money. "It was a skirmish about musical differences. There was an incident involving Alan's ears. All to do with PAs and ear tolerances. Eric tried to use it as a PR ploy in that, 'See? There are people that miss me and they want me.'" As in, 'They're nothing without me'? "Yeah, yeah, all that. But in fact that wasn't the case. The band went down just as well." Weinberg does note: "We gave the people the opportunity whether they wanted to come in and watch Alan Price sing. Most of them asked for their money back. The promoter took a real hiding that night." On the issue of whether Burdon's illness was phoney, Weinberg says, "Well it was and it wasn't. It suited Mim as well for Eric to not perform. But Eric did make mountains out of molehills, that's for sure." Though the band knew by now that the issue of the 'Rising Sun' royalties was something that was best left unaddressed, Weinberg recalls that "it came back full-force on the tour. Eric threw a book at Alan. Just missed my head and Alan ducked and it hit the reception counter. It was either Texas in Dallas or it was in Albuquerque." Of inter-band relations in general, Weinberg says, "Alan was a very private man. Alan always tried to keep himself to himself and he would go off to his room or he'd be reading a book most of the time. He really only wanted to go onstage, do his bit, come off and be by himself. He had his brother on the tour with him, John, but they never really socialised together much. Chas was the closest one to him really. Eric never saw eye to eye with anybody — the only people he spoke to was Johnny and Hilton. He never at all got on with Chas and he never got on with Alan."

September '83 finally saw the release of the first single from the recording sessions in the shape of the single 'The Night'.

Many people hearing the first Animals single for six years must have been shocked to their roots to find 'The Night' — a Burdon/Sterling/Evans composition — opening with a galloping synth line. Despite that rather unpromising and utterly un-Animals intro, 'The Night' is actually a good record. Burdon's performance in a song concerned with the horrors that afflict people in the small hours reassured anyone who had their doubts that his vocal powers had not diminished since the last Animals reunion, while the band produce a performance of a sweaty urgency appropriate to the lyric. The single's B-side was an Alan Price creation called 'No John No', of which John Steel says, "Detested that." Steel's negative feelings about the song seem a little puzzling as it's one of the best tracks from the recording sessions. The most impressive thing about it is the way The Animals reveal they are open-minded and dexterous enough to play reggae: this is authentic stuff with no hint of pastiche. The lyric is another pleasant surprise: who would have thought that Alan Price could come up with such a thoughtful tale about a lonely man's suicide? It's an injustice that it didn't feature on *Ark*, the album which followed that same month. All told, The Animals' comeback disc (which reached number 48 in America, though didn't chart in Britain) was an impressive affair.

When *Ark* did make its much delayed appearance it was credited as "Produced by Burdon/Chandler/Price/Steel/Valentine," although Steve Lipsom also got a co-producer's credit on several tracks. Weinberg claims that it was in fact produced and mixed by Chandler, which would make sense as he had produced much of Jimi Hendrix's and Slade's respective catalogues. *Ark* is as much a record of its time as *Before We Were So Rudely Interrupted* was a quintessentially mid-Seventies album. With its brittle, glistening sound, shrieks of synthesiser and helium gas backing vocals, it is of a piece with much of the music that dominated the charts (especially the British singles charts) in the early 1980s. It's debatable whether this updating is a good thing. While The Animals couldn't be accused of standing still here, once again the reunion threatens to be meaningless. Why get back together only to end up sounding like the Human League? Especially as the Human League, *et al*, never scaled the artistic heights The Animals did. Being with-it is all very well but history will show that the music of the Eighties just wasn't very good. Mercifully, John Steel opted out of this modernity by not using a click track and thus ensuring that the album isn't ruined by a metronomic beat in the way so many LPs of that era were. "I've never used a click track," he says. "As far as I'm concerned you might as well use a drum machine. You can't react to anything. If somebody does something interesting and you want to whack an accent in there, you can't do that when you're basically a backing track."

The impression of self-conscious modernism is deepened by the album's conceptualised title and its grotesque, cack-handed (and overtly American) cover art which depicts a cigar-chomping character machine-gunning some sort of sea monster that is trying to invade a sea-vessel, evidently the 'ark', a concept whose juvenile nature is emphasised by its comic book lettering and pale colouring. Said cover was drawn by Paul Power, from an idea by Burdon. Power, who has worked on the graphics side for films such as *The Goonies*, *The Terminator* and *Judge Dredd*, wasn't allowed to develop his ideas according to Zoot Money, who made friends with him. "He was given a very rough brief and that's what he put together," says Money. "He said, in fact, what you have got there is my original sketch idea which Eric saw and went, 'Yeah great.'"

Considering it features so much 'augmentation', the album has a rather sparse feel and a coldness only exacerbated by the unlovely, soulless sound of synthesiser. Where it is not self-consciously modern, the production is often feeble. The keyboards are barely audible. Alan Price is also quiet on another front, contributing no songs. Since the last Animals reunion, he had provided the score for the 1982 stage musical of *Andy Capp* and released eight solo albums, one of which (*Rising Sun*, 1980) included a re-recording of 'The House of the Rising Sun'. In a radio interview at the time, he explained of his new version that he couldn't replicate the "ignorant youthful aggression" of the '64 incarnation. This smooth, sax-heavy version, though, was surprisingly good. Though his music might have lately become increasingly middle-of-the-road and unambitious, surely he had more to offer this reunion than 'No John No'? Meanwhile, while most of the compositions are above-average, several are so sketchily and/or stiffly rendered that they feel like demos.

Steve Grant's 'Loose Change' is a poor opener to The Animals' second Second Coming, featuring a slender tune and a perfunctory sax solo. An interesting line from the lyric could be about Burdon himself: "Everybody wants to be a movie star." Things briefly threaten to get exciting towards the end of the song as it moves into double time. 'Love is for All Time' (Burdon/Everett/Wilson) is leagues better. As on 'No John No', The Animals display a surprising facility with reggae rhythms in a touching declaration of loyalty that should really have been the first single released off the album. More commercial than 'The Night' and boasting an impressively rich production, it might have given *Ark* the hit single it needed to make it a commercial success. The following 'My Favourite Enemy', another Steve Grant composition, explores the thin line that can exist between love and hate. Although this theme has been proved an interesting one in the past, the anonymous tune and lacklustre instrumentation ensure that the track wastes its subject matter. Burdon/Sterling/Raskin's 'Prisoner of the Light' is a song of paranoia. The band acquit themselves well in this atmospheric slowie. 'Being There' (Geniwells) is a very Eighties piece of pop, its unattractive technological gleam redolent of the heartless mediocrity of so much music of that decade. Its most interesting feature is some rather fine bass playing: can that really be Chandler plucking the strings with such fluidity? "None other to the best of my knowledge," says Steel. Revealing more hitherto unimagined gifts, The Animals give 'Hard Times' a nice funky feel, as well as a slight edge of menace. A fine collective performance with some particularly agreeable sleek organ on this Burdon/Sterling song about economic dire straits. Following 'The Night' comes a weird, slow reading of 'Trying To Get To You' (Singleton/McCoy). Recording this number, one of the best Elvis Presley Sun recordings, strikes one as being as futile as a Beatles cover version: what's the point in trying to top (or even match) perfection? Even as fine a singer as Burdon couldn't hope to match the gorgeous vocal quavers the Memphis Flash produced in the bridge of his rendition, nor can The Animals compete with the lovely simplicity of the backing of Scotty Moore, Bill Black and DJ Fontana. 'Just Can't Get Enough' — another Burdon/Sterling collaboration — features some attractively punchy brass but that pleasure is cancelled out by more of the dread sound of synthesiser. 'Melt Down' (Everett/Wilson) had previously appeared on the 12-inch version of the 'The Night' single. John Steel produces some powerful percussion while Burdon's emoting is doubled-up for extra effect on a song of love in crisis. A good track is slightly spoiled by cringe-worthy high-pitched backing vocals. 'Gotta Get Back To You' is another number from the team of Everett and Wilson. Burdon laments the break-up of a relationship over a staccato rhythm. Good stuff, though we are treated, as in many other places on *Ark*, to a sax solo that stops just short of being above-average. *Ark*'s closer sums up the deficiencies of a patchy album. With its nondescript melody and revolting synth shrieks, 'Crystal Nights' could be something Nik Kershaw left on the studio floor. Apparently it took no fewer than four people (Burdon/Sterling/Anthony/Lewis) to write it.

"Eric was wagging the whole dog with his idea of what he wanted to do," says Steel of *Ark*. "That's not always the best way to go but in the end sometimes the only way you can get anything out of Eric is just go with what he says because otherwise he digs his heels in or disappears. Whatever the faults are about that album, down to the cover — awful! — and the music, I'm afraid ninety per cent has to be laid at Eric's door." Valentine feels that recording new songs was a good idea and cites 'Love is for All Time', 'Prisoner of the Light' and 'Crystal Nights' as particularly worthwhile tracks. Whatever its merits or demerits, *Ark* failed to chart in Britain and only reached number 66 in America.

Burdon pins this lack of chart success directly on the Japanese leg of the tour which started in mid-September. "*Ark* was close enough to being a real attempt at a real album, as we had Copeland and his organisation at IRS behind us and it could have actually made an indentation into the charts," he says. "But unfortunately the band at the time chose to go on a worldwide tour because it had t-shirts printed up that said 'Animals Worldwide Tour'. I tried my best to get them to stay in the United States and chase up 'The Night', the single that was in the charts. My idea was to go back to travel up the West Coast and then take a week off and then go back to New York and work the album and single up the charts. But they wanted to go to Japan and in Japan we lost all the ground that we gained in America. It was gone." Weinberg scoffs at Burdon's theory and says, "The only reason Eric didn't want to go to Japan to do the four shows was that he was scared of going to Japan 'cause he thought the Yakuza were after him."

The bickering that had pocked the tour was exacerbated by the fact that in Japan the band were stuck with each other's company in a confined space for several days due to bad weather conditions. "I had a good time there," Money says of the Japan jaunt. "I was determined by this time not to be put off by all this and say, 'This is not my problem.' Japan was good. That time I managed to actually get out. I got an actual chance to go in the streets and go to places." Money and Burdon, of course, had the worry of whether the Japanese mafia had forgiven and forgotten the events of 1968. "I did bear that in mind," says Money. "It wouldn't have mattered if I had come with my own band but the fact was I was with The Animals again. I thought 'Oooh.' But I didn't really have any problems. Chas was very reassuring. He wouldn't have gone anywhere near where there was trouble and if there had have been any kind of trouble you could rely on Chas to sort it out. We did discuss this. He was very friendly with the right people."

In mid-October, The Animals played two concerts at London's Royal Albert Hall, after which they went back to the USA for forty more dates. For Weinberg, the second leg of the American tour was a bad mistake. "I told them to come out of the summer tour with a blaze," he recalls. "Ed Rubin was trying to get some extra money out of it and trying to get them to do the second tour. I'm saying, 'You shouldn't do it, because you're going from primary venues down to secondary venues into theatres', 'cause it was winter. I said, 'It's crazy. You've been doing ten-to-fifteen thousand a night and here you're going to go into theatres with two thousand. Leave it. Let's stop now, record another album for Miles — which he wanted — and let's do another summer tour next year to promote the album.' But Chas — you would have thought being such a wise guy from the music business — got the boys to agree to have a second bite of the cherry, and it wasn't there. The second tour bombed. Eric actually didn't want to go on the second tour of America but he was shanghaied into it. I don't know to this day why the hell he did it." "I don't think Japan was very successful," says Valentine. "I don't think there was enough promotion. The UK wasn't really very successful. The first leg of America was great, and Canada, and then for some reason we went back and it just seemed to be done on a different scale, different level, and that wasn't very enjoyable."

"By the time the second leg came round, I don't think anybody gave a shit anymore," says Steel. "Just blundered through. Eric was complaining for the whole tour. He ended up sacking people and putting his own people in. By the time we got to the back end of it, everybody was so bloody weary of it I don't think anybody gave a toss anymore. Just battled on to get it finished and forget it as soon as possible. Eric can be a bit wearing sometimes. In a way, it's commendable in that he's trying to get the best performance to the audience but in another way he's not always the best man to decide what's best. You're not getting a very cool-headed professional judgement. It's alright if he's just got his own little band. We weren't paid sidemen."

Not even playing to massive audiences as support to probably the biggest act in the world at that time could make The Animals stop and smell the roses. The guitarist of The Police was none other than ex-Animal Andy Summers. "They fought like cat and dog," he recalls of his old band. "They did *not* get on at all. It was a disaster basically." Not that Summers interacted much with the support act. "At that point the three of us were completely guarded and minded and then carried in and out with an entourage so we just didn't really see them at all," he reveals. "The one moment I remember — it was in Miami or Florida, a gigantic open-air stadium — and they were coming off stage and Eric was walking down the ramp and I was walking up. We sort of crossed and grinned, like, 'Fuck me, the world turns.' Amazing moment."

In November, 'Love Is For All Time/Just Can't Get Enough' was released as a single and failed to chart either side of the Atlantic. December 10 saw the start of the British tour proper. The band's performances in their home country were disappointing affairs, particularly their concert at Newcastle City Hall on December 17, which homecoming, amazingly, was not the best gig of the tour but possibly the worst. Steel: "When we first came out of Newcastle in the Sixties, we were the local heroes. Police all over the place, thousands in the street. In '83 we played the City Hall and it was crap." "I just don't think people in the UK were interested," says Valentine. "We did the gig and it wasn't a very good turn-out." There were bad omens even before The Animals stepped on stage. Dave Finlay, who had been employed by Mike Jeffery as head of security in the old days, punched Burdon in fury backstage when the singer made derogatory comments about Newcastle. "Eric wasn't even going to go on," remembers Steel. "He said, 'That's it, I've had enough of this, I'm off!' By the end of that tour, Tappy Wright seemed to be the only bloke Eric would talk to. Tappy got him calmed down and we went on and did the show." Money feels that Newcastle in general had been turned off by the re-formed Animals' attitudes. "You're presuming that people are looking at you with eyes of seventeen-years-olds," he says. "That's true to a degree but there's a certain amount of antagonism as to why they should they be lording it and doing so well and we're still here. That thing didn't affect me because I wasn't from there. They should have been all pally-pally: 'Yeah it's great to be back man, we love it, and we're going to open a blind school for Geordies' or whatever." "I told them to do it for free and give all the money to the local orphanage," says Weinberg of the Newcastle gig. "Alan Price's response to that in the dressing room at the Albert Hall was to say, 'Charity begins at home.' Which was such a big mistake they made. I'd actually been talking to the local city council and they were talking about making them freemen of the city. Eric supported me and so did Hilton but the others just outweighed us. Chas had this good knack of just being

able to manipulate everybody else." Meanwhile, the presence of
Alan Price's brother at the gig prompted Burdon to sabotage 'The
House of the Rising Sun'. The concert was being recorded and
John Price had made it known that he was particularly anxious
to get a good live rendition of the band's most famous song.
With his enduring fury over the wayward publishing royalties
of 'House', this was a red rag to Burdon. Steel: "Eric tried to
pull a fast one on 'House of the Rising Sun' by winding Hilton
up to not play the traditional Animals version of it. Eric's such
a bloody mischief maker. He loves causing trouble. Eric cranked
up Hilton into going out and starting the intro completely differently: strumming and farting about. It was embarrassing. The
audience just sat and said, 'What the hell is that?' It's not what
they wanted to hear. John Price [was] running around backstage
going, 'My publishing! My royalties!'"

The last ever proper Animals gig took place on December
31 at Wembley Arena, London with the band again supporting The Police. The occasion was broadcast in the US by MTV,
although such was the rancour in the band's ranks that not even
that impressed them at this point. Recalls Weinberg, "Eric and
Hilton didn't want to do the show. By that time, I'd fallen out with
them and I wasn't involved anymore and they all came begging
me to persuade Eric and Hilton to do the final show, which I did.
Hilton said to me, 'Rod, I'm only doing this because of you.' That
was the end. I never even spoke to Chas on the night. He was
such a bully to everybody. Chas and I fell out in the autumn of '83
because I put together a British tour and he took it away from me."

Unremarkable though the commercial performance of *Ark*
had been, it was enough to see The Animals offered another
deal to make a studio album. Weinberg reveals, "It was worth a
quarter of a million quid to us, a lot of money back in the early
Eighties. Miles phoned me at the end of the tour and said, 'We
want them to go back in the studio.' I said, 'I'm sure they'd be
delighted to.'" Unfortunately, so poisonous was the atmosphere in
the ranks now that the group spurned the offer. "They were just
stupid," says Weinberg. "So stupid you would not believe. And
you're talking about a very seasoned manager in Chas Chandler.

You would have thought he'd be very savvy. But he made so many mistakes it's not true. They couldn't agree to agree. It was such a shame. They just couldn't talk to each other. I personally think basically nobody ever got over the fact that Alan Price had nicked all the royalties from 'House of the Rising Sun' and also Eric still hated Chas for being too much of a bully. He just never got to grips with Chas. I think he blamed Chas for Jimi's death as well. I don't mean directly. Eric didn't want to work with them anymore, mainly. I think also Chas realised that he wasn't the force he used to be anymore as a manager. He made some bad decisions or he influenced some bad decisions through the others. He was being shouted down even though he tried to bully everybody. They didn't want Chas to produce the next album 'cause they didn't think he did a great job on the first one. I remember saying to them in Japan, 'You're such tossers. If you could only get on with each other and talk to each other and discuss things properly, we could go on and on for years and make good money, but you're going to blow it all.' Johnny summed it up I think in a *Daily Express* article when he said, 'We may all be in our forties but things never change. Everybody's still kids.'"

After that, all five Animals would seem to have been of the same opinion, namely: "Never Again." "It was an interesting year," says Steel. "It was an interesting thing to get round the world again and look at places I hadn't been for twenty years, apart from with Slade on business." However, the drummer adds, "I never wanted to see any of them ever again in my life. That was everybody. I didn't care." The money earned would not seem to have been enough to compensate for all the aggravation of the tour. Zoot Money observes, "If you listen to any one of them they would all say, 'Didn't make any money out of that, you know. I don't know about him, but I lost money.' I've heard that ever since. On the tour it was, 'People are taking advantage of me' and 'I don't like the way that's done.'" Offers Weinberg, "[Chandler] said to me one day, 'You've made more fookin' money out of this than we have.' I said, 'I never told you to do the second tour of America. I tried to stop you.'" Steel says, "We made a bit of money. Nothing like enough to retire on."

"I think they all should have written books about it," says Money. "They were going to keep notes and write a book. In fact Johnny Steel was the only one that actually kept notes about the tour but I'd thought it was a great idea. I'd said way, way back, 'You should all be talking, all write the book.' That would be funny stuff, that tour. You've got to get the whole set if you want to know what happened and in fact Eric was quite far-sighted in the sense that he wanted a video kept of all of it."

Last word to Burdon: "The '83 Animals reunion tour was one of the worst experiences of my life. I am sorry that I did it then, I'm sorry that I did it now. It sets the tone for the future: enough is enough."

chapter sixteen

On January 30 1984, John Steel took a train to London and met up with Chas Chandler. They then went to the offices of David, Elton & Wineman Solicitors to meet Jeffery A. Elton and from there to the chambers of Stephen Silber, the counsel instructed on their behalf. Alan Price and The Animals' accountant Colin Newman joined them there. Their collective purpose, says Steel, was "about suing Mickie Most about our lousy record deal." In his journal, Steel wrote, "In Silber's chambers we were told in a roundabout way that we hadn't a leg to stand on unless we were prepared to fight it out over several years at a cost of tens of thousands of pounds and even then that was no guarantee. Especially as Alan [sic] Klein controlled the US side of things." Some of course will raise an eyebrow at the amazing chutzpah of Alan Price thinking himself a wounded party and might consider it just as well, for his sake, that the case did not proceed to court, what with the embarrassing questions that the defendants might direct his way.

The only way for The Animals to make any money was to not look backwards but to issue new product. The live album recorded on their 1983 tour was released in September 1984. Titled *Greatest Hits Live!* (the American version was sub-titled *Rip It To Shreds*), it purports to be a record of the last-ever Animals gig at Wembley Arena on New Year's Eve 1983. In fact, it would seem to be a hodgepodge of performances from various gigs on that tour. "I think that live album was taken from the Wembley thing as well as Chipping Norton," says Money. "We did a little gig in Chipping Norton somewhere so sound-wise it sounded huge at one second and then slightly smaller." It's also possible that some of the tracks were recorded at the Royal Albert Hall. Burdon himself has even gone so far as to claim that it's not a live album at all but a forgery concocted in a studio. This, though, would seem to be typical Burdon exaggeration. "Well, it's like most albums," says Steel. "The initial tracks were recorded live at a variety of gigs and you'll find that in any live album you'll investigate on, by the time you're listening to it back you have to go into the studio and overdo this and tweak this and that and the other and you might as well have done it in the studio when you've finished the thing. It was a genuine attempt at a live recording and taken into the studio and doctored up." "It wasn't bodged," Money says. "It was for the most part what we were playing. We just took the best bits from here and there. We dubbed bits and pieces yeah, and guess who had to be dubbed? Somebody was not quite hitting it vocally." Whatever the extent of the overdubbing, it's probably fair to say that the album is representative of The Animals' 1983 tour — whatever that's worth.

For a live album, the atmosphere on *Greatest Hits Live!* is very poor, comments to the crowd and other evidence of the fact of performances in front of human beings being few and far between. Sad to report but Burdon's singing is embarrassing throughout the album, his meaningless and incessant ad-libbing ("Don'tcha know!"; "Bay-bee!"; "Yeah!") often disfiguring the tunes almost beyond recognition. The album opens in the bizarre way that gigs on the world tour did: the Burdon/Sterling 'It's Too Late' was a song that would have been completely unfamiliar to the audience, having only appeared as the B-side of a 'The Night' promotional single distributed to radio stations in America. It's a briskly-paced catalogue of modern horrors and is pretty good. The attendees at the gig, though, must have been mystified. 'The House of the Rising Sun' is inevitably disappointing — no one could match the sheer perfection The Animals captured in one take back in '64 — but does Price have to play as though he's the kind of stripy-jacketed organist who used to perform during the intervals at cinemas? The relentlessly pounding additional percussion is an awful, unnecessary piece of updating. Burdon — who sounds hoarse — alters the lyric to advise people not to try to become a rock'n'roll star. Following a nondescript 'It's My Life'

comes a rushed 'Don't Bring Me Down'. Burdon's slow, smoul-
dering singing on the original is a distant memory. 'Don't Let
Me Be Misunderstood' features a bizarrely ornate keyboard-and-
synth intro that would not be out of place on an Emerson, Lake
and Palmer record. This precedes some strained singing from an
apparently constipated Burdon who has forgotten how to use
silences for effect, him groaning and 'baby'-ing in every spare
moment. 'I'm Crying' features a drum solo. 'Nuff said. 'Bring it
On Home to Me' isn't bad, with pleasant keyboards and Burdon
relatively faithful to the original record. The difficult, shapeless 'O
Lucky Man!' is an odd choice for an Alan Price solo spot considering the presence in the keyboardist's back catalogue of catchy
crowd-pleasers like 'Rosetta', 'The House That Jack Built' and
'Jarrow Song'. The lengthy bongo playing by Nippy Noya and the
vocal extemporizing by Burdon in the intro to 'We've Gotta Get
Out of this Place' virtually constitutes a new composition grafted
onto the beginning of the song. If Cynthia Weil didn't like the
'65 version(s), God alone knows what she made of this travesty.
'When I Was Young' wasn't included on the original album but
was added as a bonus track for the CD release. This is a surprisingly faithful and sensitive version of the New Animals track. It's
also the one track on the CD that sounds dark and supple rather
than glaringly bright and rigid. The publishing credit, incidentally,
now declares the song to have been written by Burdon alone.

Valentine says of *Greatest Hits Live!*, "I was past caring. I've
maybe played it once." His apathetic feelings were reflected by
the reaction of public. The album didn't chart in the UK and even
in America only managed to struggle to number 193.

afterword

Mike Jeffery took the secrets of The Animals' accounts to his grave when on March 5 1973 a DC9 on which he was travelling was involved in a mid-air collision.

Some have claimed that Jeffery somehow faked his death or that he happened to survive by switching planes at the last minute. Kathy Etchingham scoffs at such talk. "He's in Croydon Cemetery," she says. "He's got a bloody headstone. He was identified by his father. I know exactly what happened. He was there with a friend called Tom Salt who I used to know. The pair of them were supposed to be flying back on this Iberian aircraft the next day. Tom Salt went out the night before, got thoroughly pissed, didn't wake up on time, rushed to the airport, got to the check-in thing and they said, 'Sorry, you can't get on the plane, the flight's closed.' He went to the barrier and caused all kinds of a fuss, screaming and shouting and everything — because in those days, if you didn't get your flight, you lost your ticket — and they wouldn't let him on. And he said afterwards he just could not believe it: two more minutes, he'd have been on the flight and he'd have been dead as well. There was no plane switching. It was a pre-booked flight."

Mickie Most was no flash in the pan as a producer or hitmaker. He achieved the significant feat of probably becoming more associated with the Seventies than the decade in which he first made his name, not only through issuing a string of glam rock hits on his own RAK label but by his acidic performances as a judge on television talent show *New Faces*. He did so well for himself that he was listed on the *Sunday Times* Rich List of the wealthiest people in Britain. None of that, though, could make him immune to the cancer which claimed his life in 2003 at the age of 64.

On January 19 1994, the original Animals were awarded the honour of being inducted into The Rock'n'Roll Hall Of Fame in a ceremony at the Waldorf-Astoria Hotel, New York that was marked by events entirely in keeping with their history. Eric Burdon decided not to turn up to collect his statuette, getting a spokesman in Germany (where he was then working) to issue a statement to the effect that he was looking to the future, not the past. "But," says John Steel, "at the same time the police were re-investigating the death of Jimi Hendrix and apparently they were very keen to talk to Eric. I think Eric was just keeping his head down because if he'd been in the Rock 'n' Roll Hall Of Fame they'd have known exactly where to find him." Although there is no suggestion that Burdon had anything to do with the guitarist's demise, he has given bizarre interviews about its circumstances that would have made his testimony of interest to the authorities.

Alan Price flew over with Chas Chandler, Hilton Valentine and John Steel, but declined to sit at the same table as his former colleagues during the ceremony. All of which, you might say, is typical Animals. "Isn't it?" laughs John Steel.

There will never be another reunion of the five original Animals. On July 17 1996, Chas Chandler collapsed and was taken to Newcastle General Hospital where he died of a heart attack, aged just 57. Not that it seems likely that the original Animals would have reunited had it not been for Chandler's death. They seemed content to pursue their separate paths after 1983, although, with the exception of Alan Price, the word "Animals" usually featured in their billing in some form.

Following the '83 reunion, Valentine "went back up to Newcastle and I formed a band called The Alligators which is the band that kind of developed into the Animals II." For several years he and John Steel worked the lucrative nostalgia circuit together in The Animals II. Eric Burdon seemed to be taking his cue from them when he announced in December 1998 that from the following January, his band would be known as "Eric Burdon and the New Animals." Burdon explains his reasoning for re-adopting the Animals name thus: "There's two other guys out there that retired from the business for years and now have decided they wanna get

back in and they're using the name Animals II and they're making
more money than I'm making at the moment, so why the hell not?
I have a right to call the band the New Animals. I haven't used
it up to now but the business is turning nasty. Things are getting
lean and mean and everybody always associates me with the name
anyway. They always call me 'The Animal', even against my will.
When I call my band other names, I still come up to gigs and I
find myself billed as 'The Animal'." The only surviving original
Animal who does not trade under that name lives in London and
continues to make a good living from live work, much of which is
comprised of corporate functions. Price was off the road for nearly
three years after a heart bypass operation in the 2000s, though
has reportedly recovered well. In May 2010, he was able to tell
the *Bournemouth Echo*, "My main ambition was to go on as long
as possible and I'm still going. The work is still coming in and I'm
booked right through to next spring." The following month, he
was due to play on the Acoustic Stage at the Glastonbury Festival.
"I was thrilled to bits," he said. "It is like getting knighted." In
2002, Colin Randall interviewed Price for *Down South*, a magazine for supporters of Sunderland Football Club. Price referred to
The Animals as "different people living different lives" and "really
just ships in the night," feelings — Randall suggested in what was
presumably an inference from comments by Price — stemming
from the fact that the constituent parts of the band only gravitated
towards each other out of musical convenience.

One gets the impression that Price has backed himself into an
agonising moral corner over his past behaviour. He is unable to
admit having ripped off the other band members over the 'Rising
Sun' royalties, not just for public legal reasons, but privately in
order to maintain the sense of self-worth that all human beings
must possess for the sake of self-preservation. This being no easy
task, the options are constant, exhausting self-justification, an
endless quest to not think about the issue or self-loathing —
or possibly flitting back and forth between the three. His glum
awareness that every single person who wants to interview him
will have a question about the matter of the 'Rising Sun' royalties must only add to his sense of being beleaguered and disliked

and make him want to hide away as much as a man who is a performer can. The wretched psyche of someone who knows that every moral pronouncement he makes, in life or in song, will be contrasted by people with an incident in 1965 that has come to define him can only be imagined at.

Price's Vox Continental, of course, defined The Animals for many. Yet it remains mildly astonishing that in The Animals' original career as well as their two reunions, Price never gave his all songwriting-wise.

The man who replaced Price in the original Animals, Dave Rowberry, was belatedly recruited to Animals II at the turn of the new century after they had already been touring for half a decade. "We heard that Dave was a bit of a lush," is Steel's explanation for why Rowberry hadn't been brought on board in the beginning of the Animals II venture, despite the drummer initially making an overture. "Which turned out to be true, but he was still a better player than most people in the market at the time, as we discovered when we plumped for him. We didn't know whether to take a chance. For a while, it was Dave Rowberry, me and Hilton in the band at the same time. It was working quite well." However, this line-up, probably the closest there could be to a full-scale Animals reunion, foundered on disagreement between Valentine and Steel over choice of lead vocalist. "We agreed not to work together again," says Steel.

When this author spoke to him at the turn of the 21st century, Burdon was writing his second volume of autobiography, which appeared in 2002 as *Don't Let Me Be Misunderstood*. It appears to be as controversial as *I Used to be an Animal, but I'm Alright Now*. Steel: "God. It's a novel. The second novel. Eric sent me a copy and when I challenged him about some of the content he just shrugged and said 'Never let the truth get in the way of a good story.'" Burdon also talked of other media ambitions, including screenplays. "I've got five that I want to do," he said. "But I see those projects being done in conjunction with another person. I don't think movies are written, movies are re-written. If you have a person to bounce ideas off, you end up having a much better product. One is set in New Orleans in the 1860s.

Another story that I've got is set in the tropics on the high seas.
I've another story that I want to do about Berlin. It was always
projected that I was struggling to be an actor. That's not necessarily true. I wanted to be involved in film, but when I look at
movies I don't look at the actor, I look at the production value,
I look at the costume design, I look at the graphics, whatever.
Today I still feel that there's an opportunity there for me to do
that in the future. I haven't given up on that." However, he continues to make his living from music. He claims to have turned
down the sort of career-reviving projects that have seen veterans
like Carlos Santana front all-star bands in exchange for a product of unashamedly commercial orientation. With such a purist
attitude, it's perhaps not surprising that his recording output is
sporadic, but he tours consistently. Though he wrote in *Don't
Let Me Be Misunderstood* of being "married to the road," he also
admits, "Traveling is never a pleasure no matter what anybody
says. You never get used to it." He still loves the blues: "To me
the best music in the world, when everything else dies down and
everyone's gone away and when the TV's off and I'm alone in
the hotel room, the music that I like to listen to the most is still
Howlin' Wolf, Muddy Waters, Jimmy Reed."

Burdon and Valentine worked together again in 2007-08. Valentine explains, "He was short a guitar player for this gig down
in Florida and he got in touch with me and asked me if I could
come down and sit in for that. Did the gig and as I was leaving,
I was coming down in the elevator with him and his wife. He
said, 'Got some more gigs coming up.' Ended up doing it for two
years." Steel is not amused. "That was a sorry affair," Steel says.
"Eric and me are in a dispute over the Animals name, so I'm
putting two and two together when I saw that Hilton was suddenly in Eric's band, I thought, ''ello!' He's trying to strengthen
his position in this dispute.' 'I've got another original Animal
in the band', sort of thing. But Eric's wife's a control freak and
Hilton's wife's a control freak (I should know, I'm married to one
also) and it would have made life hell on the road, so I knew it
wouldn't last ten minutes, and it didn't. Hilton by all accounts
was absolutely fucking gutted when he was dumped. I would

guess that Eric suddenly thought, 'This isn't worth the hassle.'"
Valentine says he and Burdon parted ways because, "He broke
the band up and formed another band. He does this quite a lot."
As to the idea that he was recruited by Burdon for reasons other
than musicianship or sentiment, he says, "I've heard that story. I
don't know if it's true or not. He never mentioned any of that to
me. No, I didn't think I was used." Valentine maintains he and
Burdon are still friends.

The dispute Steel mentions started in 2004 and as of 2012
is unresolved. "It came about when I was talking to the Musician's Union legal department because somebody had sent me
a bootleg Animals thing," explains Steel. "A rip-off thing, just a
pub band in the South-East somewhere. I said, 'Is there anything
you can do about this?' He said, 'Well, it's not really worth the
money it would cost in the end.' But while he was doing this, he
was looking things up on his computer and he said, 'It appears
that Eric Burdon has applied for the trademark "The Animals"
in America.' That was the first I'd heard. Immediately I thought,
'The next thing Eric's gonna do is he's going to apply for the
trademark in Europe,' 'cause he'd been making noises about me
stealing work from him. He's going to do his best to put me out
of business — that's the way I saw it. So I got an application in
before him. Then he appealed against it. I won the decision. They
gave me the name, but Eric's appealed against that."

This court case — in combination with the disappointing
1984 meetings about suing Mickie Most — has put paid to any
thoughts Steel might have had about raising a legal case against
Alan Price over the royalties for 'The House of the Rising Sun'
despite the changed legal landscape demonstrated by belated
court victories like Matthew Fisher's claim over Procol Harum's
1967 smash 'A White Shade of Pale'. Fisher was awarded royalties
in 2006. His appeal against a subsequent decision to allow him to
be recognised as co-author but not receive royalties was upheld at
the House of Lords specifically because there are no time limits
to copyright claims under English law. Steel says he is "…totally
averse to getting bogged down in a similar situation with Pricey.
It has long been water under the bridge as far as I'm concerned."

Steel described Burdon in this book's first edition as "a lovely fella." However, though he endured with good humour Burdon's eccentricities and diva-ish behaviour for several decades, he now says that even he has decided that friendship is not the nature of their relationship. "Over these past seven years, he's said some pretty offensive, nasty things and I thought, 'Well, fuck you,'" Steel says. "I can't be bothered anymore. He's slagging me off at every opportunity. Hilton and me and Dave Rowberry went over to Eric's sixtieth birthday party thing in Los Angeles. It was a small theatre with two or three hundred people, his hard-core followers. Eric had his band on as the house band of the night but [he got] everybody he could get who ever played with him to come along and do a little spot, and it culminated in the four of us — Dave, Hilton, me and Eric — on stage with Eric's current bass player doing quite a few Animals numbers: 'We've Gotta Get Out of this Place' and 'It's My Life' and 'Boom Boom'. We did a good little set. It went down a storm. A couple of months later, I see an interview somebody sent me where he said, 'Oh, these old guys came over and all they could manage was a couple of Chuck Berry numbers.' This really shitty put-down. I thought, 'Oh, fuck off.' That's just one instance of many."

Rod Weinberg also fell out with Burdon, their rupture occurring on a solo Burdon tour not long after the '83 Animals reunion. "I had him on tour in Canada, had him on tour in Europe after it, and he walked off the Canadian tour because all his mates were going to be in Los Angeles for the Olympics," says Weinberg. "He just walked off the tour after about four or five shows. He just disappeared during the night. I had to give all the promoters their deposits back. The band were very angry with him because they could have done other tours and they were counting on the money from this tour to pay their mortgages and whatever. I flew out to California to meet up with him. He wouldn't even meet with me." For Weinberg, Burdon's career subsequently "took a tumble, really." He adds, "Eric believes the last person who he's spoken to. He's great company, he can be very, very funny, lots of fantastic stories to tell, but as far as his business life goes…Every bloody girlfriend has purported to be his manager. I said, 'Eric,

you have 25 managers, seventeen tour managers, 33 agents —
you're telling me they were all wrong?' Eric was his own worst
enemy. Eric could have been a major, major, major superstar. He
had the voice for it. Somehow he just chopped and changed all
the time throughout his career: managers, agents, record companies. He's a complex person. One of the problems with Eric
was he joined the band when he was seventeen years old. He'd
never really had a normal, proper life. Eric couldn't even go to a
Laundromat and do his own washing — wouldn't have a clue.
Couldn't go to a supermarket to buy a bag of shopping. He was
lucky he had Tappy. Tappy did everything for him. Eric always
had a conspiracy theory on everything. He was totally paranoid
about everything in his life. He always thought people were
taking advantage of him. The actual truth was, it was the reverse.
Eric took advantage of everybody he came in contact with. He's
always found people that get totally besotted by him. Everybody
wants to be his manager."

Dave Rowberry passed away in 2003, aged 62. His body was
discovered by Animals II bassist Jim Rodford. Recalls Steel, "He
was such a heavy drinker. There's a condition where the stomach
lining just gives out and he just haemorrhaged. They found him
lying on the floor with a bucket half full of blood beside him.
He literally lived on alcohol and bananas. Spaghetti Bolognese
was about the nearest thing he could get to solid food because
his teeth were gone as well." It's rather ironic that Chandler and
Rowberry, two Animals who prided themselves on forswearing
drugs, were the first two to die.

The tragedy aside, Steel admits that being the only original
Animal left in Animals II made him feel insecure for a while
about the perceived validity of his continuing use of the brand
name. "But just by a fluke we got this situation where [we got]
Mick Gallagher who however briefly had been in The Animals
in 1965," he says. "When Dave died, we connected up with Mick
again. We thought, 'Well, it's the closest we're gonna get to an
Animals keyboard player other than Alan Price.'" (Asked if invit-
ing Pricey to join the band was ever on the cards, Steel says, "Nah.
He wouldn't have done it.") Steel and Gallagher now work with

various collaborators under the name Animals and Friends. Steel: "Originally it had been Animals II partly because it was not the original Animals but at least there were two of the original Animals in the band. Then when Dave and me and Hilton were in it, we did use the name The Animals for a while. Then Dave died and we restructured the band with Peter Barton as the lead vocalist. Peter and I had this idea of being able to invite friends to join us, which we've done with Spencer Davis and Mick Green and Steve Cropper. That was that conception, to not confuse the potential audience that they were going to see the original Animals and at the same time give us the flexibility of bringing other elements into the band. It's worked really well."

Valentine, now based in the States, admits he was never really fulfilled by the oldies remit of Animals II and always wanted them to write new songs. "And that's what I ended up doing," he says. "I have a band together now going under the name Skiffledog. I'm playing old skiffle stuff and old rock'n'roll stuff I used to sing back in the day when I was about thirteen, fourteen. There's also some songs I'm writing as well. Doing my own stuff, I get a chance to sing. That's how it started out and it's enjoyable. I'm quite happy with me life, me lot. I enjoy living over here." He makes a living from Skiffledog gigs, "plus whatever royalties I keep getting every now and then from CD sales and airplay and things like that." The latter was vitally important for a group like the Animals: performance royalties accruing from broadcasts of Animals material were one revenue stream not even Mike Jeffery could divert.

The New Animals had a reunion of sorts themselves in 1992, although without Burdon and the ampersand. Danny McCulloch was responsible for putting it together and persuaded Vic Briggs and Barry Jenkins to take part. Burdon scathingly talks of "those guys... pretending to be me." Briggs is just as scathing of the enterprise. "John [Weider] didn't want to do it and in some ways I wish I'd never done it," he says. "It made me realise that was it — I would never try to do anything connected with The Animals again. It felt like nothing had changed. Being on the road. Being bored. Everybody smoking and drinking. I quit drinking and doing dope in 1969. We just did a couple of gigs: one in Moscow, one in Sweden and one in some Godforsaken place in Kent, some nuclear power plant staff party. It was so grim." After he left the New Animals in 1968, Briggs produced albums for McCulloch, Hilton Valentine and Zoot Money. Later he dropped out of the music business altogether. He and his wife brought up two daughters (both remarkably born, like him, on Valentine's Day). He is now known as Antion for religious reasons. He says of his time with the band, "From the summer to the fall of '67 was actually pretty wonderful. Very few people have had an experience like that. I'm really glad I did it. I wish it had turned out a little bit differently but it's brought me where I am today." "I met my wife through that experience," says John Weider. "That's the best thing that came out of it." After the New Animals split, Weider joined British hard rockers Family before becoming a sought-after session musician. He played fiddle on several Dolly Parton records. He left performing behind to work in the copyright department of Warner/Chappell Inc. in Los Angeles, a position that coincidentally enabled him to keep an eye on New Animals royalties: Warner/ Chappell bought Sealark, the New Animals' publishing company, in the early 1980s. Weider's mid-Atlantic inflections now bear absolutely no resemblance to the cor-blimey London accent in which he is heard speaking on 'The Immigrant Lad'. Danny McCulloch made the news in the Nineties with some purported Animals activity that turned out to be anything but. A CD called *Best of the Animals* contained songs originally released by the New Animals but now re-recorded by a group of musicians featuring only him from that band, in addition to non-Animals McCulloch compositions like 'Night Fighter' and 'Frisco Queen'. He also hit the headlines for the wrong reasons via a K-Tel album that purported to be comprised of new recordings of Mott the Hoople songs by original members of the band, with the additional distasteful touch of it being claimed that these were some of Mick Ronson's last recordings before his death from cancer in 1993. In fact, it was another McCulloch project featuring no members of that ensemble. It had to be withdrawn from sale after a disgruntled consumer took the label to court, though was later legally issued with the chutzpah title *I Can't Believe It's Not Mott the Hoople!* credited to The Trybe. Though he laid low for a long while (one source joked to this author, "He's wanted in nine counties"), in October 2009, McCulloch — or somebody purporting to be him — posted a picture on *http://ericburdon.ning.com* along with a note reading, "Life Begins at 65 Still Playing." He is also said to be preparing an autobiography titled *When I Was Young*. Barry Jenkins says, "He's a bit funny Danny. He wants money all the time." McCulloch failed to respond to interview requests for this book in both 1999 and 2011. Barry Jenkins is living in England and running a guitar shop. Zoot Money lives in London and is a sought-after session musician. He has a sideline as a comedic actor. Andy Summers became the most successful of any musician to have emerged from either set of Animals. "I must have been disappointed but I don't think, 'Oh, I've missed my chance of the big time,'" Summers says of the New Animals' 1968 split. "I kept playing. I drifted into another situation." Ultimately he drifted into a situation beyond most musicians' wildest dreams. Such was the phenomenal success of The Police that it is hardly necessary to recite their CV here. Of his first proper shot at the big time back in '68, Summers says, "We stayed in pretty nice places and [played in] decent arenas and stuff. It just didn't last long. I joined up in May or something and by the end of the year it was over." Nonetheless, he has happy memories, even if those memories seem, perhaps understandably, fused with those of the times in general: "It was a great era despite everything, the ups and downs of it. It was an amazing time in the world. I look back on it with great affection actually."

Is John Steel, for all his own ups and downs, glad to have been an Animal? "What's the alternative?" he responds. "If Chas hadn't asked me that day if I was interested, I would have been plugging away in a working man's club or something, God knows what. I wouldn't have missed it for the world, really." Hilton Valentine says of The Animals' story, "I think there's a lot of things that have gone under the carpet. A lot of things that haven't been resolved — financial and personal." However, he too is glad to have been an Animal. "That's something that I wanted to do, a childhood dream to make it playing in a band, be a successful rock star," he says. "I don't know how many people have that opportunity."

That at the time of writing the four surviving original Animals are all more or less estranged from each other continues a familiar motif in the band's story. "Unfortunately, we're all sort of sulking in different corners of the world," says Steel. "You'd think at our age we'd be above that kind of stuff. It just seems to get worse."

E N D

bibliography

Wild Animals
By Andy Blackford *(Sidgwick & Jackson; 1986)*
A lightweight but enjoyable biography of the original Animals. The discography is poor (Blackford doesn't even seem to know of the existence of the US *Animalism* LP) but there are many pictures and much of the text is informative and perceptive.

I Used To Be An Animal, But I'm All Right Now
By Eric Burdon *(Faber and Faber; 1986)*
Don't Let Me Be Misunderstood
By Eric Burdon and Jeff Marshall *(Da Capo Press; 2002)*
I Used To Be An Animal, But I'm All Right Now (a paraphrasing of an old werewolf joke), Burdon's first autobiography, indicates he has a career in writing. His biographer Jeff Kent, who saw early drafts, says Burdon didn't need a ghost writer but physically wrote it himself. However, that writing career would be one in the field of fiction. Burdon's penchant for anecdotes that do not chime with established facts or the most generous notion of plausibility is taken to further extremes in his second volume (actually more a rewrite of the first). *Don't Let Me Be Misunderstood*, for example, includes a momentous mid-Fifties meeting with Louis Armstrong that Burdon supposedly managed to keep to himself for half a century despite the kudos it would have acquired him with his mates as a young man.

The Last Poet: The Story Of Eric Burdon
By Jeff Kent *(Witan Books; 1989)*
It's the story of Eric Burdon's life that when he was finally the subject of the serious biography he deserved, it was a self-published work: Kent fell out with Babylon, the publisher that

originally commissioned it. This is a crying shame, for this 400-page work is an extremely absorbing and staggeringly thorough examination of Burdon's life and work (although it has to be said that numerous dates and incidents in it conflict with those in this book). Burdon himself co-operated with the book, as did various Animals. Although the book is currently out of print, Jeff is thinking of re-printing. Those who would be interested in buying a copy of the second edition can contact him at:

> Witan Books,
> Cherry Tree House,
> 8 Nelson Crescent,
> Cotes Heath,
> via Stafford, ST21 6ST.
> ENGLAND
> (Telephone 01782 791673; *email witan@mail.com*).

Good Times: The Ultimate Eric Burdon Audio-Videography 1963-1991
By Dionisio Castello *(1991)*

Dionisio Castello is an Italian Animals superfan who seems to have bought every Animals/Eric Burdon record ever made: reissues, compilations and obscurities from any and every country. This self-published, English-language, 300-page tome lists them all up to 1991, with photographs of the covers of many. Dionisio's book was invaluable to me when researching my own one. Though its discography is out of date, it remains valid for the period it covers, as does Dionisio's chronology of Animals events. Those who would like a copy of *Good Times* should write to Dion at:

> via A. Grandi, 15
> I-04019 TERRACINA (Lt)
> ITALY

Sex, Brown Ale And Rhythm & Blues: The Life That Gave Birth To The Animals
By George Pearson *(snagaP Publishing; 1999)*

Written by a lifelong friend of John Steel, this book mixes fiction with fact as it follows a young man called Terry Molloy through the venues and landscapes traversed by the pre-Animals Burdon, Steel, Price, Chandler and Valentine. It's both an interesting documentary of what it was like to grow up in Fifties Britain (quite smelly, apparently — baths were a weekly affair) and a valuable eyewitness account of the early days of what would become a world famous band. It includes photographs of Animal Hogg, the rest of the Squatters and Doreen Caulker.

The paperback is now out of print and fetching ridiculous prices on the internet. However, George has produced an audio version (MP3 format) running to 7hrs 22mins available from him at *pagan.pearson@gmail.com.*

One Train Later: A Memoir
By Andy Summers *(Thomas Dunne Books; 2006)*
His mega-success as a Police-man has long retroactively reduced Andy Summers' stint with The Animals to the status of an outlet for his guitar juvenilia rather than the career highlight it once constituted, so the Animals element is little more than a sliver of his memoir. Nonetheless, it will be of some importance to Animals fans, with the recountings of his hardly uninteresting adventures with The Police making for a rather substantial bonus.

Rock Roadie: Backstage And Confidential With Hendrix, Elvis, The Animals, Tina Turner, And An All-Star Cast
By James 'Tappy' Wright and Rod Weinberg *(JR Books; 2009)*
Tappy Wright was preparing his autobiography when the first edition of *Animal Tracks* was being written but it took The Animals' former roadie more than a decade to get *Rock Roadie* into print. It certainly made the headlines when he did, with Wright claiming that Mike Jeffery made a drunken confession to him of murdering Jimi Hendrix, whom who he feared was going to propel him toward bankruptcy and the mercies of loan sharks by not renewing his management contract. Jeffery had recently taken out an insurance policy on Hendrix's life. Leaving aside the fact that Jeffery is said to have been in Spain at the time of Hendrix's demise in London, it's a plausible tale. Some of the rest of the book is plausible too, although Wright's recollection

of The Animals secretly recording 'The House of the Rising Sun' when Mickie Most was on a toilet break not only clashes with the memories of The Animals but with Wright's own story of the session as relayed to *Eye* magazine in a Sixties interview. This, erroneously placing Sammy Davis, Jr. in *The Dangerous Christmas of Red Riding Hood* and various wrong dates and eyebrow-raising misspellings casts doubt over the rest of Wright's recollections, which go into sometimes eye-watering detail about both his and The Animals' sexual and toiletry habits. Though the sexual kinks of the band may not be crucial to these interested in their story, Wright provides a few minor but valuable additions on the musical front such as the revelation that he played rhythm guitar on some of their tracks, though he doesn't name them. If true, that is. Steel says he has no recollection of anybody but The Animals playing on their records. This author interviewed Wright for the new version of this book and found his anecdotes so consistently at odds with either the known facts, The Animals' memories and in some cases Wright's own previous recollections that I decided not to use any of them.

Masters Of Rock
By Paul Gambaccini *(BBC/Omnibus; 1982)*

The Heart Of Rock And Soul
By Dave Marsh *(Plume; 1989)*

Are You Experienced?: The Inside Story Of The Jimi Hendrix Experience
By Noel Redding and Carol Appleby *(Fourth Estate; 1990)*

Periodicals that were of help included *Record Collector*, *Daily Mirror* and *News Of The World Sunday Magazine*.

Websites of help included:
http://en.wikipedia.org/wiki/The_Animals
http://www.chickenonaunicycle.com/Eric%20Burdon.htm

discography

The purpose of this discography is to give a clear, uncluttered picture of the material issued by The Animals. For that reason, reissues and compilations of previously issued material have been ignored. In the first edition of this book, selected reissues of albums on the then new-ish medium of compact disc were included, as well as a list of tracks not yet available on CD. This element has been dispensed with for the new edition, partly because CDs go in and out of print so frequently as to make the exercise pointless, partly because CDs are easily locatable on sites like Amazon whether in print or not, partly because at this point in history it's unclear whether the compact disc will still be in existence as a mainstream product for much longer. However Animals CD compilations useful for one reason or another are still listed in the discography's first appendix.

With the exception of *I Just Wanna Make Love To You*, EPs have been ignored as The Animals — unlike The Rolling Stones and various other groups — did not place exclusive material on their Extended Play releases.

Alternate takes are noted but not alternate mixes or edits.

Note: DNC = Did not chart

Below release credited to 'The Alan Price Rhythm & Blues Combo'
FOLLOWING BRITISH RELEASE ON GRAPHIC SOUND LABEL

I Just Wanna Make Love To You (EP)
UK: 10/63 (DNC)
UK TRACKLISTING: I Just Wanna Make Love To You; Boom Boom; Big Boss Man; Pretty Thing

Below releases credited to 'The Animals'
FOLLOWING BRITISH RELEASES ON COLUMBIA RECORDS;
US RELEASES ON MGM RECORDS

Baby Let Me Take You Home/Gonna Send You Back To
Walker
UK: 3/64 (No. 21) US: 8/64 (No. 57)

The House Of The Rising Sun/Talkin''Bout You
UK: 6/64 (No. 1) US: 8/64 (No. 1)

I'm Crying/Take It Easy
UK: 9/64 (No. 8) US: 10/64 (No. 19)

The Animals
UK: 10/64 (No. 6) US: 9/64 (No. 7)
UK TRACKLISTING: Story Of Bo Diddley; Bury My Body;
Dimples; I've Been Around; I'm In Love Again; The Girl Can't
Help It; I'm Mad Again; She Said Yeah; The Right Time;
Memphis Tennessee; Boom Boom; Around And Around
US TRACKLISTING: The House Of The Rising Sun; Blue
Feeling; The Girl Can't Help It; Baby Let Me Take You Home;
The Right Time; Talkin''Bout You; Around And Around; I'm
In Love Again; Gonna Send You Back To Walker; Memphis
Tennessee; I'm Mad Again; I've Been Around

Boom Boom/Blue Feeling
US: 11/64 (No. 43)

Don't Let Me Be Misunderstood/Club-A-Gogo
UK: 1/65 (No. 3) US: 2/65 (No. 15)

Bring It On Home To Me/For Miss Caulker
UK: 4/65 (No. 7) US: 5/65 (No. 32)

Animal Tracks
[US TITLE: *The Animals On Tour*]
UK: 5/65 (No. 6) US: 3/65 (No. 99)
UK TRACKLISTING: Mess Around; How You've Changed;
Hallelujah I Love Her So; I Believe To My Soul; Worried Life
Blues; Roberta; I Ain't Got You; Bright Lights, Big City; Let
The Good Times Roll; For Miss Caulker; Roadrunner
US TRACKLISTING: Boom Boom; How You've Changed; I
Believe To My Soul; Mess Around; Bright Lights, Big City;
Worried Life Blues; Let The Good Times Roll; I Ain't Got
You; Hallelujah I Love Her So; I'm Crying; Dimples; She Said
Yeah

We've Gotta Get Out Of This Place*/I Can't Believe It
UK: 7/65 (No. 2) US: 9/65 (No. 13)
*A-side of US single is not the same version of song as on A-side of
UK single

Animal Tracks
US: 9/65 (No. 57)
US TRACKLISTING: We've Gotta Get Out Of This Place; Take It
Easy Baby; Bring It On Home To Me; Roberta; Story Of Bo
Diddley; I Can't Believe It; For Miss Caulker; Club A Go-Go;
Don't Let Me Be Misunderstood; Bury My Body

It's My Life/I'm Gonna Change The World
UK: 10/65 (No. 7) US: 12/65 (No. 23)

FOLLOWING BRITISH RELEASES ON DECCA RECORDS; US
RELEASES ON MGM RECORDS

Inside — Looking Out/Outcast
UK: 2/66 (No. 12)

Inside — Looking Out/You're On My Mind
US: 2/66 (No. 34)

Don't Bring Me Down/Cheating
UK: 5/66 (No. 6) US: 5/66 (No. 12)

Animalisms
[US TITLE: *Animalization*]
UK: 6/66 (No. 4) US: 8/66 (No. 20)
UK TRACKLISTING: One Monkey Don't Stop No Show;
Maudie; Outcast; Sweet Little Sixteen; You're On My Mind;
Clapping; Gin House Blues; Squeeze Her, Tease Her; What
Am I Living For; I Put A Spell On You; That's All I Am To
You; She'll Return It
US TRACKLISTING: Don't Bring Me Down; One Monkey
Don't Stop No Show; You're On My Mind; She'll Return It;
Cheating; Inside — Looking Out; See See Rider; Gin House
Blues; Maudie; What Am I Living For; Sweet Little Sixteen; I
Put A Spell On You

Below release credited to 'Eric Burdon & The Animals'

See See Rider/She'll Return It
US: 9/66 (No. 10)

Below release credited to 'The Animals'

Animalism
US: 12/66 (No. 33)
US TRACKLISTING: All Night Long; Shake; The Other Side Of
This Life; Rock Me Baby; Lucille; Smokestack Lightning; Hey
Gyp; Hit The Road, Jack; Outcast*; Louisiana Blues; That's All
I Am To You; Going Down Slow
This song is a different take to previously released version

Below releases credited to 'Eric Burdon & The Animals'

Help Me Girl/See See Rider
UK: 10/66 (No. 14)

Help Me Girl/That Ain't Where It's At
US: 12/66 (No. 29)

Eric Is Here
US: 3/67 (No. 121)
US TRACKLISTING: In The Night; Mama Told Me Not To
Come; I Think It's Gonna Rain Today; On This Side Of
Goodbye; That Ain't Where It's At; True Love (Comes Only
Once In A Lifetime); Help Me Girl; Wait Till Next Year;
Losin' Control; It's Not Easy; The Biggest Bundle Of Them
All; It's Been A Long Time Comin'

FOLLOWING BRITISH RELEASES ON MGM RECORDS; US RELEASES
ON MGM RECORDS

When I Was Young/A Girl Named Sandoz
UK: 5/67 (No. 45) US: 4/67 (No. 15)

Good Times/Ain't That So
UK: 8/67 (No. 20)

San Franciscan Nights/Good Times
US: 8/67 (No.9)

San Franciscan Nights/Gratefully Dead
UK: 10/67 (No.7)

Winds Of Change
UK: 10/67 (DNC) US:9/67(No. 42)
US TRACKLISTING: Winds Of Change; Poem By The Sea;
Paint It Black; The Black Plague; Yes I Am Experienced; San
Franciscan Nights; Man–Woman; Hotel Hell; Good Times;
Anything; It's All Meat
UK TRACKLISTING: As US version

Monterey/Ain't That So
US: 11/67(No. 15)

Sky Pilot (Part 1)/Sky Pilot (Part 2)
UK: 1/68 (No. 40) US: 7/68 (No. 14)

Anything/It's All Meat
US: 3/68 (No. 80)

Monterey/Anything
UK: 5/68 (DNC)

The Twain Shall Meet
UK: 5/68 (DNC) US: 3/68 (No. 79)
US TRACKLISTING: Monterey; Just The Thought; Closer To The
Truth; No Self Pity; Orange And Red Beams; Sky Pilot; We
Love You Lil; All Is One
UK TRACKLISTING: As US version

Every One Of Us
US: 7/68 (No. 152)
US TRACKLISTING: White Houses; Uppers And Downers;
Serenade To A Sweet Lady; The Immigrant Lad; Year Of The
Guru; St. James Infirmary; New York 1963-America 1968

River Deep, Mountain High/White Houses
US: 11/68 (No. 67)

Love Is
UK: 12/68 (DNC) US: 12/68 (No. 123)
US TRACKLISTING: River Deep, Mountain High; I'm An
Animal; I'm Dying, Or Am I?; Ring Of Fire; Coloured Rain;
To Love Somebody; As The Years Go Passing By; Gemini/The
Madman (Running Through The Fields)
UK TRACKLISTING: As US version except As The Years Go
Passing By and Gemini/The Madman (Running Through The
Fields)

Ring Of Fire/I'm An Animal
UK: 1/69 (No. 35)

River Deep, Mountain High/Help Me Girl
UK: 5/69 (DNC)

*Below release credited to 'The Animals with Eric Burdon' [US]
and 'The Animals' [UK]*
FOLLOWING BRITISH RELEASE ON DJM RECORDS; US RELEASE
ON WAND RECORDS

In The Beginning
[UK TITLE: *In Concert From Newcastle*]
UK: 4/76 (DNC) US: 1973 (DNC)
US TRACKLISTING: Let It Rock; Gotta find My Baby; Bo
Diddley; I'm Almost Grown; Dimples; Boom Boom; C Jam
Blues
UK TRACKLISTING: As US version

*Below release credited to 'Sonny Boy Williamson and the Animals'
[US] and 'The Animals & Sonny Boy Williamson' [UK]*
FOLLOWING BRITISH RELEASE ON CHARLY RECORDS; US
RELEASE ON SPRINGBOARD RECORDS

Night Time Is The Right Time
[UK TITLE: Newcastle-On-Tyne, December 1963]
UK: 1/77 (DNC) US: 1974 (DNC)
US TRACKLISTING: Sonny's Slow Walk; Pontiac Blues; My
Babe; I Don't Care No More; Baby, Don't You Worry; Night
Time Is The Right Time; I'm Gonna Put You Down; Fattening
Frogs For Snakes; Nobody But You; Bye-Bye, Sonny, Bye-Bye;
Coda
UK TRACKLISTING: As US version

Below releases credited to 'The Original Animals'
FOLLOWING BRITISH RELEASES ON BARN RECORDS; US
RELEASES ON JET RECORDS

Please Send Me Someone To Love/Riverside County
UK: 8/77 (DNC)

Before We Were So Rudely Interrupted
UK: 8/77 (DNC) US: 8/77 (DNC)
UK TRACKLISTING: Brother Bill (The Last Clean Shirt); It's All
Over Now Baby Blue; Fire On The Sun; As The Crow Flies;
Please Send Me Someone To Love; Many Rivers To Cross;
Just A Little Bit; Riverside County; Lonely Avenue; The Fool
US TRACKLISTING: As UK version

Many Rivers To Cross/Brother Bill (The Last Clean Shirt)
UK: 10/77 (DNC)

Below releases credited to 'The Animals'
FOLLOWING BRITISH RELEASES ON IRS RECORDS; US RELEASES
ON IRS RECORDS

The Night/No John No*
**12 inch version also featured Melt Down*
UK: 9/83 (DNC) US: 9/83 (No. 48)

Ark
UK: 9/83 (DNC) US: 9/83 (No. 66)
UK TRACKLISTING: Loose Change; Love Is For All Time; My
Favourite Enemy; Prisoner Of The Light; Being There; Hard
Times; Trying To Get To You; Just Can't Get Enough; Melt
Down; Gotta Get Back To You; Crystal Nights
US TRACKLISTING: As UK version
Note: Some CD reissues included bonus track: No John No

Love Is For All Time/Just Can't Get Enough
UK: 11/83 (DNC) US: 11/83 (DNC)

Greatest Hits Live!
[US TITLE: *Rip It To Shreds (Greatest Hits Live!)*]
UK: 9/84 (DNC) US: 9/84(No. 193)
UK TRACKLISTING: It's Too Late; The House Of The Rising
Sun; It's My Life; Don't Bring Me Down; Don't Let Me Be
Misunderstood; I'm Crying; Bring It On Home To Me;

O Lucky Man!; Boom Boom; We've Gotta Get Out Of This Place
US TRACKLISTING: As UK version
Note: Some CD reissues included bonus track: When I Was Young (live)

Below release credited to 'Eric Burdon And The Animals'
FOLLOWING 1990 AUSTRALIAN RELEASE ON RAVEN RECORDS

Roadrunners!
Australian tracklisting: Heartbreak Hotel; The Work Song; Corrina Corrina; Jailhouse Rock; Roadrunner; Gin House Blues; Hey Gyp (Dig The Slowness); Shake, Rattle & Roll; When I Was Young; See See Rider; All Night Long*; Tobacco Road; So Long; Inside — Looking Out; Maudie; Yes I Am Experienced; San Franciscan Nights; Monterey; Paint It Black
*Incorrectly listed on sleeve as Rock Me Baby

discography appendix I

RECOMMENDED CD COMPILATIONS

The Complete Animals
(EMI CDS 79 46132) 1990
This highly useful double CD rounds up all of the Mickie Most-produced Animals tracks: that is, all the Columbia singles and B-sides plus everything from the albums *The Animals* (apart from 'Dimples' — see below) and *Animal Tracks*. In addition, several rare and/or previously unavailable tracks were included. 'Talkin' 'Bout You (Full Version)' is the unexpurgated rendition of a track which appeared in a drastically edited form on the B-side of 'The House of the Rising Sun'. At more than six minutes in length, it's an amazingly daring performance for a Sixties chart band. It's also superb, The Animals showing off the wonderful chemistry that would lead to them recording so many classic records. Price puts in a particularly sublime performance with his extended organ break. Now that this full version is considered to supersede it, the edited version will probably become difficult to get hold of. For those interested, it can be found on the (actually rather good) EMI CD compilation *The Singles Plus* (CDP 7 46605 2). 'Baby What's Wrong' (Unknown) is also previously unreleased but it's no hidden gem, merely a chugging number with a riff and lyric banal even by blues standards. 'F-E-E-L' is purely a re-write of 'Talkin' 'Bout You', the re-write presumably by the band themselves, and for that reason possibly not released before for legal reasons. *The Complete Animals* publishing credits wisely declare that the author is "Unknown." 'Don't Want Much' is another re-write of someone else's song (Rosco Gordon's 'Just A Little Bit') which turned up for the first time on *The Complete*

Animals with a coy "Unknown" publishing credit. It's as disjointed and slight as Gordon's original. Another rarity from the *Complete Animals* CD is an alternate version of 'Dimples', although this was a complete accident. EMI assumed they were simply including the version of this song that appeared on the band's first British album whereas it is in fact a different version of whose existence no one had hitherto been aware. It's not quite as polished as the previously available take, though Valentine's guitar has an attractive rawness to it.

Inside Looking Out — The 1965-1966 Sessions
(SEQUEL NEX CD 153) 1991
Nicely complementing *The Complete Animals*, this release rounds up everything else released in Britain by the original Animals (reunions excepted). In other words, the Decca singles and B-sides (including 'See See Rider'), the tracks from the *Animalisms* album and the four tracks from *In The Beginning There Was Early Animals* (i.e., the contents of the Graphic Sound EP). Also included is 'Help Me Girl'.

The Greatest Hits Of Eric Burdon & The Animals Volume II
(POLYDOR 839 522-2 – Canadian release) 1982
A typically slapdash Animals compilation mentioned only because it features a rare CD appearance of the fabulous 'When I Was Young' as well as an even rarer appearance of the A-side of the remixed single version of 'Sky Pilot'.

Gratefully Dead 1964-1968
(Raven RVCD-194) 2004
The Antipodean Raven Records have always been known for the loving knowledgeableness behind their compilations, as well as a leeway on the parts of their licensors that is not so easily granted to markets considered as out of the way as theirs. Presumably the latter is the explanation for the inclusion herein of 'Spill The Wine' — highly useful for those who are of the opinion that the War signature song was the last classic of Burdon's career. There is much else on this compilation of Burdon's first three bands that is

useful however, not so much thorugh the conscious side-stepping of obvious inclusions but because of that policy's by-product: the presence of previously extremely rare Eric Burdon & The Animals B-sides 'A Girl Named Sandoz', 'Ain't That So' and 'Gratefully Dead'.

discography appendix II

"I still think to this day, the ultimate example of what the band could do is *Roadrunners!* Definitely it's my favourite album." So says Vic Briggs of a compilation released in 1990 by the Australian label Raven Records featuring radio sessions and live recordings by the New Animals. It's a worthwhile release, although the liner notes honestly acknowledge, "Technical quality of tracks is consistent with concert recording standards in 1967/68." The album opens with five tracks recorded in BBC radio sessions in 1966, quite possibly the merest hint of a treasure trove of such recordings: both the original and New Animals recorded many of these sessions, often performing songs of which they never released a studio recording. This raises the mouth-watering possibility of an Animals equivalent of the album *The Beatles at the BBC.* The first three tracks are probably the original Animals rather than the New Animals (the album's liner notes are rather sketchy). The opening 'Heartbreak Hotel' is an unusual example of The Animals leaning more toward rock'n'roll than R&B. They can't hope to compete with the Elvis classic (written by Mae Axton and Tommy Durden) so they simply try to copy it, right down to the echo on Burdon's voice. 'The Work Song' (Adderley/Brown) is a prison song in the mould of 'Inside — Looking Out'. Its narrator is a member of a chain gang who, as far as he's concerned, is in jail because he's committed the crime of being hungry. The band's performance has such punch and power that it's inexplicable why they never recorded the song for an album. The traditional 'Corrina Corrina' features some clichéd but rollicking piano, presumably from Dave Rowberry. 'Jailhouse Rock' sees Burdon exploring Elvis territory again, this time with the New Animals. At the risk of committing sacrilege, the track is better than the version of Leiber/Stoller's song that was made famous by The King (which was, frankly, always rather too disjointed to be exciting) and this is due in no small measure to Jenkins' sprightly ride cymbal work. The instrumental break features some Jeff Beck-like blazing guitar work from John Weider. 'Roadrunner' is a live performance which is very lo-fi. The sound separation seems non-existent. Two of the four songs performed by Eric Burdon & The Animals at the Monterey Festival follow. 'Gin House Blues' is introduced as a song of "bygone days." Burdon customises the lyric to mention heroin and cocaine. It's a rather boring (7:47 long) rendition, nowhere near as good as the *Animalisms* version. 'Hey Gyp' runs for 8:10. The wonderful song from the US *Animalism* album is here interminable, way too metallic, with an atonal freak out in the instrumental break and even a drum solo. The following five tracks are taken from the Animals' appearance at Melbourne's Festival Hall during their ill-fated 1967 visit. On 'Shake, Rattle & Roll' (Calhoun), the band avoid bogging down the old rock'n'roll style in too much virtuosity, unlike many in '67. The lead guitar is most definitely in the new virtuoso era but not at the expense of the track's primal rock excitement. 'When I Was Young' is surprisingly true to the studio version with some unusually meticulous stage singing from Burdon. There is some delicious molten guitar at the end. A slightly too fast version of 'See See Rider' follows, with the guitar lick that was such an attractive feature of the old Animals' final US single buried in the mix. The next track, listed as 'Rock Me Baby', is in fact a nondescript version of 'All Night Long' from *Animalism*. 'Tobacco Road' is the slowed-down version of this song that the New Animals often did live, drained of all the excitement of the Nashville Teens' punchy effort. 'Inside — Looking Out', the first of two tracks recorded in London in 1967, is cursed with such a poor sound quality that it's actually difficult to tell whether it's a good performance. However, although 'Maudie' is almost as lo-fi, this slinky reading is clearly better than the ungainly rendition to be heard on *Animalisms*. The final four tracks on *Roadrunners!* are taken from a performance in Stockholm in 1968, before the recruitment of Money. The first is the weakest of the quartet: 'Yes I Am Experienced' is a slight song which doesn't improve in a live setting. However, the closing trio of tracks are a real treat. 'San Franciscan Nights' is, considering that the technology of the age precluded the use of acoustic guitars onstage, an amazingly faithful live reproduction of this classic. Briggs and Weider, playing their twin, undulating lines electricly, are on top form. It was even more difficult to match the grand, FX-heavy 'Monterey' on stage but The Animals prove there is a solid tune behind that ornamentation by playing it 'bare'. The lengthy instrumental break sees the guitars of Briggs and Weider coiling sinuously around each other. The closing 'Paint It Black' is the band's usual lengthy and slightly spooky version of the song, with Weider effortlessly shining on violin.

Though two of Eric Burdon & The Animals' four Monterey songs are available on the *Roadrunners!* compilation, it's worth mentioning the other two as they are legally available in various places simply because copyright law differs from country to country: in Italy, for example, copyright on a public performance expires after twenty years. On 'San Franciscan Nights', the Dragnet-style intro with the dedication "to the city and people of San Francisco" gets a predictably good reception. As with the above-mentioned Stockholm version, it is electric accompaniment heard here. John Weider's violin is pretty good on 'Paint It Black' but otherwise the festival rendition tests the limit of one's patience at 7:36 while Burdon's ad-libbed singing ("If everything is wrong, it's right…") is stream-of-consciousness gibberish. The audience seem to like it. No doubt you had to be there (and high as a kite).

SICK OF BEING ME

By Sean Egan

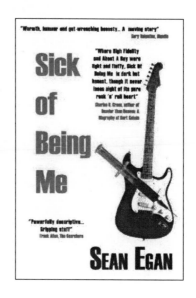

The alternately exhilarating and harrowing story of guitarist Paul Hazelwood, from his childhood on a London council estate where he nurtures his dreams of stardom to his agonising realisation on the cusp of his thirties that talent doesn't necessarily bring success. Respected music journalist Sean Egan portrays the reality of being a struggling musician and of achieving low-level success in that profession with an authenticity that spurns the sensationalism and cartoon nature of previous literary depictions of this milieu. Similar compelling verisimilitude informs the drug scenes, which reveal the touching pain that can be hidden beneath an unpleasant junkie exterior. Vulnerable, truthful, moving and beautiful, *Sick of Being Me* is one of the great coming-of-age tales of our times.

"Few rock'n'roll novels are as dead-on in their realism and few writers are able to describe both drugs and rock with such vivid and compelling language. Where 'High Fidelity' and 'About A Boy' were light and fluffy, Egan's 'Sick Of Being Me' is dark but honest, though it never loses sight of its pure rock'n'roll heart."

Charles R. Cross

author of *Heavier Than Heaven: A Biography Of Kurt Cobain*

ISBN:0954575008

DON'T MESS WITH THE BEST

By Sean Egan

"Interesting, intelligent and well-written…
These are clever, strong stories about a group we rarely come across"
Stanley Middleton, Booker Prize Winner 1974

"I was struck by their authenticity and, almost paradoxically,
their sensitivity"
David Storey, Booker Prize Winner 1976

Barry Hines' *A Kestrel for a Knave*, Stan Barstow's *Joby*, Bill Naughton's *The Goalkeeper's Revenge*, Keith Waterhouse's *There Is A Happy Land*, David Storey's *Saville*…In the esteemed tradition of British working class childhood depicted through fiction comes Sean Egan's superb collection *Don't Mess With The Best*.

In these fifteen tales describing the adventures, escapades, high jinks and set-backs of children and teenagers, Egan captures the 1970s as acutely as did the aforementioned writers their eras. Whether writing about a skinhead who realises that his hard-man status means nothing to a woman interviewing him for a job, a ten-year-old tomboy whose kindness nullifies the embarrassment produced by peer pressure in her new, male best mate, a 13-year-old who realises to his horror that a girlie magazine he has hidden in his mother's flat has disappeared, a boy who is swept up by the illusion of being as tough as his playmate with humiliating results, or a football hooligan whose crushing anonymity is replaced by exhilarating fame on match days, Egan's powers of observation, flawless ear for speech and technical dexterity make for a collection bursting with life and studded with pleasures.

ISBN:0954575024

DON'T MESS WITH THE BEST
"Interesting, intelligent and well-written. These are clever, strong stories about a group we rarely come across"
- Stanley Middleton
"I was struck by their authenticity and, almost paradoxically, their sensitivity"
- David Storey
Sean Egan

ALSO FROM ASKILL PUBLISHING

THE GUYS WHO WROTE 'EM

By Sean Egan

Leiber & Stoller. Mann & Weil. Greenwich & Barry. Bobby Hart. Chip Taylor. Holland-Dozier-Holland. Tony Macaulay. Stock, Aitken & Waterman.

Few would recognise them in the street but they are responsible for some of the best-selling and most famous songs of all time. From *Jailhouse Rock* to *You've Lost That Lovin' Feelin'* to *Leader of the Pack* to *(Theme From) The Monkees* to *Reach Out I'll Be There* to *Wild Thing* to *Build Me Up Buttercup* to *I Should Be So Lucky*, their

melodies and lyrics are embedded in the minds of music lovers worldwide.

With the aid of lengthy and exclusive interviews with some of the biggest names in the history of rock and pop songwriting, including all the names mentioned above, Sean Egan's *The Guys Who Wrote 'em* seeks to put right the lack of recognition for compositional geniuses who for most of their careers have chosen to use their musical skills to help not themselves but others achieve stardom. The result is a recounting of the history of post-Elvis popular music from an intriguing and delightful lateral angle.

The Guys Who Wrote 'em *is the fascinating untold story of popular music.*

ISBN:0954575016